Chapter 1
Relationships Among Organisms

The giraffe does not seem to notice the birds, but the birds are doing the giraffe a favor. They are picking pesky insects and other organisms from the giraffe's skin. In return, the birds get a meal. Both animals benefit from their close relationship.

The lessons in this chapter will help you identify different ways that organisms live together.

D1529508

UNIT ONE
BALANCE AND INTERDEPENDENCE

Still . . . suddenly it
Springs to life killing its prey
With one swift death blow.

Ryan Jones *age 10*

3

UNIT EIGHT The Universe

UNIT SEVEN
Water on the Earth

UNIT SIX
Energy Sources Today and Tomorrow

2 How Do Some Organisms Live Together?

symbiosis (sim/bē ō/sis), a relationship where two unlike organisms live closely together.

Imagine a group of hunters living thousands of years ago, cooking their food over a campfire. They might have tossed aside a few scraps of meat. Wild dogs were attracted by the odors and came to the campfire to feed on the scraps. After a while, the wild dogs began to depend on the food and stayed near the campsite. The hunters began to depend on the dogs' barking to scare away dangerous animals. Many years later, people tamed the wild dogs and developed the close relationship they have with their pet dogs today.

Symbiosis is a special relationship where two unlike organisms live closely together. Sometimes both organisms benefit from living closely together. The bird on the crocodile's mouth looks as if it might be in trouble. But the crocodile does not harm the bird. The crocodile keeps its mouth open as the bird feeds on wormlike organisms, called leeches, inside the crocodile's mouth. The leeches attach to the inside of the crocodile's mouth and suck its blood for food. The crocodile and bird both benefit from their close relationship. The bird gets food, and the crocodile gets rid of the leeches.

Bird picking leeches from the mouth of a crocodile

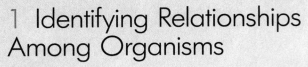

1 Identifying Relationships Among Organisms

All organisms live near other organisms. They have special relationships with each other. A bird might eat other kinds of organisms, such as insects or plants. Frogs and fishes might share some of the things they need to live, such as food and water. But a herd of sheep might have to try hard to get enough food to eat.

The picture includes many kinds of organisms. Some organisms might be hard to find. List the organisms you see. Write briefly about how these organisms might live together. For example, what do you think the organisms eat? What kinds of things might some organisms share or compete for?

Think About It

1. What do you think would happen if all the trees in the forest disappeared?
2. **Challenge** What kind of relationships might people have with the organisms in the picture?

Scott, Foresman

Science

Series Consultant

Irwin L. Slesnick
Department of Biology
Western Washington University
Bellingham, Washington

Program Consultant

Ronald D. Anderson
Laboratory for Research
in Science and Mathematics Education
University of Colorado
Boulder, Colorado

Reading Consultant

Robert A. Pavlik
Reading-Language Arts Department
Cardinal Stritch College
Milwaukee, Wisconsin

Special Writers

Laboratories
Alfred DeVito
Science Education
Purdue University
Lafayette, Indiana

Enrichment Features
David Newton
Department of Chemistry
Salem State College
Salem, Massachusetts

Authors

Michael R. Cohen
School of Education
Indiana University
Indianapolis, Indiana

Bette J. Del Giorno
Science Consultant
Fairfield Public Schools
Fairfield, Connecticut

Jean Durgin Harlan
Education Division
University of Wisconsin, Parkside
Kenosha, Wisconsin

Alan J. McCormack
Science and Mathematics
Teaching Center
College of Education
University of Wyoming
Laramie, Wyoming

John R. Staver
College of Education and
College of Liberal Arts and Sciences
University of Illinois at Chicago
Chicago, Illinois

Cover: Mountain sheep live in very
rugged mountain areas. Their range
includes the Rocky Mountains and
the California Sierras.

Scott, Foresman and Company
Editorial Offices: Glenview, Illinois

Regional Offices: Palo Alto, California
Tucker, Georgia • Glenview, Illinois
Oakland, New Jersey • Dallas, Texas

Reviewers and Contributors

Gretchen M. Alexander
Program Coordinator
Museum of Science and Industry
Chicago, Illinois

Daniel W. Ball
Division of Education
Northeast Missouri State University
Kirksville, Missouri

Mary Coban
Teacher
Divine Savior School
Norridge, Illinois

Thomas Graika
Science Chairman
School District 102
LaGrange, Illinois

Robert G. Guy
Science Teacher
Big Lake Elementary School
Sedro Woolley, Washington

Irma G. Hamilton
Science Teacher
Oglethorpe Elementary School
Atlanta, Georgia

Judy Haney
Teacher
East Noble School Corporation
Kendallville, Indiana

Garth P. Harris
Teacher
Lincoln Elementary School
Evanston, Illinois

Edwina Hill
Principal
Oglethorpe Elementary School
Atlanta, Georgia

LaVerne Jackson, Sr.
Science Teacher
Medgar Evers Elementary School
Chicago, Illinois

Hollis R. Johnson
Astronomy Department
Indiana University
Bloomington, Indiana

Irene S. Kantner
Teacher
Lincoln Elementary School
Evanston, Illinois

Sol Krasner
Department of Physics
University of Chicago
Chicago, Illinois

Dolores Mann
Teacher
Glenview Public Schools
Glenview, Illinois

Phillip T. Miyazawa
Instructional Consultant
Science Education
Denver Public Schools
Denver, Colorado

Anita E. Moore
Principal
George Howland Elementary School
Chicago, Illinois

Janet Ostrander
Teacher
Indian Trail School
Highland Park, Illinois

Barbara Scott
Teacher
Crown Magnet School
Chicago, Illinois

Elaine R. Seaman
Teacher
Greenbrier Elementary School
Arlington Heights, Illinois

R. A. Slotter
Department of Chemistry
Northwestern University
Evanston, Illinois

Anita Snell
Coordinator of Primary Education
Spring Branch Independent
School District
Houston, Texas

Lois Spangler
Teacher
Central School
Great Meadows, New Jersey

Carol Leth Stone
Biology Writer
Stanford, California

Johanna F. Strange
Model Laboratory School
Eastern Kentucky University
Richmond, Kentucky

William D. Thomas
Science Supervisor
Escambia County Schools
Pensacola, Florida

Dorothy Wallinga
Christian Schools International
Grand Rapids, Michigan

Les Wallinga
Science Teacher
Calvin Christian Junior High School
Wyoming, Michigan

ISBN: 0-673-14006-7

Copyright © 1984, Scott, Foresman and Company, Glenview, Illinois. All rights Re-served. Printed in the United States of America.

345678910VHJ929190898887868584

When You Read This Book

1 Read the question.

3 Find the answer.

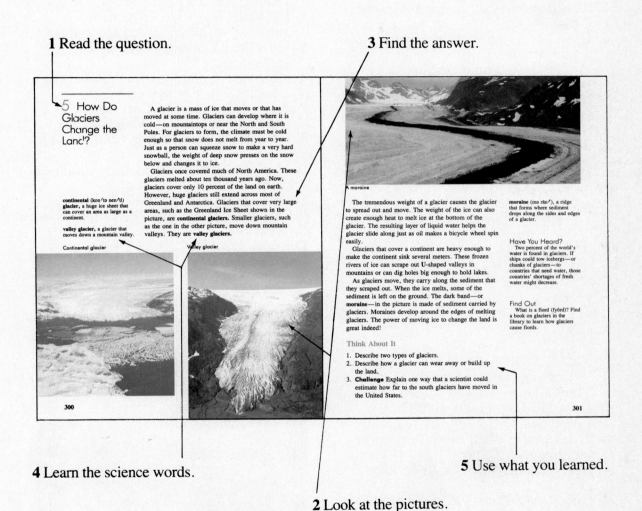

4 Learn the science words.

2 Look at the pictures.

5 Use what you learned.

UNIT ONE Balance and Interdependence

Remora fish attached to a shark

Some organisms live closely together, but only one of the organisms seems to benefit. The other organism is neither harmed nor helped by the relationship. The orchids in the picture are growing on the tree. The orchids have no stem, so they use the tree for support. The orchids do not seem to harm or to help the tree by growing on it.

If you look closely at the picture of the shark, you will see a smaller fish attached to the shark. The smaller fish is a remora fish. As the remora swims along with the shark, it eats small pieces of food that the shark leaves behind. The remora also protects itself from enemies by attaching itself to the fierce-looking shark. The shark does not seem to be hurt or helped by the remora fish swimming along with it.

Orchids growing on a tree

Have You Heard?

Male orchid bees collect liquid perfume from orchids. The male bee then changes the fragrance of the liquid and uses it to attract female bees.

parasite (par′ə sīt), an organism that lives in or on another organism and feeds on it.

host, an organism on which a parasite feeds.

How Do Some Organisms Harm Other Organisms?

The tapeworms in the pictures live in the intestines of animals and harm the animals. In this relationship one partner benefits while the other organism is harmed. A **parasite** is any kind of organism, such as the tapeworm, that lives in or on another organism and feeds on it. The organism that a parasite feeds on is called a **host.**

The tapeworm needs a host, because a tapeworm does not have a mouth or stomach. The host digests food that the tapeworm then takes in through its skin. Hosts that have tapeworms in their intestines can become ill but usually do not die.

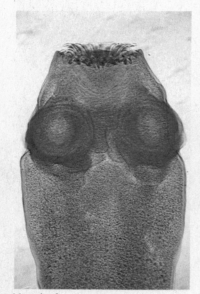

Head of a tapeworm parasite

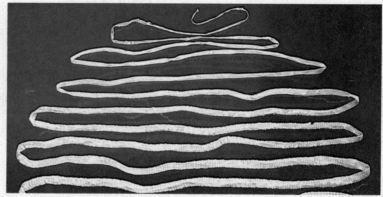

Body of a tapeworm parasite

Other parasites, such as the flea in the picture, live on the host's skin. The parasites suck the host's blood for food. These kinds of parasites often spread diseases as they move from host to host.

Think About It

1. Describe three ways some organisms live closely together.
2. How does symbiosis help some organisms survive?
3. **Challenge** What kind of relationship do the crocodiles and the leeches in their mouths have?

Flea

UNIT TWO Plant Processes

UNIT THREE
Your Body: Support and Transport

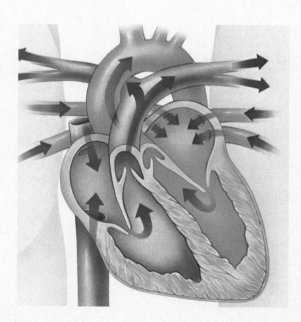

UNIT FOUR
Your Body: Regulation and Response

UNIT FIVE Energy and Its Use

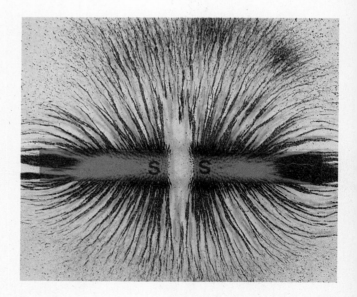

Do You Know?

Some Ants Are Farmers

The ants in the picture are collecting food from their own "farm animals." The animals are tiny insects called aphids that live on plants. They have no way of fighting off enemies that may want to make a meal of them.

But aphids have one unusual characteristic: their bodies can store any excess food that they eat. Aphids get food by sucking sap from the stems of plants. When the aphids take in more sap than their bodies need, they change the sap into a sweet, nutritious liquid called honeydew.

Ants like to eat sweet things, so they are very fond of the honeydew that aphids make. When ants are hungry, they visit a group of aphids. The ants stroke the backs of the aphids with their antennae. The aphids release drops of honeydew through special openings at the back of their bodies.

Ants taking care of aphids

Then, the ants feed on the honeydew.

But how do the aphids benefit from this relationship? The ants protect the aphids by building special shelters that keep other insects away from the aphids. The ants also move the aphids to more nourishing parts of a plant where the aphids can get more food. In winter, ants carry the aphids underground so that they do not freeze. In spring, ants carry the aphids to good feeding places.

By taking good care of the aphids, the ants have a supply of food that they can count on. In return the aphids get protection from insects and from bad weather.

3 How Do Organisms Compete for Resources?

The picture shows a group of cats eating from four dishes of food. They have enough food to share. But what would happen if the cats were given only one dish of food? Each cat might have to try hard to get some food. The quicker cats might get the food first. Then, stronger cats might push aside the weaker cats.

All organisms need food, water, space, and other things to live and grow. A **resource** is anything that an organism uses to live. Different kinds of organisms often get resources in different ways, because they have different lifestyles—or **niches.** But sometimes resources become scarce. As a result, organisms sometimes have to try to get resources also needed by other organisms—or **compete.**

The lion and wild dog in the picture will be competing for food. When organisms compete for a resource, one of the organisms may have a characteristic that gives it a better chance of getting the resource. When lions and wild dogs compete for food, the stronger lions usually win the food.

resource (rē′sôrs), something an organism uses to live.

niche (nich), the way an organism lives, including the things it needs and how it uses them.

compete, try to get something also needed by other organisms.

Cats sharing food

Lion and wild dog will be competing for food

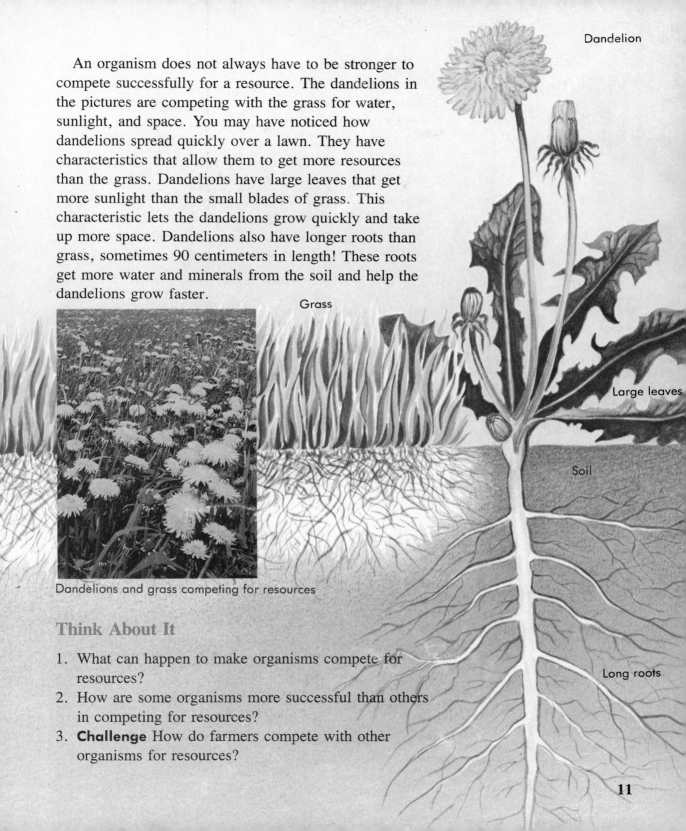

An organism does not always have to be stronger to compete successfully for a resource. The dandelions in the pictures are competing with the grass for water, sunlight, and space. You may have noticed how dandelions spread quickly over a lawn. They have characteristics that allow them to get more resources than the grass. Dandelions have large leaves that get more sunlight than the small blades of grass. This characteristic lets the dandelions grow quickly and take up more space. Dandelions also have longer roots than grass, sometimes 90 centimeters in length! These roots get more water and minerals from the soil and help the dandelions grow faster.

Dandelion

Grass

Large leaves

Soil

Long roots

Dandelions and grass competing for resources

Think About It

1. What can happen to make organisms compete for resources?
2. How are some organisms more successful than others in competing for resources?
3. **Challenge** How do farmers compete with other organisms for resources?

4 How Are Predator-Prey Relationships Important?

Sometimes many organisms of the same kind live in the same place. These groups of organisms are **populations.** The picture shows a population of killer whales.

The killer whales might eat animals from other populations, such as seals or porpoises. A **predator** is an organism that captures other animals for food. The organisms that predators eat are **prey.** The hawk in the picture is a predator. The mouse is its prey.

Some plants also are predators. The plant in the picture uses its leaves to capture and eat insects. The leaves release juices that digest the prey.

population (pop′yə lā′shən), many organisms of the same kind living in the same place.

predator (pred′ə tər), an organism that captures animals for food.

prey (prā), an animal that predators eat. [Plural: prey.]

Population of killer whales

Predator hawk capturing its prey

Venus's-flytrap capturing its prey

12

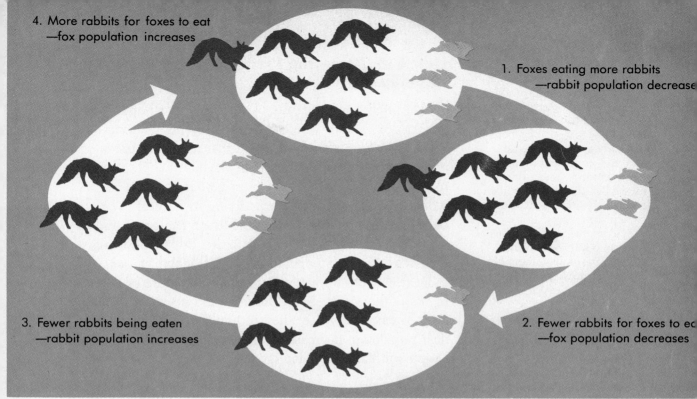

4. More rabbits for foxes to eat
   —fox population increases

1. Foxes eating more rabbits
   —rabbit population decrease

3. Fewer rabbits being eaten
   —rabbit population increases

2. Fewer rabbits for foxes to ea
   —fox population decreases

Balanced population sizes

A **community** of organisms is all the plants, animals, and other organisms that live in the same place. A community can have many kinds of predators and prey. Most of the time, the number of predators and prey remains in a steady balance. The drawing shows how this balance is kept.

Imagine a population of foxes feeding on a population of rabbits. If the foxes began eating more rabbits, the number of rabbits would decrease slightly. Then, the foxes would have less to eat. Some foxes might die from hunger. Soon, there would be fewer foxes eating rabbits. The size of the rabbit population would increase slightly. Then, more food would be available for the foxes. The fox population would increase slightly, and more rabbits would be eaten. The cycle would continue. In this way the sizes of some populations can stay in balance for a long time.

community (kə myü′nə tē), a group of different populations living together in the same place.

Find Out

Find a book on sea animals to learn how the sea anemone uses poison "harpoons" to capture its prey.

How Can Removing Predators Harm a Community?

You might think that removing a predator population from a community would help the prey population. Some people in Arizona learned that removing predators could actually harm a community. These people decided to protect a deer population from predators, such as wolves, cougars, and coyotes, living in a forest. The people killed the predators in the area. The graph shows what happened to the deer population in the following years. At first, the population grew quickly. But as more deer were born, they ate more and more of the plants in the forest. Soon, the deer did not have enough food to eat. Many deer died of hunger. The size of the deer population decreased greatly. Other plant-eating animals in the forest also died.

Changes in size of deer population

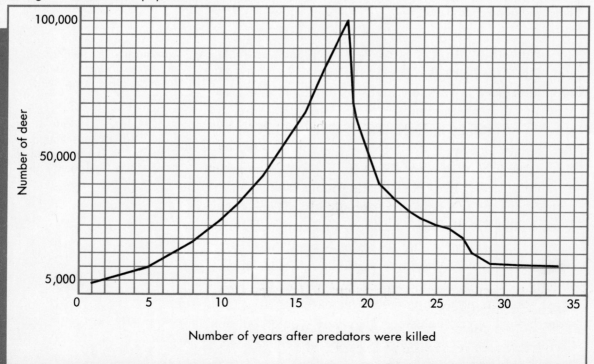

Hunting predators

Spraying insecticides

It is important to remember that the balance between predators and prey is easy to disturb. Think of how the human activities in the pictures disturb these balances. Today, people are protecting communities by limiting activities that can be harmful, such as hunting certain animals or spraying insecticides.

Think About It

1. How do predator-prey relationships affect population sizes in a community?
2. Do only predator populations benefit from a predator-prey relationship? Explain.
3. **Challenge** Think of predators that also are prey.

15

Activity

Playing the Predator-Prey Game

Purpose
To infer how predator-prey relationships affect population sizes.

You Will Need
- chalk
- meter stick
- 50 index cards with "rabbit" written on each
- 20 sheets of heavy construction paper with "fox" written on each
- graph paper

Directions

1. Using chalk, mark a 1-m square on the floor.
2. Work in groups of 3. One student will toss fox cards. Another student will pick up captured rabbit cards. A third student will be the recorder.
3. Evenly spread 10 rabbit cards inside the square. These cards represent your rabbit population. The rabbit cards should not touch each other.

4. Stand about 1/2 m away from the square. Begin with a population of 2 foxes. Toss both fox cards on top of the rabbit cards, as shown.
5. The rabbit cards touched by the fox cards are "captured" rabbits. Remove the fox and captured rabbit cards.
6. Determine the number of rabbits left in the population by counting the number of rabbit cards on the floor. Pretend that these rabbits have babies, and the population size doubles. Record the new number of rabbits in the population.
7. Determine the number of foxes in the population. Foxes that do not capture any rabbits die from hunger. Foxes that capture 1 rabbit live. Foxes that capture 2 or more rabbits live and have babies. Pretend that their number doubles. Record the final number of foxes.
8. Ask the next group of students to repeat steps 4–7. They should begin with the fox and

rabbit population sizes with which you ended.
9. Have each group record its final rabbit and fox population sizes on the chalkboard. Graph the class results on a bar graph.

Think About It

1. What happened to the fox population when the rabbit population decreased?
2. How does the feeding relationship between the predators and prey keep the populations from getting too large or too small?
3. **Challenge** What might happen to the fox and rabbit populations if a new animal population joined the community?

Tie It Together

Sum It Up

1. Write a short story about organisms that live together in the ways described below. To help you write your story, you may use the examples of organisms given in the chapter or do library work to learn about other organisms that live together.
   a. Both organisms benefit.
   b. One organism benefits; the other organism is harmed.
   c. One organism benefits; the other organism is neither helped nor harmed.

2. Imagine a fox population feeding on a rabbit population in a community. What would happen to the sizes of the populations at steps *a, b,* and *c?* Explain your answers.

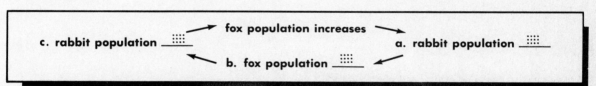

c. rabbit population _____ → fox population increases → a. rabbit population _____
← b. fox population _____ ←

3. Unscramble the underlined science words in the following sentences.
   a. ibyssioms is a relationship where two unlike organisms live closely together.
   b. A tsieraap is an organism that lives in or on a ohst.
   c. A ceoserru is something an organism uses to live.
   d. When resources become scarce, organisms sometimes etemcop for these resources.
   e. Plants, animals, and other organisms that live in the same place make up a numcmtyio. Many kinds of rreotpdas and eypr live in a community.

Challenge!

1. The sea anemone is a sea animal that has poison stingers, but it cannot move around. Sometimes this animal attaches itself to the shell of a crab. How do the sea anemone and the crab benefit from this relationship?

2. How might bad weather increase competition among organisms?

3. How would removing a prey population from a community affect the predators in that community?

4. How can people help keep balances between predators and prey in communities?

Science Words

community	population
compete	predator
host	prey
niche	resource
parasite	symbiosis

Chapter 2
Food Chains and Webs

The farmer in the picture is busy gathering food for people to eat. The wheat in the field is making its own food. Neither the wheat nor the farmer would have food if there were no sun.

The lessons in this chapter describe how organisms, including yourself, depend on other organisms for food.

1 Classifying Organisms by the Food They Eat

2 How Do Organisms Get Their Food?

3 What Is the Feeding Order Among Organisms?

4 How Does Energy Flow Through a Community?

1 Classifying Organisms by the Food They Eat

All organisms need food to live and grow. Some organisms eat plants. Others eat animals or both animals and plants. Some organisms make their own food. Identify the organisms on this page. Draw their pictures on index cards, and write their names. Use library books to find out what each organism feeds on to stay alive. Write this information on the cards. Classify the organisms into groups by the kinds of food they eat.

Think About It

1. Describe how you classified the organisms.
2. Could you classify the organisms in a different way? Explain.
3. **Challenge** How do organisms in a community benefit by eating different kinds of food?

2 How Do Organisms Get Their Food?

producer (prə dü′sər), an organism that makes its own food.

consumer (kən sü′mər), an organism that eats food.

herbivore (hėr′bə vôr), an organism that eats only plants.

carnivore (kär′nə vôr), an organism that eats only animals.

omnivore (om′nə vôr), an organism that eats both plants and animals.

Every year, people in the United States eat millions of kilograms of vegetables, fruits, and meats. People need this food for energy and growth. The organisms we eat also needed food when they were alive. But plants and animals get their food in different ways. Plants make their own food. Animals must eat other organisms.

Plants use energy from the sun to make food. Because plants make, or produce, their own food, they are **producers.** Other kinds of organisms that make food, such as some bacteria and algae, also are producers.

Animals cannot use energy from the sun to make their own food. Animals are **consumers** because they must eat food already produced. The pictures show animals that are different kinds of consumers. Some consumers, such as rabbits, eat only plants. They are called **herbivores.** A **carnivore,** such as a tiger, eats only animals. Other consumers, such as bears, eat both plants and animals. These consumers are **omnivores.**

An animal is not the only kind of organism that has to eat food. Many bacteria, other single-celled organisms, and fungi also are consumers.

Carnivore

Herbivore

Omnivore

Organisms decomposing a plant

The dead plant in the picture is decaying. Some consumers, called **decomposers,** feed on dead organisms. Certain bacteria and fungi are decomposers. They live in the soil, water, and air. While feeding, decomposers break down complex chemicals in the bodies of dead organisms. They change these complex chemicals into simpler ones and return them to the soil. These chemicals help plants live and grow.

Without decomposers, dead plants and animals would pile up on the earth. Chemicals needed for new growth would be trapped in the bodies of dead organisms. Eventually, the earth would run out of the chemicals that organisms need to live.

decomposer (dē′kəm pō′zər), an organism that breaks down the complex chemicals of dead organisms into simpler chemicals.

Think About It

1. What is the difference between a producer and a consumer?
2. What are the names of the different kinds of consumers, and what do they eat?
3. **Challenge** What kind of consumers are people?

3 What Is the Feeding Order Among Organisms?

Imagine that you are a cattle rancher, such as the one in the picture. You raise cattle to provide meat for yourself and other people. But you would not have this food if the cattle did not eat their own food first.

Rancher raising cattle for food

food chain, the feeding order of organisms in a community.

Every community has a feeding order among organisms. The pictures show the feeding order in the ranch community. Notice how the organisms are linked to each other. This feeding order forms a **food chain.** Plants are the first organisms in the food chain. They make their own food. The cattle are the second link in the food chain because they eat the plants. Humans are the third link because they eat the cattle.

Food chain in a ranch community

Meadow food chain

Some food chains are longer than others. Imagine that plants, frogs, hawks, insects, and snakes live in a meadow community. The pictures illustrate a meadow food chain. The insects eat the plants. The frogs feed on the insects. The snakes swallow the frogs. The hawks eat the snakes. Notice that some animals are both predators and prey.

All food chains begin with plants, the producers, because they make their own food. Animals, the consumers, follow the producers in a food chain. Herbivores, such as some insects, are the first consumers in a food chain because they eat only plants. Carnivores, such as frogs, snakes, and hawks, come after the herbivores because they eat only animals. Omnivores can follow either producers or other consumers. Decomposers have a special position in food chains. Decomposers can feed on all producers and consumers.

Have You Heard?

Grasshoppers are herbivores. Sometimes billions of grasshoppers fly together in swarms. In just one day a large swarm can eat about 70 metric tons of food!

Find Out

Explore gardens, abandoned lots, or parks near your home to learn what food chains might be found there.

food web, all the food chains that are linked in a community.

Two food chains

Decomposers

How Are Food Chains Connected?

Some organisms belong to more than one food chain. The diagram on the left shows how insects in a meadow community can belong to two different food chains. You can trace each food chain with a continuous line. In one of the food chains, frogs eat the insects. In the other food chain, birds eat the insects.

In a community many food chains are linked to form a **food web.** You can think of a food web as a net that connects all the feeding relationships in a community. In the food web of the forest community shown below, you can see that animals eat many kinds of food. Trace the food chains that make up the forest food web. Notice where the food chains are linked.

Think About It

1. What are the positions of carnivores, producers, herbivores, omnivores, and decomposers in a food chain?
2. How do food chains make up a food web?
3. **Challenge** What kind of food chain might be found in a jungle community?

Forest food web

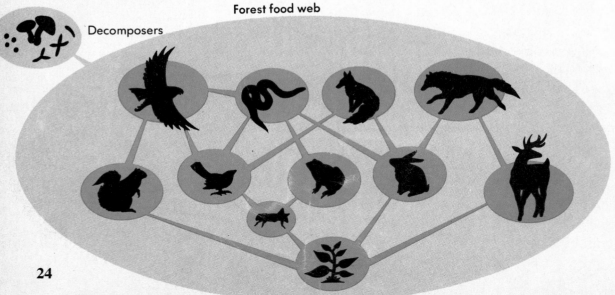

Decomposers

24

Activity

Making a Food-Web Model

Purpose
To identify feeding relationships among producers, consumers, and decomposers.

You Will Need
• 5 sheets of drawing paper
• yarn
• tape
• chalkboard

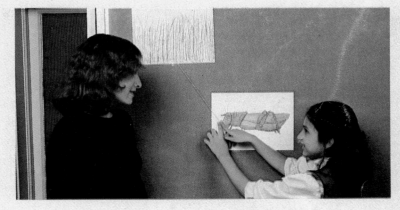

Directions
1. Select a producer, herbivore, carnivore, omnivore, and decomposer to represent populations in a pond community. For example, you might pick a water lily, grasshopper, fish, duck, and decomposing bacteria. Draw these organisms on paper. You will need these picture cards to play the food-web game.
2. The teacher will divide the class into 2 teams. One student from each team will be the scorekeeper for that team.
3. The teacher will begin by taping a plant card in the center of the chalkboard.
4. A member of the first team will tape a herbivore on the board and link it to the producer with a piece of yarn, as shown.
5. The first person on the second team either (a) adds to the chain by linking a carnivore or an omnivore to the herbivore, or (b) starts another chain in the web by linking a second herbivore to the original plant, or (c) starts a different food chain with another kind of plant.
6. Team members continue taking turns, and the entire class discusses the accuracy of each food link. The teacher makes final decisions about accuracy.
7. When a team member makes a correct link, the scorekeeper will record 1 point. After all the students have had their turns, the team that has the most points wins.

Think About It
1. Where were carnivores, herbivores, producers, omnivores, and decomposers in the food web?
2. Why did the food web begin with a producer?
3. **Challenge** What effect would reducing the amount of sunlight have on the food web?

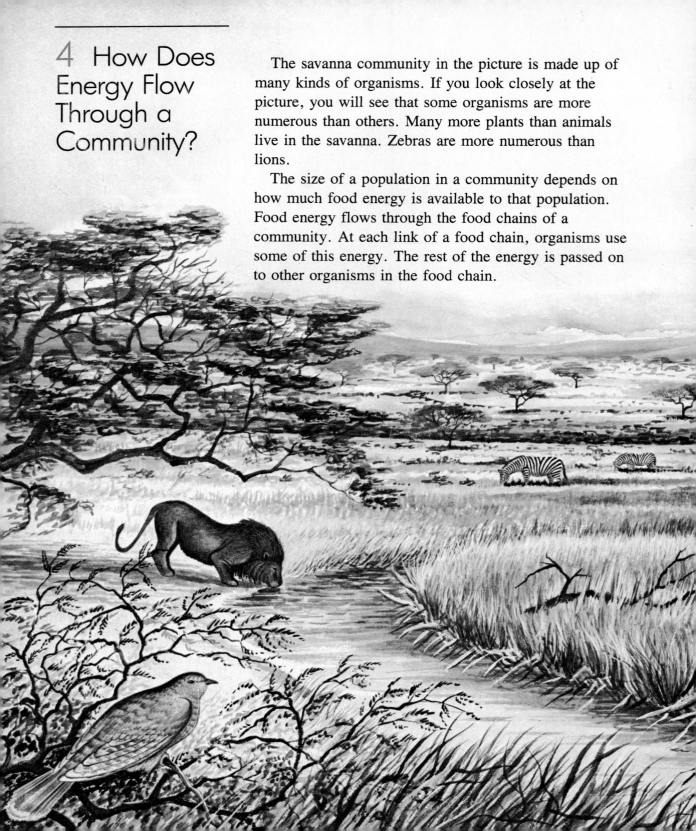

4 How Does Energy Flow Through a Community?

The savanna community in the picture is made up of many kinds of organisms. If you look closely at the picture, you will see that some organisms are more numerous than others. Many more plants than animals live in the savanna. Zebras are more numerous than lions.

The size of a population in a community depends on how much food energy is available to that population. Food energy flows through the food chains of a community. At each link of a food chain, organisms use some of this energy. The rest of the energy is passed on to other organisms in the food chain.

Plant populations begin the flow of energy by using sunlight to make their food. They use some of the food energy to live and grow. The leftover energy is stored in the leaves, stems, and other plant parts. The plants' stored energy is passed to the zebras and other herbivores as food. The herbivores use some of the food energy and store the rest in their bodies. The herbivores' stored energy passes on as food to the lions and other consumers in the community.

Also, the energy stored in dead plants and animals is passed on to decomposers that feed on the dead matter. In these ways, leftover energy continues moving through the food chains.

Have You Heard?

Organisms use about nine-tenths of the food they eat to live and grow. One-tenth of the food energy is stored in their bodies.

What Does an Energy Pyramid Show?

Because some energy is used at each link of a food chain, less and less energy is available for the organisms at each of the following links. The pyramid shows how much energy is available for the different populations in a community. The producers have the most energy available because they get their energy directly from the sun. Less energy is available for the frogs because the plants and insects in the community have already used much of the energy for their own needs. The least amount of energy is available to the hawks, shown at the top of the pyramid. The hawks are many links away from the sun in the food chain.

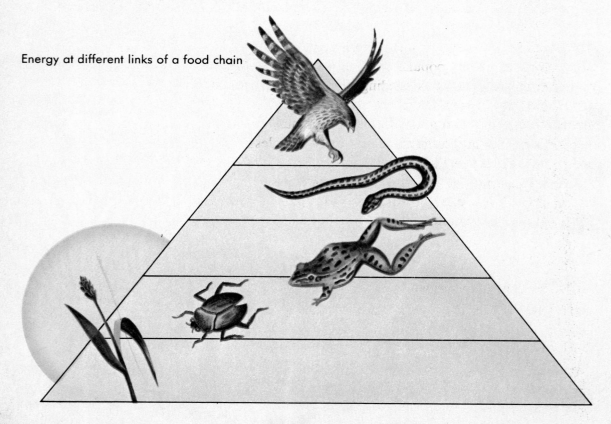

Energy at different links of a food chain

Population sizes in a community

The amount of energy available to a population affects the size of that population. The pyramid shows population sizes at different feeding links in a community. Plant populations are very large because the sun provides them with a lot of energy. The number of frogs in a community is much fewer. They have less energy available to them for living and growing. The hawks at the top of the pyramid are even fewer in number. Much less energy is available for these organisms in the community.

Think About It

1. Where does the energy that flows through food chains come from?
2. Why do carnivore populations have less energy available to them than do the herbivore populations in a community?
3. **Challenge** How do we get energy from the sun by eating a hamburger for lunch?

Do You Know?

Poisons Can Pass Through Food Chains

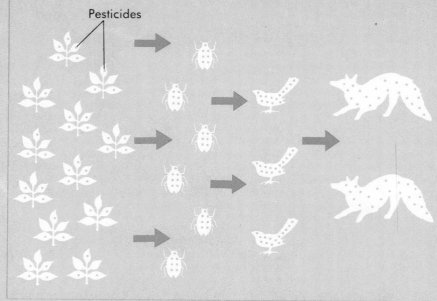

Pesticides

Pesticides in a food chain

"Pass it along" is a good motto for food chains. Passing energy is really what food chains are about.

But other things can pass through food chains too. Pesticides are chemicals that many people use to kill weeds or organisms that destroy crops. Most farmers are careful to use only the amounts of pesticides that are absolutely necessary. Some pesticides are not harmful because they break apart quickly in the soil and change into harmless wastes. Other pesticides can be harmful because they become part of food chains. When these pesticides get into the soil, they remain there for months or years and become part of plants that grow from the soil. When herbivores eat the plants, the pesticides become part of the herbivores and can harm them. When other animals eat the herbivores, the pesticides become part of their bodies. The pesticides can continue to pass through food chains and harm organisms.

The drawing shows that the amount of pesticides that passes to an organism in a food chain increases with each link in the chain. For example, a bird does not eat just one insect; it eats hundreds. The pesticides in all these insects become part of the bird. Now, if a fox eats a bird, the fox will take in much more pesticide than if it had eaten an insect. The fox will probably eat many birds during its lifetime. The amount of pesticide in the fox will be greater than that in a bird. At the end of a food chain, organisms can collect pesticides that have passed from hundreds or thousands of organisms!

Even if people do not come in direct contact with pesticides, they can take in harmful amounts of pesticides with the foods that they eat. Scientists try to prevent this indirect contact by warning people not to eat certain kinds of food, such as ducks that had been feeding on plants sprayed with pesticides. Also, farmers are not allowed to use some pesticides that do not break down into harmless products. For example, since 1972 farmers have not been allowed to use the pesticide DDT.

Tie It Together

Sum It Up

1. Place the following types of organisms in their proper order in a food chain: carnivores, herbivores, decomposers, producers, and omnivores.

2. List the differences between producer and consumer populations. Be sure to include (a) how these populations get their food, (b) how much energy is available to them in the community, and (c) the sizes of the populations. Explain the reasons for these differences.

3. Use the information in the chart to order the populations in the left column into an energy pyramid.

Population	What the organisms eat
Wolves	Small birds
Worms	Small plants
Small birds	Worms
Small plants	Make food

Challenge!

1. When people can food, they boil the food and jars before sealing them. Why do you think they do this?

2. How is the plant *Venus's-flytrap*, described on page 12, both a producer and a consumer?

3. What might happen to a food web if one of the animal populations were removed?

4. Where do decomposer populations belong in an energy pyramid?

Science Words

carnivore

consumer

decomposer

food chain

food web

herbivore

omnivore

producer

Chapter 3
Ecosystems

The campers in the picture seem well prepared for their vacation. They brought sleeping bags, tools, flashlights, and other things to help them live in the forest. The campers will use other nonliving things that can be found in the forest. They will collect dead wood to build campfires or to support tents. Of course, the campers will breathe air and drink water. The sunlight will keep them warm during the day.

The lessons in this chapter will help you identify the many ways that you and other organisms use nonliving things from your surroundings. You need these nonliving things to survive.

1 Identifying Nonliving Things People Need to Live

2 In What Ways Do Organisms Interact with Nonliving Resources?

3 How Are Resources Reused in Ecosystems?

4 How Are Organisms and Resources Balanced in Ecosystems?

5 How Do Communities Change with Time?

1 Identifying Nonliving Things People Need to Live

Imagine that you have been shipwrecked near the deserted island in the picture. Your boat is sinking rapidly, so you have to decide which things to take from the boat to help you survive. The boat has the items listed in the chart, but you have time to take only five items. Make a list of the items you would want to save.

Now, imagine that you are on the island. Think of things on the island that can help you survive. Include these items on your list. Be sure that your list is complete, including such items as the air you will breathe.

Discuss with your classmates your reasons for choosing the items on your list.

Think About It

1. Which items were necessary for your survival?
2. Which items would make life easier for you on the island?
3. **Challenge** Which nonliving things on your list are also needed by other organisms?

Items on the boat	
Games	Radio
Knives	Dishes
Clothes	Spoons
Blankets	Forks
Flashlight	Tools
Medicines	Books
Lotion	Rope
Jug of fresh water	Food

A deserted island

2 In What Ways Do Organisms Interact with Nonliving Resources?

The snake in the picture is using sunlight to warm its body. The deer is drinking water to quench its thirst. The runners are using oxygen from the air with every breath they take. All of these organisms are using a nonliving thing, or resource, to live.

Deer using water resource

Snake warming itself in the sun

Runners breathing the air

An elephant, mosquito, and bird use the same kinds of resources

No matter where organisms live, they need certain
nonliving resources. Air, water, space, proper
temperature, and minerals are some resources that living
things need. These resources are part of the organisms'
surroundings—or **environment.**

Air and water contain the gases carbon dioxide and
oxygen. Plants use carbon dioxide, water, and sunlight
to make food. Organisms use oxygen to get energy from
food. Plants use water and minerals from the soil to
grow. All organisms need water to keep them alive. The
elephant in the picture is thousands of times bigger than
the insect. But both organisms need many of the same
things to live, such as oxygen, water, and space.

environment (en vī′rən mənt),
all the living and nonliving
things that make up the natural
surroundings.

Swamp organisms and nonliving resources

A fish tank

Decomposers growing on a log

Where Can Ecosystems Be Found?

All organisms and the nonliving resources around them act upon—or **interact** with—each other. Your body interacts with the air by taking in gases when you inhale and releasing gases when you exhale. All the interactions among the organisms of a community and their nonliving surroundings make up an **ecosystem.**

Ecosystems can be found in any area of land, water, or air where living things interact with each other and with nonliving things. The swamp, fish tank, and log shown in the pictures are examples of ecosystems. Think of ways in which the organisms in the pictures interact with nonliving resources.

interact (in′tər akt′), to act on each other or influence each other in some way.

ecosystem (ē′kō sis′təm), the interaction of organisms with each other and with nonliving things in any area of land, water, or air.

36

The ecosystems in the pictures look very different because they have different amounts of some resources. The tropical rain forest has a great deal of rain and heat. The tundra has little rain and heat.

The kinds of organisms that are part of an ecosystem depend on the resources available. Fish could not live in most tundras because they must live in liquid water. A cactus could not grow from the soil of a rain forest because the excess water in the soil would rot its roots.

All organisms interact with the resources in their environment. Only those organisms that are adapted to use those resources will survive.

Think About It

1. What are some nonliving resources that organisms need to live?
2. What is an ecosystem?
3. How do resources affect the kinds of organisms that make up an ecosystem?
4. **Challenge** A city is an ecosystem. How do its resources affect people and other organisms?

Tropical rain forest

Tundra

3 How Are Resources Reused in Ecosystems?

The people in the picture can see their breath. At one time, the water in their breaths may have been part of the food they ate. Now it is in the air. Someday, it might become part of a tree. Water is a resource that moves around and around. It continuously passes from one part of the environment to another.

Water vapor in breath becomes part of the air

You can trace a resource as it moves through an ecosystem. The diagram on the next page will help you follow the movement of water in a forest. Begin with water from the soil that is moving up the stem of a plant. Some water moves up to the leaves. There, the water can change into a vapor and be released through the leaves. Now, the water is part of the air.

Air currents might lift the water vapor high up in the atmosphere where it cools. The cooling will change the water into liquid form. Tiny drops of water might become a cloud in the sky. When enough water gathers in a cloud, rain or snow might fall.

Imagine that the water you are tracing falls as rain into a stream. Perhaps a squirrel will drink the water. It may later pass with the squirrel's wastes and become part of the soil for the plants to use. Another possibility is that the water in the stream will flow eventually into an ocean and become part of another ecosystem. The water can continue moving through ecosystems in many ways and be used again.

Water moving through ecosystems

Rain or snow

Water evaporates from land and bodies of water

Plants and animals take in and give off water

Stream

cycle, the continuous
movement of resources to
different parts of ecosystems to
be used again.

Find Out

Use a library to learn how
organisms use nitrogen and
how nitrogen cycles through
ecosystems.

What Is a Cycle?

Water is a reusable resource. You saw that the
movement of water in the forest had no beginning or
end. The continuous movement of a resource to different
parts of ecosystems is called a **cycle.**

Other resources also cycle in ecosystems. The pictures
show that oxygen and carbon dioxide make up a gas
cycle. Plants, animals, decomposers, and other
organisms use oxygen to get energy from food. This
process produces carbon dioxide. Animals exhale the
carbon dioxide. Plants release some of it through their
leaves, stems, and roots. Decomposers release large
amounts of carbon dioxide as they break down the
bodies of dead organisms into simpler materials.

Plants take in the carbon dioxide that organisms
produce. They use the carbon dioxide, along with water
and sunlight, to make food. This process produces
oxygen, which plants release through their leaves and
other plant parts. The oxygen is then used by organisms
to get energy from food. The cycle is repeated.

Carbon dioxide and oxygen cycle in ecosystems

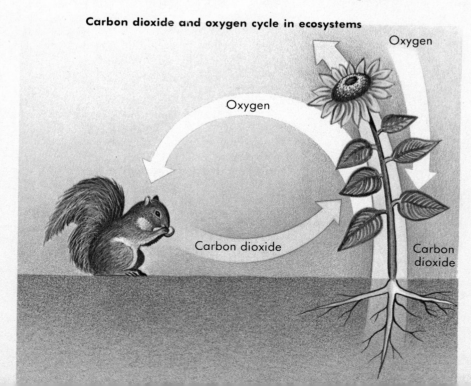

Oxygen

Oxygen

Carbon dioxide

Carbon
dioxide

Plants are an important part of the gas cycle in ecosystems. Plants take in the carbon dioxide that organisms produce and release the oxygen that organisms need to live.

Water and gases are not the only resources that can be reused. Minerals and other chemicals also cycle through ecosystems. If these resources could not be used over and over again, organisms would run out of the things they need to live.

Think About It

1. What are some reusable resources in ecosystems?
2. How is water cycled in ecosystems?
3. How do plants, animals, and other organisms help cycle gases in ecosystems?
4. **Challenge** What happens to resources that cannot be reused in ecosystems?

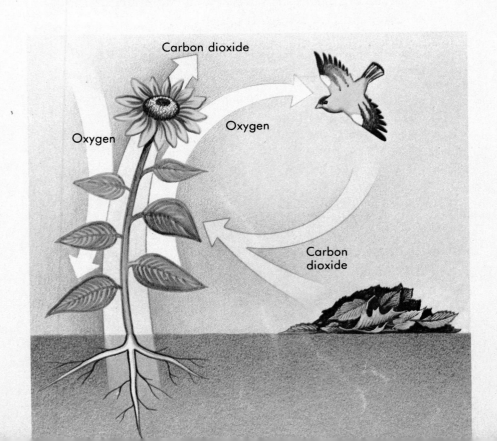

4 How Are Organisms and Resources Balanced in Ecosystems?

A scientist studied a population of starfish living on the seacoast. He was interested in learning how large a starfish population might get if nothing stopped it from increasing. He estimated that a population of 100 starfish could increase to a size of 25 trillion in just 2 years. The drawings illustrate how the starfish population might grow to be so large. The growing starfish population would soon fill all the seas in the world.

But a starfish population would not increase that much in two years. No ecosystem has enough resources to support so many organisms. Many starfish would starve or run out of oxygen and space to live.

Populations are kept from getting too large in a number of ways. Diseases or accidents kill many organisms before they have a chance to reproduce. Predators also keep down the sizes of some populations. Some organisms die because they are unsuccessful in competing for limited resources.

Starfish population with nothing limiting its growth

100 starfish

1 year — If all starfish survived

50 million starfish

1 year — If all starfish survived

25 trillion starfish

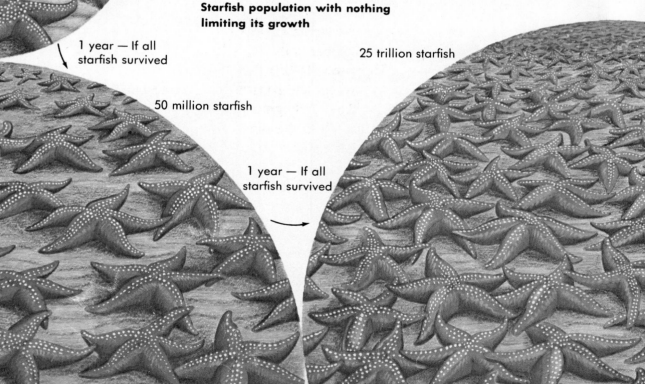

Desert plants do not grow close together | Rain-forest plants grow close together

The resources in an ecosystem can support only a certain number of organisms. This number is the ecosystem's **carrying capacity.** Suppose a 40-liter fish tank has enough hiding places and oxygen for 10 fish. If you add 5 more fish to the tank, without adding more hiding places or oxygen, you will soon discover that some of the fish die. The number of organisms and the amount of resources in an ecosystem usually are balanced with each other. This balance is sometimes called the "balance of nature."

The plants in the pictures are in balance with the resources in their ecosystem. Desert ecosystems have enough water to support only a small number of plants. Only when the plants are spaced far apart can each plant get enough water from the soil. Plants in rain forests are closely spaced because the soil has much water.

carrying capacity
(kə pas′ə tē), the number of organisms that an ecosystem can support.

43

How Can Human Populations Disturb Ecosystems?

The number of people living in the world increases every year. In 1850 about one billion people lived in the world. In 1982 there were more than four billion people. Some people estimate that the earth might have more than six billion people by the year 2000.

The pictures show how the increasing needs of human populations can disturb the balance in some ecosystems. Increasing populations have dumped more and more wastes into some bodies of water. This pollution has decreased the amount of oxygen available to the water organisms. Cutting trees, without planting new trees, destroys forests where many organisms live. As humans use more and more resources from some ecosystems, other organisms do not have the resources they need to live.

Some scientists think the world could eventually have more people than its resources can support. Others think that if we learn to use our resources more wisely, fewer ecosystems will be disturbed. Then, there will be more resources for the people on earth.

Think About It

1. What is an ecosystem's carrying capacity?
2. What can disturb the balance of nature in some ecosystems?
3. **Challenge** The International Pacific Salmon Fisheries Commission controls salmon fishing in some parts of the world. Give reasons why it is important to control fishing.

Some industries dump wastes

Cutting trees for lumber and paper

Activity

Inferring the Carrying Capacity of an Ecosystem

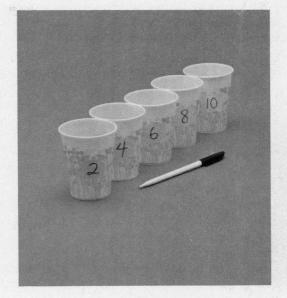

Purpose
To infer how space can affect the carrying capacity of an ecosystem.

You Will Need
- 5 paper cups
- marker
- spoon
- soil
- centimeter ruler
- 30 beans that have soaked in water overnight
- water

Directions
1. Label the cups as shown in the picture.
2. Using a spoon, place a 3-cm layer of soil into each cup.
3. The number on each cup indicates the number of beans to be planted in the soil. Place 2, 4, 6, 8, and 10 beans into the proper cups. Space the beans on the soil as far apart as possible as shown in the picture.
4. Completely cover the beans with soil. A 2-cm layer of soil should be enough. Each cup, with the planted beans, will represent the same kind of ecosystem.
5. Water the beans every day with the same amount of water to keep the soil moist, but not soaked.
6. Continue watering the beans for a week. Record the number of beans that grow in each cup. Record any differences in the plants' appearances.
7. Compare your results with those of your classmates.

Think About It
1. In which cups did many of the beans not grow into plants? Why do you think this happened?
2. Can you tell what was the carrying capacity of the ecosystem?
3. What resource determined the ecosystem's carrying capacity?
4. **Challenge** How could you increase the ecosystem's carrying capacity?

45

5 How Do Communities Change with Time?

Many things change with time. Your body looks different as you grow older. Rocks and mountains wear away over many years. Communities of organisms can also change with time.

As organisms interact with one another and with nonliving things, they sometimes cause changes. The resources available to the organisms change. As a result, the kinds of organisms that make up a community also change. In time, the pond community in the picture might become a forest community.

Most ponds begin as small bodies of water with small organisms living in them. A young pond usually has a sandy bottom. Algae, snails, and other small organisms live in the pond. When the organisms die, they sink to the bottom of the pond and decompose. The dead matter builds up and forms a thick, muddy soil. Water plants begin to grow from the muddy soil. The mud provides a home for new kinds of organisms. The drawings show how the pond continues to change over many years.

Pond community

Changes in a pond community over many years

a

b

46

Crayfish, clams, and worms from surrounding areas find the pond and burrow in the mud. Small fish from nearby streams enter the pond and feed on the plants. Soon, large fish enter and feed on the small fish. The muddy pond bottom gets thicker as organisms die and sink to the bottom.

More kinds of organisms live in the pond as it gets older. Ducks, frogs, and taller plants enter the pond. As the muddy bottom continues to rise with dead matter, less water is available for fish. Eventually, all the fish die. The drawings show that the edges of the pond fill up faster than the center of the pond. Grasses and other small land plants begin to grow on the drier edges of the pond. The muddy bottom continues rising until the whole pond is filled in. The frogs and ducks disappear. Larger plants, such as shrubs and trees, can now grow in the area. Herbivores, such as rabbits and squirrels, move in. The area that was once a pond can become a forest, such as the one in the picture.

Forest community

c

d

succession (sək sesh′ən), gradual changes in a community that occur as it grows older and some kinds of organisms are replaced by others.

What Is Succession?

The pond went through a series of changes over time. As organisms moved in, they changed their environment. The pond eventually dried up. As a result, some organisms could no longer live there. Different kinds of organisms that could live in the new environment moved in. **Succession** is the changes that take place in a community as some kinds of organisms are replaced by others. Sometimes these changes take only a few years. Other times, the changes occur slowly, over hundreds of years.

A pond community is not the only kind of community that changes as it gets older. The pictures below and on the following page show the succession of a beach community. The first plants to live on the beach are some small grasses that grow well in sand. They are followed by a community of shrubs and bushes with long roots that get water from deep in the sand. When these organisms die, they decompose and make the soil rich enough for trees to grow. After many years of changes, a forest covers the area. The kinds of animals that live in the area also change with time.

Succession of a beach community

a

b

Eventually, communities change so little that they appear to have stopped changing. The organisms and the rest of the environment remain the same for a long time. Such a community is a **climax community.** Forests, deserts, and rain forests are examples of climax communities. Usually, a wide variety of resources and organisms are found in a climax community. For example, a forest may include many different kinds of trees such as birch, maple, oak, and poplar. The kinds of organisms that make up a climax community depend on the resources available.

climax (klī′maks) **community,** a stable community that is made up of the same kinds of organisms over a long time.

Have You Heard?

The redwood forests in California are climax communities. Some of the trees are almost 2,000 years old.

Think About It

1. What causes some pond communities to change into forest communities?
2. What is succession?
3. **Challenge** How is a climax community different from a younger type of community?

c

d

Do You Know?

Disasters Can Change Communities

When you think of a community, such as a forest, you may not think that community will change very much with time. The kinds of organisms that make up a forest usually stay the same for a long time. But sometimes things can happen that cause a community to change.

The area in the picture used to be a forest. A fire destroyed the forest a few years earlier, leaving a cleared area with burned trees and tree stumps.

Plants are beginning to grow in the cleared area in the picture. Succession has begun. Small herbs and shrubs are the first plants to grow after the fire. Then, insects, rabbits, snakes, and other organisms move in. Later, birches and pine trees begin to grow. They are the first trees to make up the new, young forest. As the resources change in the area, so do the organisms living there. Eventually, the birches and pines might be replaced by trees, such as oaks. A new community will form.

Will the new community be the same as the old one? The answer to that question depends on the conditions in the area, such as the amount of rainfall or sunlight. If the conditions are the same as those before the fire, the same kind of forest will probably form.

A fire is not the only kind of disaster that can change a community. Earthquakes, volcanoes, and storms also can bring change. On May 18, 1980, the eruption of Mount St. Helens in Washington destroyed forests in the surrounding area. Trees were blown down or scorched. Many populations of organisms were killed or decreased in number.

Two years later, scientists studying the area around Mount St. Helens found a variety of plants, animals, and other organisms that had moved into the area. Succession had begun. New life was beginning to inhabit the area.

Fires can destroy communities

Tie It Together

Sum It Up

1. Explain how organisms interact with the following nonliving resources: water, oxygen, carbon dioxide, sunlight, and space.

2. Draw two diagrams to show how water and gases cycle through ecosystems.

3. The pictures illustrate two kinds of ecosystems that show a balance of nature. Describe the balance of plants and resources in these ecosystems. Which ecosystem has a greater carrying capacity for plants?

4. Write a paragraph explaining how a pond can change into a forest. Be sure to include how the organisms and resources change over time. Draw pictures to help show the changes that occur.

Challenge!

1. Your mouth has bacteria that live on the food you eat. What are the resources that the bacteria interact with in this ecosystem?

2. How is it possible that the next glass of water you drink might contain water that was in a lake while a dinosaur drank from it?

3. In Chapter 1 you learned how the deer population increased when the predators were removed. How did this change affect the balance of nature?

4. Describe the succession that might take place in an abandoned lot in the city.

5. Why do climax communities have a large variety of organisms?

Science Words

carrying capacity

climax community

cycle

ecosystem

environment

interact

succession

Laboratory

Observing Decomposition

Purpose
To observe the effects of temperature and moisture on populations of decomposers.

You Will Need
- slice of white bread
- table knife
- spoon
- soil
- 4 clear-plastic bags with twist ties
- masking tape
- marking pen
- water
- brown paper bag
- refrigerator
- magnifying glass

Stating the Problem
Decomposers, such as bacteria and fungi, live on dead animal and plant matter. Decomposers can also live on food and cause the food to spoil. Decomposer populations grow more rapidly in some conditions than in others. Predict how temperature and moisture affect the growth of a decomposer population on food. Record your prediction.

a

Investigating the Problem
1. Cut a slice of white bread into 4 pieces. Use a spoon to sprinkle a thin layer of soil on each piece of bread. See picture a.

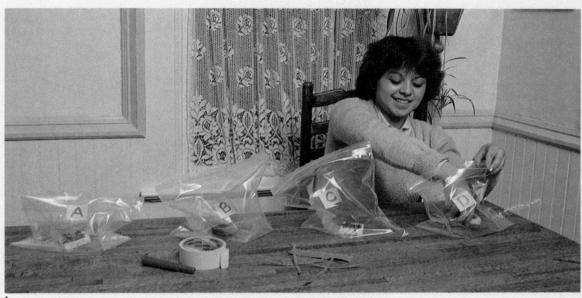

b

2. Label the plastic bags *A, B, C,* and *D*. Put each bread piece inside a plastic bag, as shown in picture *b*.
3. Add 5–10 drops of water to bags *A* and *B*.
4. Seal all the bags. Place bags *A* and *C* inside a refrigerator.
5. Place bags *B* and *D* inside a brown paper bag, and put the bag in a warm place.
6. Examine bags *A, B, C,* and *D* daily. Use a magnifying glass to observe the bread through the plastic bags. Record your observations for at least 4 days. Discard the bags after you record your observations on the last day of the experiment.

Making Conclusions
1. What was the reason for putting bags *B* and *D* in the paper bag?
2. What caused the bread to decompose?
3. How did temperature affect the growth of decomposer populations? How do you know?
4. How did moisture affect the growth of decomposer populations? How do you know?
5. Which bread sample showed the greatest decomposition? Was your prediction correct?
6. Where would you expect decomposer populations to increase in size most rapidly—in a desert, in the arctic, or in the tropics? Explain your answer.

Careers

Tree Trimmer

"Some of our busiest days are right after a bad thunderstorm," says John. "Branches lying on the road and hanging on power lines are dangerous to the community."

John is a tree trimmer. He trims and sprays trees. "When we remove branches from wires, we usually work with electric company crews. We often have to trim a tree whose branches are growing toward the wires. We may have to cut a big V out of the tree branches. This shape might look silly. But it allows several power lines to pass safely through the tree."

After John graduated from high school, he started working with the tree-trimming company as a trainee. "When you go out with a crew, it is a lot of hard, physical work. Trainees carry tools and logs, drag branches, and rake up the area.

"After a while, I became a trimmer. The company has its own school in Ohio. I learned about tree diseases, pesticides, and identifying trees. I also learned how to trim a tree so it will grow in certain ways.

Now, I am in charge of my own crew.

"Tree trimming can be dangerous. I have a safety meeting with my crew every Monday morning. Workers must wear a hard hat and safety glasses. We also wear earmuffs when using some equipment."

John enjoys working outside, even during the cold winters. "The weather does not bother me because I wear many layers of clothing. The worst kind of weather is rain. It is very difficult to climb wet bark."

Most of the loose branches are put into a machine that grinds them. "But I get permission to use some of the stumps and pieces of logs for my hobby—making wood sculptures."

Landscape architect

Wildlife control agent

Many careers are concerned with the environment. Some people try to make sure humans do not disturb the balance of organisms and resources.

A **landscape architect** plans and designs outdoor areas. This person tries to make land in a park or around a building as beautiful and useful as possible. A landscape architect consults with engineers, landscapers, and other architects before making any final decisions. The landscape architect then recommends where trees, shrubs, and flowers should be placed.

People who want to become landscape architects go to college for four or five years.

Soil conservationists help protect one of our greatest natural resources—soil. This person discovers ways to better use the soil so that it does not lose minerals and other chemicals plants need to grow. The conservationist also gives farmers advice on how to prevent rainwater from wearing away their soil and crops.

Soil conservationists learn about the soil and farming methods in college.

Other people help protect our *living* natural resources. A **wildlife control agent** protects wildlife by enforcing fishing and hunting laws. The agent will also try to relocate an animal, such as a bear or cougar, if it becomes a threat to people. The agent knows a lot about animals and the places where they live.

Park management technicians help care for lawns, trees, and other plants in a park or recreation area. They are also needed at ski and hotel resorts, golf courses, industrial centers, garden centers, and sports stadiums. Some technicians work as guides in National Parks.

Park management technicians have usually gone to college for two years.

55

On Your Own

Picture Clue

The picture on page 2 shows a plant and an insect. This unusual plant can *eat* food. What do you think is happening to the insect?

Projects

1. Set up an ecosystem in an aquarium or jar. You may want to add some soil, grass seeds, worms, insects, or other organisms. Be sure to water the soil occasionally. Watch how the organisms interact with each other and with nonliving resources.

2. Dig up some different weeds from an empty lot. Compare their roots and leaf shapes. Determine which weed has the best characteristics for competing for resources in that lot.

3. Get soil samples from different places. Use a magnifying glass to observe small organisms or decayed matter in the soil. Record any differences you see. Add some soil from each sample to a jar of water. Leave the soil in the water for a few weeks. Watch for plants that might begin growing from seeds in the soil. Be sure to wash your hands after touching the soil.

Books About Science

Animals and Their Niches by Lawrence Pringle. Morrow, 1977. Learn how animals in the same community share resources in order to survive.

Animal Rescue by William Wise. Putnam, 1978. Explore ways in which people can prevent endangered wildlife from becoming extinct.

How the Forest Grew by William Jaspersohn. Greenwillow, 1980. Learn how a farm field can change into a forest.

Islands and Their Mysteries by George Laycork. Four Winds, 1977. Discover unusual plants and animals that live on faraway islands.

Tall Grass and Trouble by Ann E. Sigford. Dillon, 1978. Read about the destruction of prairie ecosystems and what people can do to help keep balances in prairies.

Unit Test

Matching

Number your paper from 1–7. Read the description in Column I. Next to each number, write the letter of the word or phrase from Column II that best matches the description in Column I.

Column I

1. a special relationship where two unlike organisms live closely together

2. an organism that lives in or on another organism and feeds on it

3. an organism that captures animals for food

4. something an organism uses to live and sometimes obtains by competing with other organisms

5. the feeding order of organisms in a community

6. an organism that eats both plants and animals

7. changes that take place in a community over a long period of time

Column II

a. predator

b. omnivore

c. symbiosis

d. herbivore

e. parasite

f. resource

g. food chain

h. succession

Multiple Choice

Number your paper from 8–11. Next to each number, write the letter of the word or phrase that best completes the statement or answers the question.

8. Energy is transferred at each link of a
   a. food chain.
   b. symbiosis.
   c. population.
   d. resource.

9. Which of the following is a nonliving resource that is part of a cycle in ecosystems?
   a. oxygen
   b. water
   c. carbon dioxide
   d. all the above

10. An ecosystem's carrying capacity is
    a. the size of a population in the ecosystem.
    b. how long the ecosystem will last.
    c. the number of organisms that an ecosystem can support with the resources available.
    d. always the same.

11. Removing a predator population from a community
    a. might disturb the balance of population sizes in the community.
    b. will benefit the predator population.
    c. will always help the community.
    d. will always help the prey population.

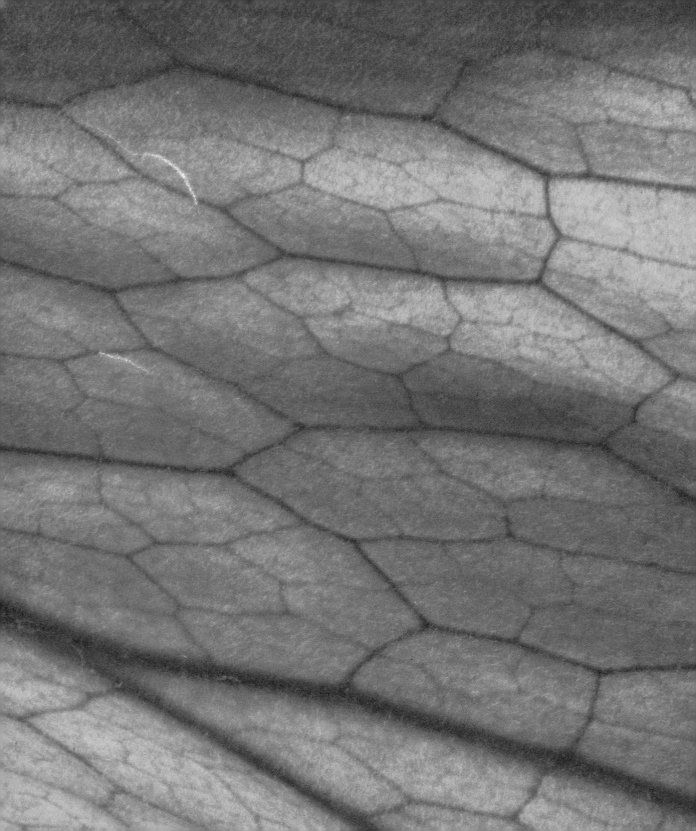

UNIT TWO
PLANT PROCESSES

Chapter 4 Leaf Structure and Function

Chapter 5 Storage and Transport in Plants

Lots of little, tiny, veins
Green and wet
    when it rains.
Starts from a seed,
    then gets tall.
Changes colors
    in the fall.

Leslie Aylsworth *age 10*

59

Chapter 4
Leaf Structure and Function

Workers bring raw materials to the food factory in the picture. The workers prepare the food in the workrooms. The factory is a very busy place. When the workers finish preparing the food, the waste materials are taken out of the factory.

Another kind of food factory also is very busy. It has entrances and exits and places where the food is made. You cannot go inside this factory, but you can see many like it every day. This food factory is a green leaf.

The lessons in this chapter describe how plants make food and use this food for energy to live and grow. When you eat plants, you use the food the plants have made for your own energy to live and grow.

1 Separating Leaf Colors
2 What Are the Colors and Parts of a Leaf?
3 How Do Plants Make Food?
4 How Do Plants Use Food?

1 Separating Leaf Colors

The people in the picture are playing football. Their clothes are smudged with green stains from the coloring material in the grass leaves.

You can see the different coloring materials that are in some leaves. Place some chopped leaves in a small jar. Add enough rubbing alcohol to cover the leaves. Mash the mixture with a metal spoon. Cover the jar with clear plastic wrap and let it stand for 15 minutes. Then, tape a strip of white paper towel 2 centimeters wide to a pencil. Hang the paper strip into the jar, letting the bottom of the strip just touch the liquid as shown in the picture. Carefully cover the jar with plastic wrap again. Let the strip soak up liquid for about 30 minutes. Observe and list the colors on the paper strip. Compare them with the colors other students find using different leaves.

Think About It

1. Which colors did you see on each strip?
2. **Challenge** Did your paper strips show any colors that you could not see in the leaves? Why do you think you could not see some colors in the leaf?

Football players with grass stains

61

2 What Are the Colors and Parts of a Leaf?

pigment (pig′mənt), coloring material.

chlorophyll (klôr′ə fil), green coloring material found in plants and some other organisms.

The picture shows the many colors of autumn leaves. Some leaves are red, orange, or brown. Other leaves are green with yellow spots. Some leaves are still green. Coloring material—or **pigment**—determines the color of a leaf. Most leaves are green because they contain the green pigment called **chlorophyll.**

Many leaves also contain red or yellow pigments. The red or yellow coloring is usually not visible because the leaf has so much chlorophyll. The green chlorophyll masks the other pigments.

In autumn, when the amount of daylight decreases, the chlorophyll in green leaves breaks down and fades. As the chlorophyll fades, other pigments can be seen. Leaves that were green then appear red or yellow.

Some leaves never look green. They may be red, purple, or yellow all year long. These leaves also contain chlorophyll, but the other pigments mask the green color because these leaves have more of the other pigments than of chlorophyll.

Autumn leaves showing color pigments

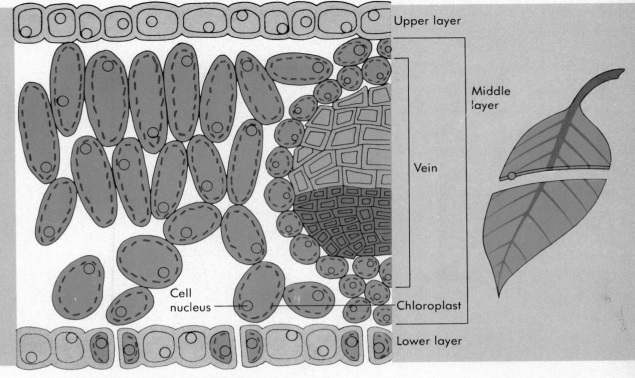

Upper layer

Middle layer

Vein

Cell nucleus

Chloroplast

Lower layer

Layers of a leaf as seen through a microscope

Chlorophyll is contained in tiny structures—or **chloroplasts**—that are in the cells of a leaf. A single leaf cell might have forty to fifty chloroplasts. Each leaf has many cells, so the number of chloroplasts in a leaf might be in the thousands or millions. Green stems also contain chloroplasts.

The drawing shows a cut leaf as seen through a microscope. You can see that the leaf has three layers with different kinds of cells. The upper and lower layers are each one cell thick, but the middle layer is several cells thick.

The cells in the middle layer contain most of the chloroplasts. These cells are oval shaped. Air space is between the cells in the bottom part of this layer. The veins of the leaf run through the middle layer. The veins are like tubes that branch into smaller and smaller tubes.

chloroplast (klôr′ə plast), an oval-shaped structure that contains chlorophyll and is found in a plant cell.

Have You Heard?

A corn plant can lose as much as 2 L of water from its stomata in a day. While the plant loses water through its leaves, it takes up more water from the soil through its roots.

nlargement of af surface

Guard cells

Stoma

What Is in the Outer Layers of a Leaf?

Openings in the leaf are found in the upper and lower layers of cells. The picture shows that each small opening—or **stoma**—is a space between two cells. A leaf might have millions of stomata. A stoma is like a doorway in the leaf's outside layers through which gases can come and go. These gases include water vapor, carbon dioxide, and oxygen.

Like a doorway, a stoma can be open or closed. **Guard cells** control the opening and closing of the stoma. The drawings show two sausage-shaped guard cells on either side of the stoma. When the guard cells are full of water, they bend away from each other. The cells leave a space between them—the stoma. Then, gases can enter and exit the leaf. When the guard cells contain little water, they come together and close the stoma. By opening and closing the stomata, guard cells control the amount of gases that enter and exit the leaf.

Guard cells open and close a stoma

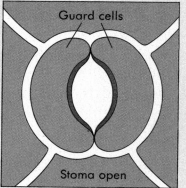
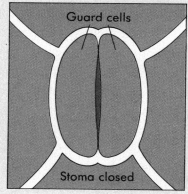

Guard cells — Stoma open

Guard cells — Stoma closed

Think About It

1. What is chlorophyll?
2. Describe the three layers of a leaf.
3. How do guard cells open and close the stomata?
4. **Challenge** What might happen if a leaf did not have stomata?

64

Activity

Collecting Water from Leaves

Purpose
To observe that leaves give off water.

You Will Need
- celery stalk with leaves
- scissors
- 2 plastic bags
- string
- paper cup
- water

Directions
1. Trim the bottom of the celery stalk so that it has a cleanly cut edge, as shown.
2. Cover the top half of the celery stalk and the leaves with a plastic bag. Tie the open end of the bag around the stalk, leaving some air in the bag.
3. Half-fill the paper cup with water. Place the bottom of the stalk in the cup as shown.
4. To see how much moisture collects in an empty plastic bag, tie off the second bag,

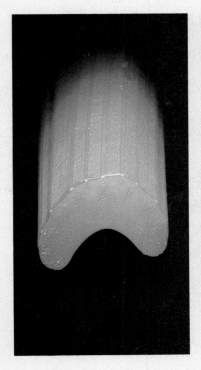

leaving some air in the bag.
5. Let both bags sit overnight.
6. Compare both bags. Record your observations.

Think About It

1. Explain any differences you observed in the 2 bags.

2. Compare what happened with the celery stalk to what happens with a tree.
3. **Challenge** What do you think would happen if petroleum jelly were smeared on the leaves before the leaves were put in the bag? Why?

65

3 How Do Plants Make Food?

photosynthesis
(fō′tō sin′thə sis), a process by which plants use sunlight, chlorophyll, carbon dioxide, and water to make food.

glucose (glü′kōs), a sugar.

Look at some green plants around you. If they are in the sunlight, they probably are making food right now. Plants produce the food they need. Each leaf of a plant is like a tiny food factory.

The food-making process in plants is **photosynthesis.** *Photo* means "light," and *synthesis* means "putting together." Plants use light from the sun to put together carbon dioxide and water to make food. The food that plants make is **glucose,** a kind of sugar.

The picture describes the process of photosynthesis in a leaf that takes place when the sun shines on the leaf. The light shines through the transparent upper layer of the leaf and reaches the chloroplasts in the middle layer. In the chloroplasts the chlorophyll traps the light energy from the sun. Carbon dioxide gas enters the leaf through the stomata and then moves into the chloroplasts. Water comes up from the roots of the plant, through the stem and the leaf, and then into the chloroplasts.

In the chloroplasts, carbon dioxide and water go through a chemical change to produce glucose and oxygen. This process requires light energy. Most of the oxygen leaves the cells and escapes from the leaf through the stomata. The leaves and other parts of the plant use the glucose for food. The word equation describing photosynthesis is shown.

Have You Heard?

Organisms in the ocean that carry on photosynthesis live near the surface because sunlight cannot reach the deeper waters.

Oxygen

Carbon dioxide

Photosynthesis

Carbon dioxide + Water → (Chlorophyll / Sunlight) → Glucose + Oxygen

Water

Glucose

Which Colors of Light Do Plants Use?

The chloroplasts in a leaf must absorb light in order to get energy for photosynthesis. Chlorophyll is one substance that absorbs the light. But chlorophyll does not absorb light of every color.

White light, such as sunlight, is made of many colors of light, as the picture shows. Chlorophyll reflects green light, which is why chlorophyll appears green to our eyes. The green light that is reflected cannot be used for photosynthesis. A plant in green light does not absorb any more light than a plant in the dark.

The graph shows that, when a plant is placed in sunlight, the chloroplasts absorb mostly violet and red-orange light. Light of these colors is used for photosynthesis. If you want to grow a plant under artificial light, you might use a lamp that gives off violet-colored light, like the one in the picture.

Plants grown under violet light

Colors of light used by green plants

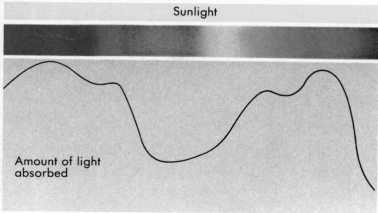
Sunlight

Amount of light absorbed

Think About It

1. Describe photosynthesis, stating where it occurs and how it is important.
2. Write the word equation for photosynthesis.
3. **Challenge** Design an experiment to show which colors of light are used in photosynthesis.

Discover!

Leaves Can Fight Back

Gypsy-moth caterpillars feed on leaves

About every ten years, gypsy-moth caterpillars attack large sections of forests in the eastern United States. The picture shows a forest after an attack of gypsy-moth caterpillars. For two or three years the caterpillars attack every leaf in sight. By feeding on the leaves, the caterpillars destroy millions of trees.

Recent studies show something surprising about plant adaptation. Plant scientists have learned that oak trees make a chemical which might be helpful in fighting off caterpillars. They discovered that leaves growing on red-oak trees change the year after an attack by gypsy-moth caterpillars. The leaves contain less water and greater amounts of a chemical called tannin. The extra tannin in the second-year leaves seems to make the leaves harder for the caterpillars to digest and less nutritious to eat. Because of this change in the leaves, fewer caterpillars survive during the second year; and even fewer survive during the third year.

After producing more tannin in their leaves, the red-oak trees in the forest have a better chance of surviving a caterpillar attack. Some oak trees win their battle against the caterpillars, but only for a while. In about ten years the battle begins once more.

4 How Do Plants Use Food?

Redwood tree

Like all living things, plants need energy to grow. Plants get energy from the glucose they make. The stored food in a bean seed provides energy for sprouting. The redwood tree in the picture has used a great deal of energy from glucose to grow. It is as tall as a thirty-story building! Even a tiny moss plant needs energy for growth. New cells are produced, and dead cells are replaced all the time.

Plants also use energy from glucose to produce new plant parts, such as new leaves, roots, seeds, or flowers. The wildflowers in the picture get energy from food that is stored in their roots.

Plants produce other substances besides glucose. They produce proteins, fats, starches, and vitamins. These substances are used for building new plant tissues or for other plant processes. Plants need glucose to make these substances.

Plants store food in roots

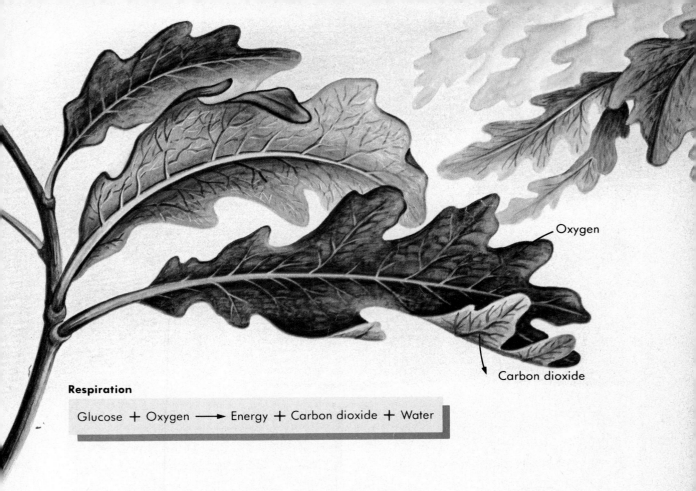

Oxygen

Carbon dioxide

Respiration

Glucose + Oxygen ⟶ Energy + Carbon dioxide + Water

The process by which plants get energy from glucose is **respiration.** When respiration occurs, glucose and oxygen go through chemical changes and produce carbon dioxide, water, and energy. Respiration takes place in every cell of a plant. The word equation for respiration is shown.

During respiration, plants use glucose that was produced during photosynthesis. Plants get oxygen for respiration in two ways. The oxygen could be left over from photosynthesis. Or the oxygen could come from the air through the stomata of the leaves. The carbon dioxide and water produced during respiration can be used for photosynthesis. Or the carbon dioxide and water can leave the plant through the stomata.

respiration (res′pə rā′shən), a process in which glucose and oxygen in cells go through chemical changes to produce energy, carbon dioxide, and water.

Have You Heard?

Evergreen trees save energy by not making all new leaves in spring. Their leaves have a heavy waxy layer to keep them from drying out during winter. So new leaves do not have to be made in the spring.

71

Find Out

Find a book on plants to learn how underwater plants get oxygen and carbon dioxide.

How Do Photosynthesis and Respiration Differ?

Compare the word equations for photosynthesis and respiration. Notice that the equation for respiration is like the equation for photosynthesis, except it is reversed. In photosynthesis, food is made. But in respiration, food is used. Another difference is that photosynthesis requires sunlight and chlorophyll. Respiration can happen in both light and dark, and chlorophyll is not needed. Photosynthesis stores energy in food. Respiration releases energy from food.

Since all organisms use energy, they all carry on respiration. You get energy from glucose in the same way plants do. But photosynthesis occurs only in plants and in some other organisms that also contain chlorophyll.

Photosynthesis

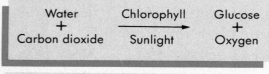

Respiration

Think About It

1. Write the word equation for respiration.
2. How do plants use energy from glucose?
3. **Challenge** Draw a diagram using word equations to show that photosynthesis and respiration make up a cycle.

Tie It Together

Sum It Up

The following are some imaginary reports written by a gardener in a spacecraft orbiting earth. Copy the reports in your notebook. Use the words below to complete the reports.

glucose   photosynthesis
chlorophyll   respiration
water   guard cells
chloroplasts   carbon dioxide
oxygen   stomata

May

"We are sending this report to let you know that the plants you sent have arrived. They are still in the plastic bags. But you forgot something. If the plants are to carry on the process of ___1.___ to make food, they need ___2.___ and the gas ___3.___ . Please send extra supplies right away. Then, we can take the plants out of the plastic bags and let them grow in the tanks."

June

"The plants are now growing very well. We open the shades so the plants get sunlight, which is trapped by the pigment ___4.___ inside the ___5.___ of the leaves. We are studying how the leaves take in gases through the ___6.___ when the ___7.___ are separated. We plan to do some experiments to see how much of each gas the plants use. Please send more supplies."

July

"We think it is time to add some fish to the tanks. The plants produce enough of the gas ___8.___ for the animals to use. The fish can also eat the plants. Both the animals and plants will use the process of ___9.___ to get energy from the sugar ___10.___ ."

"After you send the animals, you can send us fewer supplies. The plants will provide the oxygen and food the animals need. And the animals will provide some of the carbon dioxide the plants need."

Challenge!

1. What would happen if the upper layer of a leaf were not transparent?

2. In which types of places on earth would plants not be able to carry on photosynthesis?

3. What might happen to other living things on earth if photosynthesis did not occur?

4. Can respiration take place in green light?

5. Why do seeds need to use stored food for their early growth?

Science Words

chlorophyll   guard cells   respiration
chloroplast   photosynthesis   stoma
glucose   pigment

Chapter 5
Storage and Transport in Plants

Notice how the foods in the picture vary in color, size, and shape. But they also have some characteristics in common. Each of these fruits, seeds, and vegetables is like a storage cabinet for food. Two of the foods stored in these living "cabinets" are sugar and starch.

The lessons in this chapter tell which plant parts are good to eat and what happens to the water you add to the soil when you water a plant.

1 Testing Plants for Stored Food
2 Where Do Plants Store Food?
3 How Do Plants Transport Food and Water?

1 Testing Plants for Stored Food

The fruits, seeds, and vegetables in the picture provide food that we need to live and grow. One of the substances in these foods is starch. You can find out which plant parts store starch by performing a test.

Place a few drops of iodine on a piece of bread. Observe the color change. The picture shows that iodine will turn dark purple when it comes into contact with the starch in the bread. Next, place a few drops of iodine on a piece of carrot, a root. Repeat the test with pieces of a stem such as a potato, a leaf such as lettuce, a seed such as a peanut, and a fruit such as an apple. Observe any color changes in the plant parts. Compare these changes with the color change in the bread. *CAUTION: Do not taste any food tested with iodine.*

Think About It

1. Which plant parts store starch? How do you know?
2. **Challenge** Which plant part did the starch in the bread come from?

2 Where Do Plants Store Food?

Tapioca plant has large roots

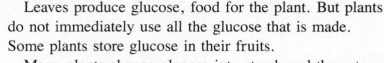

Leaves produce glucose, food for the plant. But plants do not immediately use all the glucose that is made. Some plants store glucose in their fruits.

Many plants change glucose into starch and then store the starch for later use. Notice that the roots of the plant in the picture are quite large. These roots are full of starch. A white potato, which is a swollen, underground stem, also contains a large amount of starch. A seed stores starch for use by the new plant that will grow from the seed.

Some plants store more food than others, and different plants store food in different plant parts. How much food a plant stores and where it stores the food depends on the needs of the plant.

Some plants that live through the winter store starch in their roots. During the winter these plants do not need very much glucose because their growth is slowed down. In the spring the plants need glucose to make new leaves and flowers, as shown in the drawing of the apple tree branch. At this time the plants change the stored starch back into glucose. The plants use glucose to carry on respiration to get energy for growth and for the production of new plant parts.

Flowering apple tree

Bean plants

Bean seed with stored starch

Other plants, such as these bean plants, live only for one growing season. So, these plants do not store much food in their roots for later use.

The seeds of plants store starch to provide food for the new plants that will grow from the seeds. Notice where starch is found in the seed in the drawing. The new plant that grows from the seed needs the starch because the plant does not yet have leaves to produce the glucose it needs. The starch in the seed is changed to glucose, which the new plant uses for respiration.

Animals use the stored food in plants. The food animals eat includes leaves, roots, stems, seeds, and fruits. Each of these plant parts contains sugar or starch that the plant has stored.

Think About It

1. Where is starch stored in a plant?
2. How does a plant use stored starch?
3. **Challenge** What would happen to a seed if it did not store starch?

Have You Heard?

We use plant parts for many other things besides food. For example, we make rubber, oil, medicines, perfumes, dyes, and textiles from different plant parts.

77

3 How Do Plants Transport Food and Water?

Find Out

Rabbits gnaw on the outer layers of some woody stems. Find out why this sometimes causes the plants to die. Find a book on plants, and look up the structure of woody stems.

Glucose is made in leaves and in green stems, but it is used in all parts of the plant. The glucose gets to the other plant parts by moving through narrow tubes—or **phloem.** A phloem tube is made of long cells connected end to end. The cells in phloem are living cells. Notice the holes in the phloem cells that allow substances to pass from one cell to the next. Phloem runs through the veins of leaves, into the stem, and down to the roots.

Glucose travels in the phloem from the leaves to the stems, roots, or seeds where it is changed into starch and is stored. When the plant needs glucose, the starch changes back into glucose, which then travels through the phloem to the other parts of the plant. Phloem carries glucose both up and down through the plant.

Phloem and xylem tubes in a plant

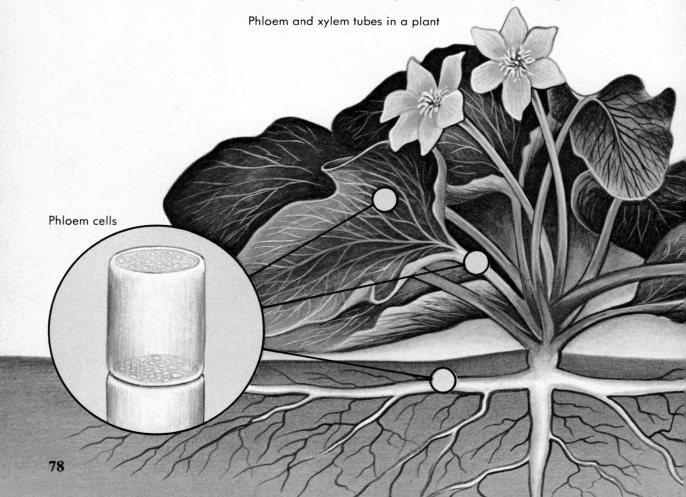

Phloem cells

Glucose is not the only substance that moves through plants. Water and minerals move through another kind of tube — **xylem.** Like phloem, xylem is made of cells connected end to end. But in xylem, the cells are not living, and the ends of the cells dissolve, leaving one cell open to the next, as the picture shows. Xylem runs from the roots, through the stems, to the veins of the leaves. Xylem only transports substances up the plant, while phloem transports substances both up and down. Notice the rings of the tree, which are bundles of xylem. Every year the tree forms a new ring of xylem. You can find the age of a tree by counting its rings.

Water and minerals are taken into the roots of a plant. These substances move up through the xylem, into the stems, and then into the leaves. As water moves through the xylem, all parts of the plant get the water they need for photosynthesis. Minerals dissolved in the water are also transported to parts of the plant where they are used for building new plant tissues.

Soft green plants need water in the xylem to hold them upright. The water in xylem is similar to the water in a garden hose that makes the hose stiff. Plants that do not have enough water become limp or wilted.

xylem (zī′lem), tubes in plants that transport water and minerals.

Have You Heard?

Tree rings are wide in years of wet and warm weather, and narrow in years of dry and cool weather. By measuring the width of the rings in old trees, scientists can tell what the weather and climate were like hundreds of years ago.

Xylem rings in a tree stem

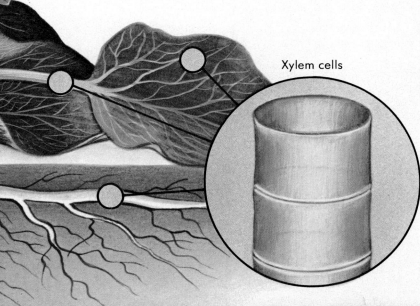

Xylem cells

transpiration
(tran′spə rā′shən), the loss of water through the stomata of a leaf.

Transpiration in a birch tree

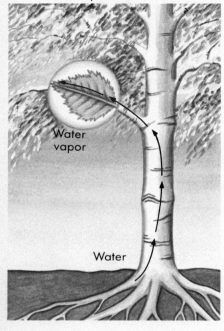

Water vapor

Water

How Do Leaves Lose Water?

A great deal of water travels up from the roots into the rest of the plant. Some of the water is used by the plant, but much of the water escapes as water vapor from the leaves through the stomata. In the birch tree shown, water keeps moving up through the xylem to take the place of the water lost from the leaves. **Transpiration** is the loss of water through the stomata of leaves. A large tree can transpire about 3400 liters of water on a hot day—enough to fill about 10 bathtubs!

The rate of transpiration of a plant depends on the needs and habitat of the plant. A birch tree in a damp environment gets a great deal of water through its roots, so it can lose much water without being harmed. The transpiration rate of the birch tree is high. The cactus in the picture grows in a dry desert and must save water. The stomata of many desert plants stay closed during the day to keep in water. The rate of transpiration in desert plants is much lower than in birch trees.

Think About It

1. What is phloem? Xylem?
2. Describe the structure of phloem and xylem.
3. What is transpiration?
4. **Challenge** How could you measure the amount of water a plant loses in transpiration in a day?

No transpiration in a cactus during the day

Water

Activity

Observing Transport in Plants

Purpose
To observe and measure transport of water in celery.

You Will Need
- water
- cup
- medicine dropper
- blue or red food coloring
- shallow bowl
- celery stalk
- scissors
- clock or watch
- centimeter ruler

Directions
1. Add water to the cup until the cup is at least one-quarter full. Use a medicine dropper to add enough food coloring to the water to give it a dark color.
2. Fill the bowl with water. While holding the celery stalk underwater in the bowl, trim the bottom of the stalk, making a clean cut. Also, cut a notch in the celery stalk about 10 cm from the bottom.
3. Quickly remove the stalk from the bowl, and place the bottom of the stalk in the cup of colored water as shown. Do not let the cut end of the stalk get dry. Record the time.
4. Check the celery stalk every 10 minutes. Notice any color change. After 30–45 minutes, remove the stalk from the colored water, and record the time.
5. Measure and record how far the colored water moved up the stem.
6. Notice any color change above and below the notch.

Think About It
1. Explain any color changes you observed.
2. Did you see a color change above the notch? Explain.
3. Find the transport rate in centimeters per minute by dividing the number of centimeters the water traveled by the number of minutes it took to travel that distance.
4. **Challenge** Must a plant be alive to transport water? Explain.

Do You Know?

Maple Syrup Comes from Trees

Without maple trees you might not be able to enjoy the taste of maple syrup on pancakes. Sugar-maple trees produce sap that is used to make maple syrup.

American Indians were the first people in the United States to cut holes into trees to draw out the sap. Later, they showed the early settlers this process, which is called tapping.

The pictures show trees being tapped. Getting sap from a sugar-maple tree might look easy, but it is not. First, you must be able to tell the age of the tree. Only mature trees give sap. Young maple trees can be damaged if they are tapped.

The tapper cuts a hole in the bark of the tree. The hole must be deep enough to reach into the phloem, through which the sap flows. The tapper inserts a spout into the hole and hangs a bucket from the spout. The sap drips out of the hole, down the spout, and into the bucket. The bucket is emptied once or twice a day.

Sap consists of about 97 percent water and only 3 percent sugar. The syrup you pour on pancakes is sap from which most of the water has been removed. The water is taken out by boiling the sap for a long time. You need a lot of sap to get a little bit of syrup. One liter of sap is used to make enough syrup for just one pancake!

In the United States only the sugar-maple trees that grow in the northeastern states, such as Vermont and New York, produce enough sap to collect for syrup. Sometimes, after making maple syrup, people give maple-syrup parties. They pour hot maple-syrup over snow or ice. The syrup cools to a waxy, taffylike candy and is then eaten.

Tapping maple trees

Tie It Together

Sum It Up

Copy the outline of the plant, including the roots, stem, leaves, fruit, and seeds. Using two different colored markers, draw the direction of transport of 1) water and minerals and 2) food throughout the plant. Label the plant parts where starch is stored.

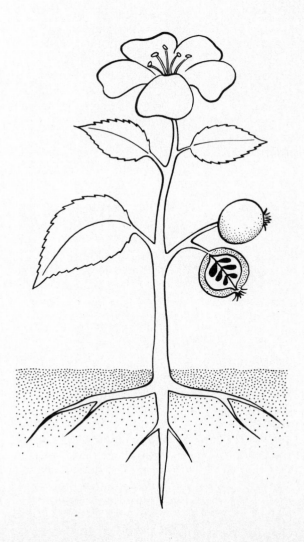

Challenge!

1. Explain why the seeds of some types of plants might store more starch than others.

2. Why do you think wheat, corn, and rice are three of the most important foods for people?

3. What might happen to a plant if the phloem were blocked? If the xylem were blocked?

4. Make a chart showing how phloem and xylem are different. Include the kinds of substances they transport, the direction in which the substances are transported, and the types of cells that make up the transport tubes.

5. Under which weather conditions might transpiration cause problems for a plant?

Science Words

phloem

transpiration

xylem

Laboratory

Transpiration in a Desert Plant and in a Forest Plant

a

b

Purpose
To compare the transpiration rate of a desert plant to that of a forest plant.

You Will Need
- cardboard
- scissors
- aluminum foil
- clear-plastic wrap
- centimeter ruler
- leaf from a forest plant
- stem with leaves from a desert plant, such as a jade plant
- 6 clear-plastic cups
- petroleum jelly
- water
- 3 rubber bands

Stating the Problem
Water transpires from the tiny openings—or stomata—in a plant's leaves. Plants of different types transpire at different rates. Which plant transpires at a faster rate, a desert plant or a forest plant? Write down your prediction and the reason for your prediction.

Investigating the Problem
1. Cut 3 squares of cardboard, each large enough to fit over the top of a clear-plastic cup. Cover each square with aluminum foil.
2. Cut 3 squares of plastic wrap, each about 4 cm larger than one of the cardboard squares. Lay a piece of plastic wrap on top of each aluminum-covered square.
3. Poke a small hole through the center of the plastic wrap, aluminum foil, and cardboard of 1 square. Insert the stalk of a leaf through the hole, as in picture *a*. The leaf stalk should fit tightly in the hole.
4. Poke a hole through the center of a second piece of plastic wrap, aluminum foil, and cardboard. The hole should be just large enough to hold the stem of a desert plant. The stem should fit tightly. See picture *b*.

c

d

5. Poke a small hole through the center of a third piece of plastic wrap, aluminum foil, and cardboard. Cover the hole with petroleum jelly.
6. Smear petroleum jelly around the leaf stalk and stem of the desert plant to seal the holes.
7. Fill 3 plastic cups with water. Set the squares over the cups as shown in picture c. Make sure both the leaf stalk of the forest plant and the stem of the desert plant are in the water.

8. Place an empty clear-plastic cup upside down on top of each square. Secure the plastic wrap over the mouth of each upside down cup with a rubber band, as shown in picture d.
9. Place all 3 setups on a window ledge in bright light. Observe the top cups for several days. Keep a record of your observations.

Making Conclusions

1. What is the purpose of the setup without a plant?

2. Which plant, the forest plant or the desert plant, transpired at a faster rate? How do you know? Was your prediction correct?
3. How does the transpiration rate of the desert plant indicate that the plant is adapted to its desert environment?
4. Would you expect a plant that lives in water to transpire at a faster or a slower rate than a desert plant? Explain your answer.

Careers

Florist

Allen smiles proudly as he puts the finishing touches on his bouquet of flowers. "Like many people, I enjoy having flowers around my home," he says. "To me, working with flowers and other plants is a wonderful career."

But as a floral shop owner, Allen must be able to do more than grow and arrange plants. He has to know how to run a business. Each morning, he calls his wholesalers. "The wholesalers are the people who sell much of the flowers to floral shops. Most florists do not grow their own flowers because they do not have enough space. Florists order the flowers for their customers from wholesalers or from the people who grow the flowers."

Once florists get their flowers, they must be able to care for them properly. Although Allen's background is in art, he took some classes on plants to learn about plant care.

"I really enjoy the challenges and freedom I have in my work. A customer might order a

bouquet of flowers and want me to decide what kinds of flowers to use. This gives me the opportunity to use my talents and creativity to make something that will please the customer. I feel good knowing that our flowers help beautify a room and brighten someone's day."

Plants provide people with jobs in many different areas.

Botanists are scientists who are interested in how plants grow. Most botanists are experts in specific fields of botany. For example, one botanist might study plant structure. Another botanist might be an expert in breeding plants. Some botanists study the use of plants as medicines.

Most botanists need one or more **research assistants** who assist the botanist in the laboratory. Research assistants might collect and classify plants. They also search for information in a library.

Research assistants attend college for four years. Botanists usually go to college for four to seven years.

If you enjoy the outdoors, you might like to be a **forestry aid.** This person works with foresters to protect and care for forests. A forestry aid might mark trees that need to be cut. He or she might also replant a forest that has burned down or been cut into lumber. Some forestry aids work in research. They develop safety gear, test new equipment, or experiment with fire-fighting chemicals.

Besides liking the outdoors, forestry aids must have a good background in biology. Most forestry aids go to college.

Plants of all kinds are very useful. They provide oxygen that we need to breathe. Many medicines come from plants. We also use plants for food. A **produce clerk** keeps a supply of fruits and vegetables in the grocery store. The clerk displays the produce and checks to see that it does not spoil. Produce clerks can train on the job during or after high school.

Botanist

Forestry aid

Produce clerk

On Your Own

Picture Clue

You might think that you are looking at a stained-glass window on page 58. But the lines you see are not connecting panes of glass. They are tubes that carry water and food through a living organism.

Projects

1. Compare the leaves of a desert plant, a water plant, a conifer, and a leafy vegetable. Look at their shapes and thicknesses. You might want to cut the leaves and look at them through a hand lens. How are the leaves adapted to their habitats?

2. Grow plants under different light intensity and moisture conditions to see how their growth is affected.

3. Look at the roots of a variety of plants, such as a carrot, a cactus, a fern, and a weed. How does the thickness, the length, and the branching of the roots differ among these plants? How are these characteristics related to food storage and water transport?

Books About Science

Gardening Without Soil by Sarah R. Riedman. Watts, 1979. Learn how some people grow plants without using soil and how this method of gardening can be useful.

How Plants Grow by Ron Wilson. Larousse, 1980. Explore the many ways that plants on earth grow and develop.

Play with Plants by Millicent E. Selsam. Morrow, 1978. Discover how you can grow plants from the roots, stems, leaves, and seeds of a variety of plants.

Watch It Grow, Watch It Change by Joan Elma Rahn. Atheneum, 1978. Learn how plant parts, such as stems, leaves, roots, flowers, and buds, form and grow.

Unit Test

Matching

Number your paper from 1–8. Read the description in
Column I. Next to each number, write the letter of the word
from Column II that best matches the description in Column I.

Column I

1. green coloring material in plants
2. tubes in plants that transport water and minerals
3. loss of water through the stomata of a leaf
4. a process by which plants make food
5. a pore or opening in a leaf that allows gases to move in and out of the leaf
6. a tiny structure that contains chlorophyll and is found in a plant cell
7. tubes in plants that transport food
8. a sugar made during photosynthesis

Column II

a. photosynthesis
b. phloem
c. stoma
d. chlorophyll
e. chloroplast
f. xylem
g. glucose
h. starch
i. transpiration

Multiple Choice

Number your paper from 9–14. Next to each number, write
the letter of the word or phrase that best completes the
statement or answers the question.

9. Which of the following do plants use during photosynthesis to produce glucose and oxygen?
   a. sunlight and chlorophyll
   b. carbon dioxide
   c. water
   d. all the above

10. During respiration organisms produce
    a. glucose, oxygen, and water.
    b. energy, carbon dioxide, and water.
    c. energy and glucose.
    d. chlorophyll.

11. Phloem transports food
    a. down the plant.
    b. up the plant.
    c. both up and down the plant.
    d. only through the leaves.

12. When the guard cells of a leaf are full of water, they bend away from each other and
    a. open the stomata.
    b. close the stomata.
    c. let in chlorophyll.
    d. let in glucose.

13. Xylem is found in
    a. leaves.
    b. roots and stems.
    c. roots, stems, and leaves.
    d. stems.

14. Soft, green plants need water in the xylem to
    a. get more chlorophyll.
    b. hold themselves upright.
    c. transport food.
    d. store starch.

UNIT THREE
YOUR BODY: SUPPORT AND TRANSPORT

They help us move
        to run and play
We sleep with them
        both night and day.
Even though
        we do not know
They are growing
        very slow.

Cirrus Mayahara *age 11*

Chapter 6
Skin, Bones, and Muscles

The scarecrow in the *Wizard of Oz* wished for a brain. If the scarecrow in the picture could think, it might wish for several other things as well. Skin might keep it from getting soaked through by rain. Bones could help it hold up its neck and head. With muscles, it could shoo the crows off its arms. If the scarecrow only had skin, bones, and muscles like a person, it would have no trouble scaring off the crows.

The lessons in this chapter describe how your skin, bones, and muscles work together to protect you, support you, and help you move.

1 Observing Skin's Protective Role
2 What Does Your Skin Do?
3 How Does Your Skeleton Work?
4 How Do Your Muscles Work?

1 Observing Skin's Protective Role

Unless you fall down and scrape your knee, you might give little thought to your skin. But your skin is an important part of your body. Skin keeps harmful organisms from entering your body and making you ill. You can use the skin of an apple to show how skin provides protection.

You will need two healthy apples, one rotten apple, and a bobby pin. Label the healthy apples so you can tell them apart. Poke the bobby pin into the rotten apple as shown. Now, poke the bobby pin into one of the healthy apples so the pulp from the rotten apple gets into the good apple. Poke the bobby pin into the rotten apple again. Then, gently rub the bobby pin across the skin of the second healthy apple. Be careful not to break the skin. Throw the rotten apple away. Observe how the labeled apples change during one week.

Think About It

1. What happened to the apple with the broken skin? What happened to the other apple?
2. How does the skin protect the apple?
3. **Challenge** How is your skin like the apple skin?

UNBROKEN SKIN   BROKEN SKIN

2 What Does Your Skin Do?

epidermis (ep/ə dėr/mis), the top layer of skin.

Find Out

Your skin has tiny ridges that you see as your fingerprints. Four basic fingerprint patterns are common. Compare your fingerprint pattern with those of your classmates. Try to find the 4 basic patterns.

The night is dark. You are walking alone. Suddenly you hear a noise. You stop, frozen with fear. You shiver. Goose bumps form on your skin. When you get scared, your skin reacts. Tiny muscles in your skin might contract to give you goose bumps. Your skin is a living organ.

The drawing on the following page shows that skin is made of two layers. The top layer called the **epidermis** keeps harmful organisms from entering your body. The epidermis also keeps water out of your body when you get wet.

The top cells of the epidermis are not alive. When you take a bath or get a sunburn like the person in the picture, these dead skin cells peel off easily. These cells must be replaced often. Beneath the dead cells in the epidermis are living cells. When the dead cells are shed, the living cells below them die and take their place. Your body is always making new epidermal cells so you will never be without your protective covering, the epidermis.

Sunburned skin

Notice the many structures in the second layer of skin—the **dermis.** One square centimeter of dermis has about one meter of blood vessels, one hundred sweat glands, fifteen oil glands, and ten hairs, each hair connected to a tiny muscle. The structures shown in the dermis help you in many ways.

dermis (dėr′mis), the second layer of skin.

Layers of the skin

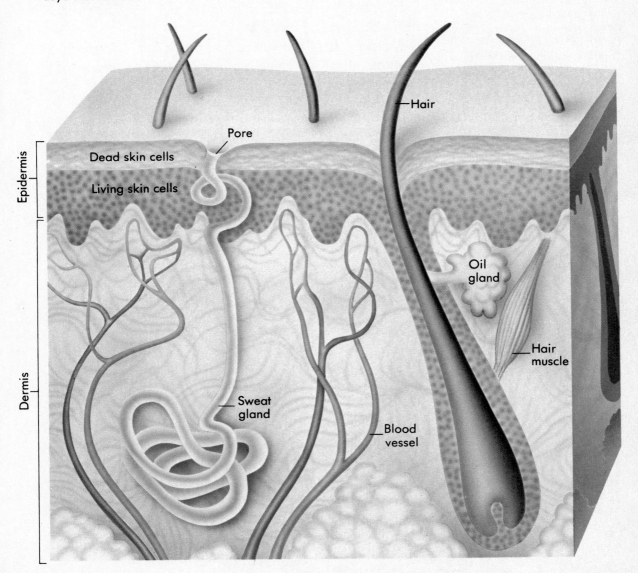

Epidermis

Dermis

Hair

Pore

Dead skin cells

Living skin cells

Oil gland

Hair muscle

Sweat gland

Blood vessel

What Does the Dermis Do?

Oil glands in your dermis layer supply oil to the top of the epidermis. If you rub a tissue along the side of your nose, you can see this oil on the tissue. If you cover your arms with lotion, water will bead up on your skin as shown in the picture. The oil produced by your dermis works the same way as lotion. It keeps water from entering or leaving your epidermal cells and makes your skin soft and moist.

Each oil gland is connected to a hair sac. Oil travels from the gland, up along the hair, and out to the top of the epidermis.

Porcupine raising quills

Oil prevents water from entering the skin

Tiny hairs cover the surface of your skin. The hairs are connected to tiny muscles in your skin. When you get goose bumps, these muscles contract, raising your skin hairs. The raised hairs trap a small amount of your body's heat next to your skin. A furry animal, such as a polar bear, also uses tiny skin muscles to fluff its fur when it gets cold. Its thick coat of fur can hold in more heat than the tiny hairs in your skin.

Pores in the skin

Skin reddens when blood vessels enlarge

Tiny blood vessels in your dermis also help control your body temperature. When your body temperature is high, the blood vessels in your skin get larger. More blood flows to your skin to be cooled by the air outside your body. Enlarged blood vessels made the basketball player's skin red. When you get cold, the blood vessels in your skin become very small. In this way, your blood is kept away from the colder air outside your body.

Sweating is another way your skin controls your body temperature. Sweat, produced in sweat glands, passes to the outer layer of your skin through openings called pores. Find the pores in the skin in the picture. When sweat passes through the pores and evaporates on your skin, you feel cooler.

Sweat glands perform another important function. Your sweat glands take excess water and salts from your blood and pass these wastes out of your body.

Think About It

1. What is the top layer of the skin called? Describe its functions.
2. Name the skin's second layer. Describe four of its structures and what they do.
3. **Challenge** Your face might get warm when you exercise. Discuss what happens to your skin.

3 How Does Your Skeleton Work?

Have You Heard?

When you hit your "funny bone," you feel a tingle all the way up your arm. You do not really have a "funny bone." But you have a nerve in your arm that is unprotected in a small spot at the end of your elbow. When you hit your "funny bone," you really hit this nerve.

Bones buried beneath the ground might look the same for several years. Because bones seem so durable, you might not think of your bones as being made of living tissue. But your bones are as alive as your skin, muscles, and brain. Your bones work together to form a living system that gives you support, helps you move, and makes blood cells.

The picture shows the three parts of a living bone. The outer layer is a tough, protective coat for your bones. If a bone breaks, this coating helps mend it.

Just inside the bone coat is the bone itself. Bone is made of bone cells. Blood vessels from the outer coat penetrate the bone. Minerals, such as calcium, from your blood are arranged in rings, as shown in the picture. These rings of minerals make your bones sturdy. The center part of your bone is filled with soft tissue called **marrow.** Many of your blood cells are made by the marrow.

Layers of a bone

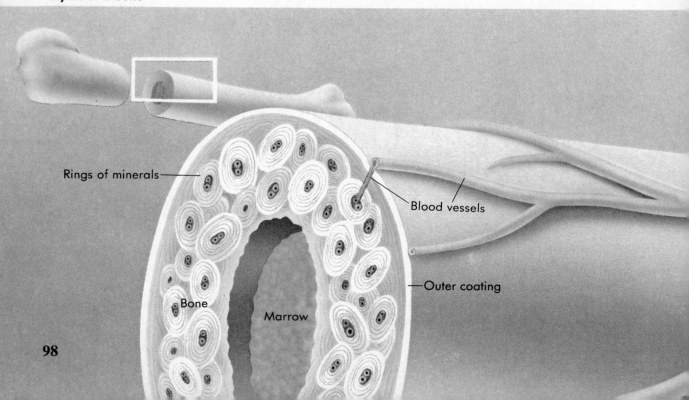

Rings of minerals

Blood vessels

Outer coating

Bone

Marrow

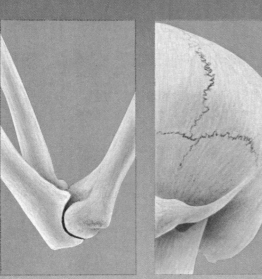

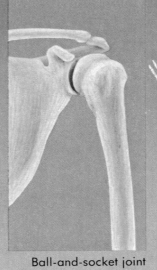

Hinge joint   Fixed joint   Ball-and-socket joint

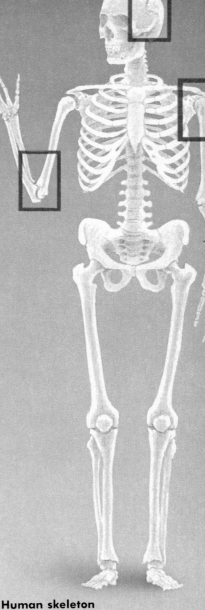

Human skeleton

Bones have different shapes. The shape of a bone is a clue to what the bone does. Your curved skull bones enclose your brain and protect it from injury. The hip or pelvic bone, shown in the skeleton picture, supports the weight of the upper body. Its wide, dishlike shape is perfect for giving this support. Your long, thin arm bone acts as a lever. The arm bone's shape makes it easy for you to lift and move things.

Your bones are connected to each other at the **joints.** Fixed joints do not allow your bones to move. The bones in a fixed joint fit together like puzzle pieces. Notice how the skeleton's skull bones join at fixed joints.

Other kinds of joints allow your bones to move in different ways. Your elbow allows your lower arm to swing back and forth like a door hinge. Find a hinge joint in the picture. Your upper arm can rotate in a circle. The ball-and-socket joint in your shoulder allows this circular motion. All moving bones are connected at joints by sheets of material—or **ligaments.**

joint, connection of two or more bones.

ligament (lig′ə mənt), a sheet of material that holds bones together at the joint.

99

cartilage (kär′tl ij), tough, flexible material that forms part of your skeleton.

Have You Heard?

Cartilage cushions the ends of your bones. It also gives you support. You can feel rings of cartilage that support your windpipe at the front of your neck. If you did not have this cartilage, your windpipe would close after you breathed out.

Baby's bones

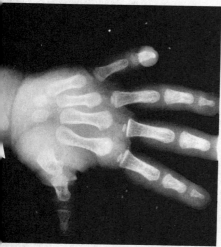

How Do Bones Grow?

Cartilage is a tough but flexible material found at the ends of many bones. Cartilage is softer than bone. You can feel the soft cartilage in your nose and ears. The cartilage at the ends of your bones keeps the bones from rubbing at the joints.

When you were very young, your bones were made almost entirely of cartilage. As you grow, bone cells replace most of the cartilage in your bones. Compare the X-ray pictures of the baby's bones, the 13-year-old's bones, and the adult's bones. Notice the small circle of bone next to the baby's larger arm bone. This part of the arm bone is surrounded by cartilage. Notice that the end of the 13-year-old's arm bone has enlarged, leaving a thin plate of cartilage between the two parts of the bone. In the adult's arm bone, the two parts of the arm bone have grown together.

Think About It

1. What are the three parts of your bones? What do they do?
2. Draw and label three types of joints. Describe how they move.
3. How do your bones grow?
4. **Challenge** What might happen to the bones of someone who does not get enough calcium?

13-year-old's bones

Adult's bones

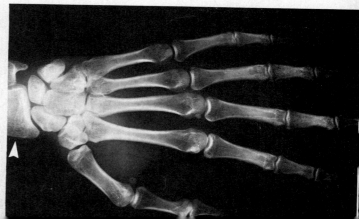

Discover!

Artificial Joints Help People Move

Pick up a pencil. Lift your foot. Raise your arm. These directions may sound simple, but many parts of your body must work together for you to make these movements. Your joints are parts of your body that help your bones move. With little effort, joints move bones in different directions. But some people's joints do not work well because of illness or injury. Their joints sometimes have to be replaced with artificial ones.

Joints look simple. You might think that scientists would have no trouble making artificial joints that work as well as real joints. After nearly a century of trying, scientists are just beginning to find ways of making artificial joints that work well.

What problems have to be solved in building an artificial joint? First, some joints have to be strong enough to support most of a person's weight. The first artificial hip-joint, built in 1891, failed because it

Artificial knee joint

could not hold up a person's weight.

Second, joints have to be flexible to allow movement in different directions.

Third, joints must be made of materials that the body will not reject. Usually, the body reacts to foreign substances by producing cells that attack and destroy the substances. To the body an artificial joint is a foreign substance that should be destroyed.

Scientists have finally found ways to solve these problems. The artificial

knee-joint in the picture is made of a special metal and plastic. The metal is a combination of silicon and stainless steel. The metal is strong, so it can support the weight of the body. The plastic is a strong, flexible material. It allows the joint to move easily. Medicines have been discovered that will prevent the body from rejecting the artificial joint. People who have lost the use of a joint may soon be able to get an artificial joint that works almost as well as the original one.

4 How Do Your Muscles Work?

Riding a bicycle, eating a peach, and watching a movie have something in common. They all require you to use your muscles. You feel your leg muscles pushing as you pedal a bicycle. When you eat a peach, your stomach muscles help break down your food. You use your eye muscles to follow action across a movie screen. If the movie is long, you might feel stiff when you get up to leave. Your muscles have worked hard the whole time to support you in your seat.

Muscles are made of thin strands called **muscle fibers.** The fibers of a muscle are cells that get shorter—or contract—when the muscle is being used. Notice how the upper arm muscle bulges as the person lifts the dumbbell. When the person lowers the dumbbell, the muscle relaxes. The muscle fibers return to their original length. All the movements of your body result from the contracting and relaxing of your muscles.

Many of your muscles are attached to bones. Strong connecting tissues—or **tendons**—attach the ends of your muscles to bones. You can feel the tendons that connect your upper arm muscle to your lower arm bone. Rest your elbow on your desk with your palm up. Raise your hand. The tendons feel like small, thin bones on the inside of your elbow.

Contracted upper arm muscle

Muscles that you decide to contract, such as your arm muscles, are **voluntary muscles.** Place the back of your hand on your desk. With your elbow on the desk, try to straighten your arm by pushing down on your desk with the back of your hand. Feel the contracted muscle in the back of your upper arm.

Voluntary muscles that are attached to bones, such as the ones in the pictures, usually work in pairs. The muscle on the back of the arm contracts to lower the bone. The muscle in front of the arm contracts to raise the bone.

Involuntary muscles that work without your thinking about them are in your stomach, your heart, your blood vessels, and other organs. If you did not have involuntary muscles, you would have to tell your heart when to beat and tell your stomach when to churn your food. You would have to think about your body so much that you would not have time to do anything else.

voluntary (vol′ən ter′ē) **muscle,** muscle that you can control.

involuntary (in vol′ən ter′ē) **muscle,** muscle that you need not control.

Find Out

The tendon that connects your calf muscle to a bone in your foot is called your Achilles' (ə kil′ēz) tendon. Look in an encyclopedia to find out why the tendon was said to be the downfall of the legendary Greek hero Achilles.

Think About It

1. What do muscle fibers do?
2. What kind of muscles move your bones? How?
3. What do involuntary muscles do? Why is it important that you do not need to control them?
4. **Challenge** Draw and label pictures of muscles bending and straightening your lower leg bone.

Muscles that work in pairs

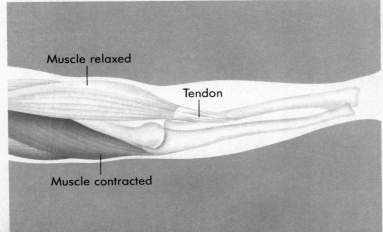

Muscle relaxed

Tendon

Muscle contracted

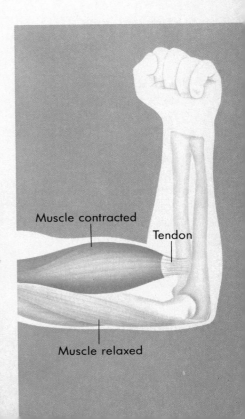

Muscle contracted

Tendon

Muscle relaxed

Activity

Making a Model of Arm Muscles

Purpose
To infer how muscles work in pairs by making a model of upper arm muscles.

You Will Need
- cardboard
- scissors
- paper punch
- paper fastener
- string
- tape

Directions
1. Ask a partner to trace your lower arm and hand on a piece of cardboard. Draw a rectangle about the same length and a little wider than your lower arm on another piece of cardboard. The rectangle will represent your upper arm. Cut out the shapes.
2. Punch holes in the upper and lower arm shapes as shown in picture *a*.

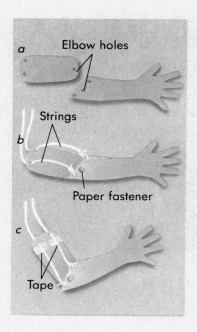

Elbow holes

Strings

Paper fastener

Tape

3. Join the 2 elbow holes with the paper fastener.
4. Thread the strings through the holes as shown in picture *b*. Secure the lower end of each string in a loop. Place a piece of tape over each string as in picture *c*. Pull the strings to loosen the tape.
5. Hold on to the back edge of the upper arm. Pull up on the string on the inside of the elbow, as shown in the picture.

6. Hold on to the front edge of the upper arm. Pull up on the string on the backside of the elbow.

Think About It
1. What happens when you raise the string at the inside of the elbow? What happens when you raise the other string?
2. Compare your arm muscles to the model, and explain how muscles work in pairs.
3. **Challenge** How does the lengthening and shortening of the string "muscles" compare to the length of your arm muscles when you move your lower arm?

Tie It Together

Sum It Up

1. Unscramble the names of the numbered structures in the skin. Describe what each structure does.

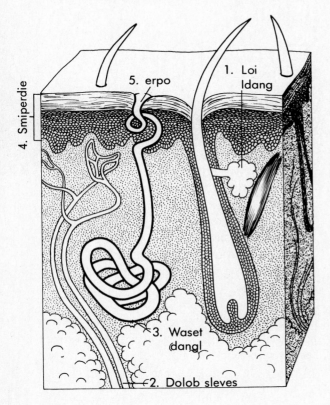

4. Smiperdie

5. erpo

1. Loi ldang

3. Waset dangl

2. Dolob sleves

2. Imagine you are a scientist who studies fossils. You have just found these two bones. Compare the bones with the skeleton picture on page 99. Draw a picture of how you think the bones you found fit together. Indicate the location of the muscles that would move the long bone in one direction and the location of the muscles that would move the bone in the opposite direction.

Challenge!

1. If you wear rubber gloves, you might notice moisture on your hands when you take off the gloves. Where does the moisture come from?

2. Even though small children often fall down, they seldom break their bones. Explain why their bones break less often than those of adults.

3. What kind of joint is your hip joint? How can you tell?

4. Why is it incorrect to say that you can ''stretch'' your muscles?

5. Name two places where voluntary muscles are not attached to bones. To what are these muscles attached?

Science Words

cartilage	ligament
dermis	marrow
epidermis	muscle fiber
involuntary muscle	tendon
joint	voluntary muscle

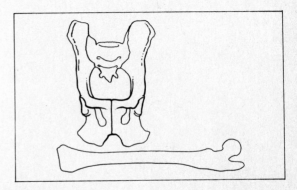

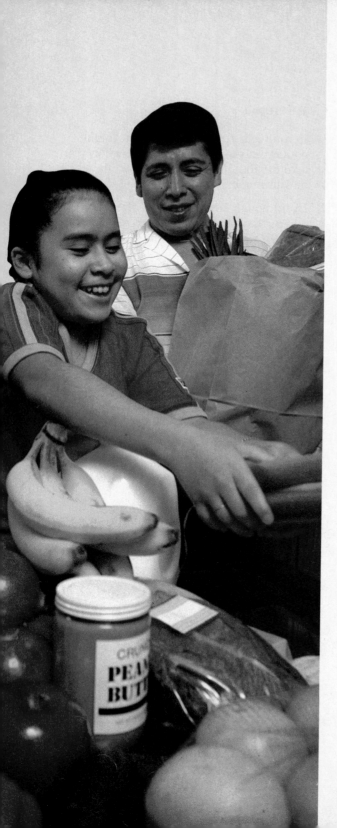

Chapter 7
Digestion and Excretion

This family has just come home from the grocery store. Most of the food that the family will eat this week is in the shopping bags. Compare these foods to the foods that your family eats. Most of the foods you eat are broken down by your digestive system. Digested food materials are absorbed into the blood. Your cells use the food materials to keep you healthy.

The lessons in this chapter will help you learn how your body processes the foods you eat.

1 Testing the Action of Saliva
2 How Does Your Body Digest Food?
3 How Does Your Body Get Rid of Wastes?

1 Testing the Action of Saliva

If you keep a soda cracker in your mouth for a while, the taste of the cracker changes. A chemical in your saliva changes the starch in the cracker into sugar. Find out how your saliva changes the tastes of foods.

First, use a paper towel to dry the tip of your tongue, as in the picture. Then, touch a small part of the cracker to your tongue, as shown. Notice how the cracker tastes. Now, remove the cracker from your mouth, and run your tongue along the side of your mouth to moisten your tongue with saliva. Touch the cracker to your tongue again. Note any changes in the taste of the cracker.

Hold a piece of cracker in your mouth without chewing it. Note any changes in the cracker.

Think About It

1. Compare the taste of the cracker when your tongue is dry to its taste when your tongue is wet.
2. Describe two ways the cracker changes after it has been in your mouth for a little while.
3. **Challenge** What does this lesson tell you about the way your taste buds work?

 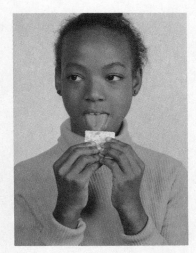

2 How Does Your Body Digest Food?

Think of what you ate for lunch yesterday. Perhaps you had a peanut butter sandwich, a glass of milk, and an apple. Like the people in the picture, you eat a wide variety of foods.

Foods are made of **nutrients**—or chemicals that your body needs. **Carbohydrates**—or starches and sugars—are one kind of nutrient. Bread is made mostly of carbohydrates. Peanut butter contains other nutrients, such as fats and proteins. Most foods also contain vitamins and minerals. Water is another nutrient found in most foods. Your body needs carbohydrates, fats, proteins, vitamins, minerals, and water to work properly and stay healthy.

Most nutrients are complicated chemicals. For example, notice the long chain that makes up the starch molecule in the picture. Before your body can use this molecule, the starch must be broken down to the simple molecule glucose. Compare the starch molecule's shape to the simple shape of the glucose molecule that your body actually uses.

Digestion is the process of breaking down complicated chemicals in nutrients into forms that the body can use. Special substances—**enzymes**—aid digestion by speeding up the chemical breakdown of your food.

Healthful lunches

nutrient (nü′trē ənt), a food chemical that the body needs. Carbohydrates, proteins, fats, vitamins, minerals, and water are all nutrients.

carbohydrate (kär′bō hī′drāt), starch or sugar.

enzyme (en′zīm), substance that speeds up chemical changes.

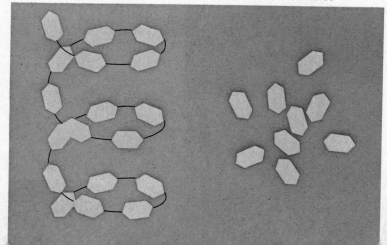

Starch molecule   Glucose molecules

Digestion begins in your mouth. When you chew, your teeth break your food into smaller pieces. Saliva mixes with the food to make it soft and moist. An enzyme in saliva begins breaking down the carbohydrates in the food. Your tongue moves the food around and forms it into a soft ball that you swallow.

When you swallow, food moves from your throat down a muscular tube—or **esophagus**—to your stomach. Find the stomach in the picture. Your stomach is a thick-walled, muscular pouch that stretches when full and folds up when empty. The wrinkled inner surface of the stomach in the picture stretches and becomes smooth when the stomach is full of food.

Glands in the walls of your stomach release different substances that help you digest your food. Some glands release hydrochloric (hī/drə klôr/ik) acid that kills many harmful organisms in your food. The hydrochloric acid also clumps proteins together and begins breaking them down. Other glands make enzymes that further digest proteins.

The muscular walls of your stomach contract and relax, mixing your food with fluids from your stomach's glands. The lining of your stomach is coated with a sticky body fluid—**mucus**—that protects your stomach from strong acids and enzymes.

Have You Heard?

The gurgling sound in your stomach can be quite loud at times. This sound is caused by gases that form during digestion and get trapped in your stomach.

esophagus (ē sof/ə gəs), passage for food from the throat to the stomach.

mucus (myü/kəs), a sticky body fluid.

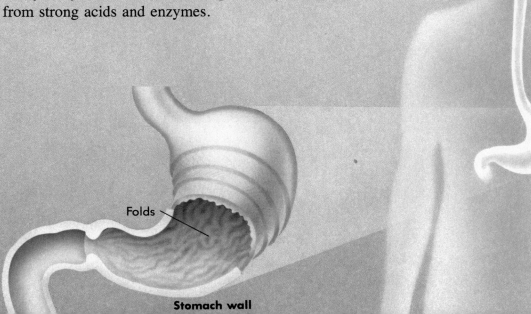

Stomach

Folds

Stomach wall

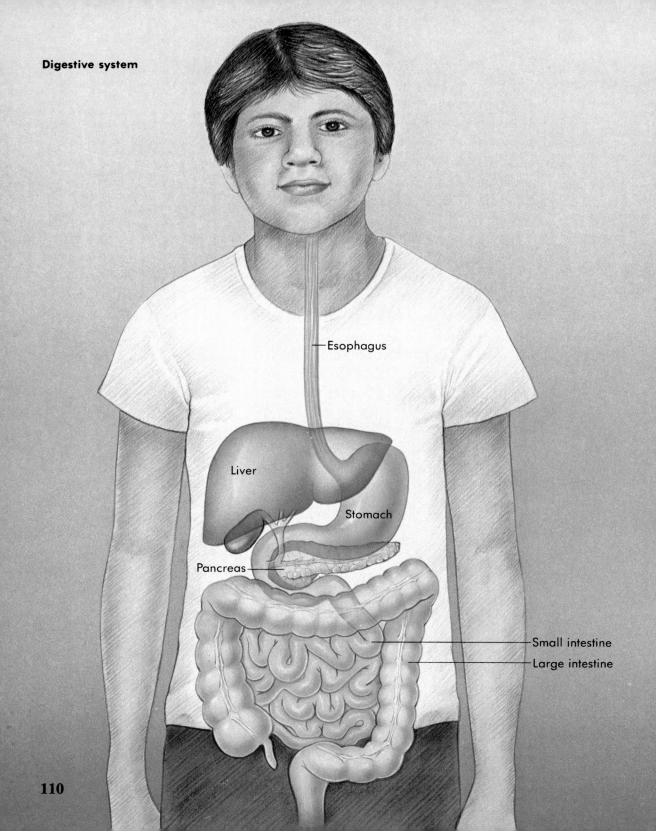

Digestive system

Esophagus

Liver

Stomach

Pancreas

Small intestine

Large intestine

What Happens to Food in Your Small Intestine?

After digesting in your stomach for several hours, your food becomes a pastelike mixture. Muscles in your stomach squeeze a small amount of the mixture into a long tube—the **small intestine.**

Glands in the walls of your small intestine make enzymes that continue the breakdown of carbohydrates and proteins that began in the mouth and stomach. Another organ—the **pancreas**—releases other enzymes into the small intestine. The picture of the digestive system shows the pancreas behind the stomach and intestines. The pancreas's enzymes enter the small intestine through an opening beneath the stomach. These enzymes help digest carbohydrates, proteins, and fats.

Notice the liver, the large, red organ above the stomach. The liver makes **bile**—a fluid that breaks fats into small droplets which can be digested. Bile is released into the small intestine.

The breakdown of food in the small intestine takes four to eight hours. When digestion is completed, food materials are in a thin, watery form that can be absorbed into the bloodstream. Notice the inner surface of the small intestine in the picture below. Each of the tiny fibers of this carpetlike surface has tiny blood vessels that absorb nutrients.

small intestine (in tes′tən), the narrow, winding tube where digestion of foods is completed.

pancreas (pan′krē əs), a large gland that releases digestive enzymes into the small intestine.

bile (bīl), a liquid made by the liver that helps break up fats.

Have You Heard?

The length of the small intestine is about 5 times your height. The small intestine is coiled and folded, so it can fit in a space smaller than the size of this book.

Inner surface of small intestine

111

large intestine, the wide tube of the digestive system where water, vitamins, and minerals are absorbed and wastes are eliminated.

What Happens to Undigested Foods?

Food that is not absorbed from your small intestine moves on to a wide tube—your **large intestine.** Vitamins, minerals, and water from your digestive fluids are absorbed by the large intestine. Much water is used to make digestive fluids. If your large intestine did not absorb the water, your cells would dry up, and you would die.

The remaining unabsorbed materials are in the form of solid wastes. Your large intestine passes the wastes out of the body.

With your finger, trace the path the student's peanut butter sandwich would take through the digestive system in the picture. From the moment you begin to eat, your digestive system starts breaking down your food. Even when you are not eating, your digestive organs continue to absorb nutrients that help keep you healthy.

Think About It

1. Why does the food you eat need to be digested?
2. Describe how the organs of the digestive system help digest food.
3. **Challenge** Are the liver and pancreas part of the digestive system? Explain your answer.

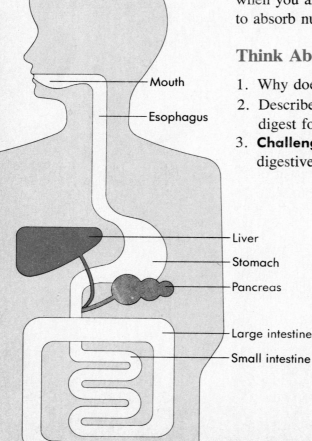

Mouth

Esophagus

Liver

Stomach

Pancreas

Large intestine

Small intestine

Eating lunch

Activity

Observing Acid and Enzyme Action on Milk

Purpose
To observe the breakdown of proteins by an acid and by an enzyme.

You Will Need
- unseasoned meat tenderizer (an enzyme)
- white vinegar (a weak acid)
- small glass of whole milk
- 3 small plastic cups
- medicine dropper
- drinking straw
- plastic wrap
- 3 rubber bands
- small plastic spoon

Directions
1. Number 3 small plastic cups 1 through 3.
2. Fill each cup half full of milk, as shown in the pictures.
3. Cover cup 1 with plastic wrap, and secure the plastic with a rubber band.
4. Put 20 to 30 drops of vinegar into cup 2, as in the picture. Stir the milk and vinegar with a straw. Observe and record any changes in the milk. Cover the cup with plastic as in step 3. Throw away the straw.
5. Put a spoonful of meat tenderizer into the milk in cup 3 as shown. Stir the milk and meat tenderizer. Observe and record any changes in the milk. Cover the cup with plastic as you did before.
6. Let the cups of milk sit overnight. Observe the changes in the milk, and record your observations. Throw away the milk.

Think About It
1. What happened when you stirred the milk and vinegar?
2. What happened when you stirred the milk and meat tenderizer? How did the milk in cup 3 change overnight?
3. What difference did you notice in the ways the vinegar and the meat tenderizer acted?
4. **Challenge** Which substance in your stomach is like the vinegar? Which substance is like the meat tenderizer?

3 How Does Your Body Get Rid of Wastes?

Poison! The skull and crossbones in the picture warns you that the chemicals in the bottle are harmful. Even a small amount can kill you. But any chemical, even a nutrient, can be poisonous if too much enters your blood at one time.

You can digest and absorb many substances that would harm you if they reached all of your cells. Your liver removes these harmful substances from your blood. The liver can change weak poisons that are absorbed by the blood into chemicals that cannot harm you. Alcohol in liquor is one poison that, in small amounts, the liver can change.

The liver also removes the excess glucose that your blood absorbs and stores the glucose until it is needed by your cells. Notice the compartments in the liver. The blood flows through these compartments to be cleaned of weak poisons and excess glucose.

Find Out

You can find out what the liver looks like. Your grocer probably sells fresh beef liver in the meat department. Notice the size and weight of the liver, and its dark-red color.

Poisonous substance

Liver compartments

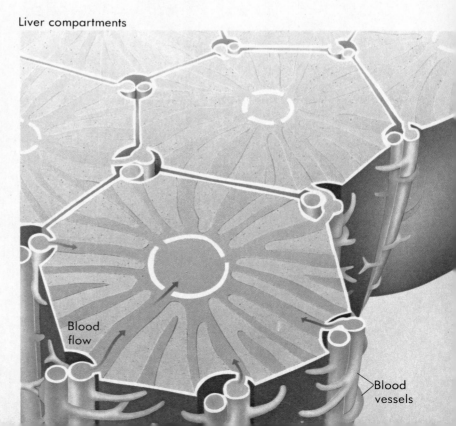

Blood flow

Blood vessels

The liver also removes old blood cells and uses them in making bile. After the bile helps break up the fats in the small intestine, it passes to the large intestine and then leaves your body with the rest of the solid wastes.

Your liver cleans your blood after the blood has absorbed nutrients from the digestive system. Your body cells use these nutrients and produce wastes that dissolve in the blood. Your kidneys remove—or **excrete**—the dissolved wastes.

Find the bean-shaped kidneys in the picture. Tiny blood vessels in your kidneys carry your blood through very small, tubelike filters. Extra minerals, vitamins, water, and other body wastes pass from the blood into the filters. The wastes are collected by the filters in the form of **urine,** a liquid waste.

Urine leaves each kidney through a tube that leads to a thin-walled, expandable sac—the **bladder.** When the bladder is full, tiny muscles in the wall of the bladder contract. Then, urine is released into a small tube that leads out of the body.

Think About It

1. What are three materials your liver removes from your blood?
2. Trace the path that body wastes take through your kidneys and out of your body.
3. **Challenge** How do poisons that have been made harmless by the liver leave the body?

excrete (ek skrēt′), to remove from the body the wastes that are dissolved in the blood.

urine (yür′ən), liquid waste produced by the kidneys.

bladder (blad′ər), sac that stores urine until the urine passes out of the body.

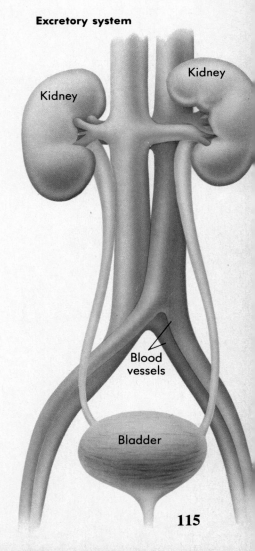

Excretory system

Kidney

Kidney

Blood vessels

Bladder

Do You Know?

Machines Can Clean Blood

Your kidneys work day and night, removing wastes from your blood. An adult's kidney cleans about 180 liters of blood every 24 hours! But sometimes a person's kidneys do not work as well as they should. More than 13 million people in the United States have kidney problems. Many people with kidney disease must use a machine, such as the one in the picture, to do the work that their own kidneys can no longer do.

The drawing shows how the kidney machine works. Special plastic-tubes are inserted into a person's blood vessels. These tubes carry blood to and from the kidney machine. The blood is pumped from the person's blood vessel into coiled tubes in the machine that are bathed in a liquid similar to the liquid part of the blood. The walls of the coiled tubes are made of a thin material with tiny holes. The holes allow some substances to pass out of the coiled tubes and into the surrounding liquid.

As blood moves through the coiled tubes, wastes move out of the blood, through the holes, and into the solution. Proteins, sugars, and other essential substances remain in the blood. The cleaned blood is returned to the person through another blood vessel. All of the blood in the person's body must pass through the machine many times before the treatment is finished.

People who use kidney machines must do so twice a week. Most people go to hospitals for treatment. However, engineers are now making smaller kidney-machines that people can use at home.

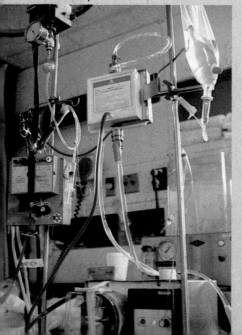

Kidney machine

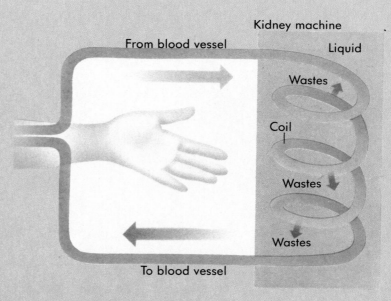

Kidney machine

From blood vessel

Liquid

Wastes

Coil

Wastes

Wastes

To blood vessel

Tie It Together

Sum It Up

1. Write a story describing the journey a peanut butter sandwich would take through your digestive system. Try to include the science words in lesson 2 and the words *fats, protein, mineral, vitamin, mouth, saliva, stomach, liver, and water*. Draw pictures to go with your story.

2. Several hours later, the peanut butter sandwich has been digested and absorbed into your blood. Write a second chapter to your story. Include the answers to the following questions. What happens to your blood when it reaches your liver? What happens to your blood after your cells have used the nutrients you digested? How is your blood cleaned by your kidneys? What happens to the wastes that are removed by your kidneys? Include drawings.

Challenge!

1. Why do your stomach cells need protection from digestive enzymes?

2. The inner surface of your small intestine is covered with tiny fibers that absorb food. If the inner surface were flat, would it take more time or less time for your small intestine to absorb food? Explain your answer.

3. Severe liver damage can be fatal. Explain why.

4. How does drinking large amounts of water affect your urine? Explain.

5. How do digestion and excretion work together in your body?

Science Words

bile

bladder

carbohydrate

enzyme

esophagus

excrete

large intestine

mucus

nutrient

pancreas

small intestine

urine

Chapter 8
Respiration and Circulation

On your mark! Get set! Go! The potato-sack race is on. You feel your heart pounding as you hop toward the finish line. Your face gets flushed. It is a close race. You breathe faster and faster. You cross the finish line, panting and laughing at the same time.

The lessons in this chapter describe how your body gets energy for all your activities.

1 Measuring the Air You Exhale

When you take a deep breath to blow up a balloon, you realize how much air your lungs can hold. You can compare the amounts of air you exhale during normal and deep breathing.

Press a plastic bag flat to get out all the air. Put a drinking straw halfway into the bag, and secure it with a rubber band, as in the picture.

Breathe out normally through the straw. Then, quickly clasp the plastic bag just below the straw so that no air escapes. Push the exhaled air to the bottom of the plastic bag, as shown. Tie off the bag. Remove the straw and rubber band.

Take a second plastic bag, and insert the straw as before. Breathe deeply, and then exhale all the air you can into the plastic bag. Push the air to the bottom of the bag, and tie off the bag.

Think About It

1. Compare the sizes of the blown up parts of the two plastic bags.
2. **Challenge** Estimate the difference between the amounts of air you exhale during normal and deep breathing.

119

2 How Do You Breathe?

Have You Heard?
Most of the time, your diaphragm moves automatically with a natural rhythm. However, sometimes this rhythm is interrupted. The diaphragm's uneven movement might give you the hiccups.

You can live for weeks without food and for days without water. But you can only live for minutes without oxygen. Your respiratory system helps get oxygen from the air into your blood.

Several muscles help you breathe. Notice the dome-shaped muscle beneath the lungs. This muscle—the **diaphragm**—lowers as it contracts, and you begin to inhale. At the same time, muscles between your ribs pull your ribs up and out. Feel your ribcage move as you take a deep breath.

As your diaphragm lowers and your ribcage expands, the space inside your lungs enlarges. Air from outside rushes in to fill the space. When your lungs are full of fresh air, your diaphragm and the muscles between your ribs relax. The space inside your lungs becomes smaller. The air inside your lungs is squeezed out and you exhale.

Respiratory system

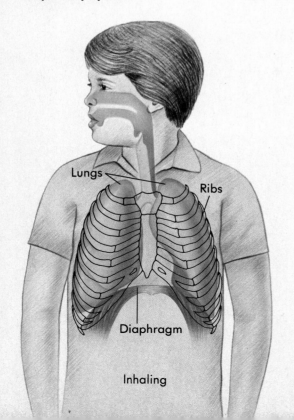

Inhaling

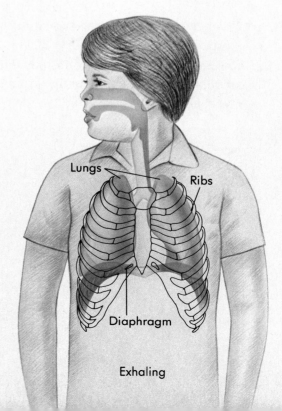

Exhaling

With your fingers, trace the path air would follow in the picture. Air normally enters your respiratory system through your nose. Small hairs in your nose filter out dust. A sticky lining of mucus coats the inside of your nose. Mucus captures some bacteria and the dirt in the air you breathe. In your nose the air becomes warmed to the temperature of your body.

Next, the cleaned, warm air travels through the back of the mouth and down your throat. Food and air travel together down the throat for part of the way. Then, the windpipe—or **trachea**—and the esophagus branch off from the throat passage. Notice the flap of cartilage—the **epiglottis**—above the trachea. The epiglottis covers the trachea and prevents food from getting into your lungs when you swallow. When you are not swallowing, the epiglottis rests above the trachea allowing air to move in and out of the lungs.

The voice box—or **larynx**—is the next structure the air passes through. When you swallow, you can feel your larynx move up and down. Two soft folds of tissue—the vocal cords—are inside the larynx. When exhaled air passes up through the larynx, the vocal cords vibrate. If you hold your fingers on your throat, like the person in the picture, you can feel your vocal cords vibrating as you talk.

trachea (trā′kē ə), windpipe.

epiglottis (ep′ə glot′is), the flap of cartilage that covers the entrance to the trachea during swallowing.

larynx (lar′ingks), the upper end of the human trachea, containing the vocal cords.

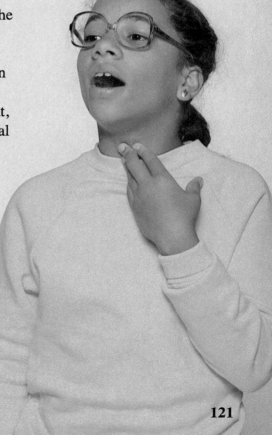

Feeling vocal cord vibrations

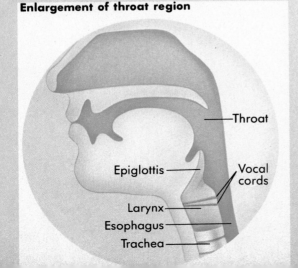

Enlargement of throat region

—Throat

Epiglottis—

Vocal cords

Larynx—

Esophagus—

Trachea—

Find Out

The chemicals in cigarette smoke can damage the lungs. Write to your local chapter of the American Lung Association for information on how cigarette smoke can affect the lungs.

What Happens in Your Lungs?

From the larynx, air continues down the trachea which divides into two main tubes leading to the lungs. Follow these air tubes as they branch into smaller and smaller tubes inside the lungs. Each tiny tube ends in a cluster of tiny air sacs, as shown in the picture. When you inhale, the air rushes into the air sacs, which expand like tiny balloons.

Each lung contains about a million air sacs. Even when you exhale, your air sacs are not totally empty. The air that is always in your air sacs helps you float when you swim.

Enlarged view of air sacs

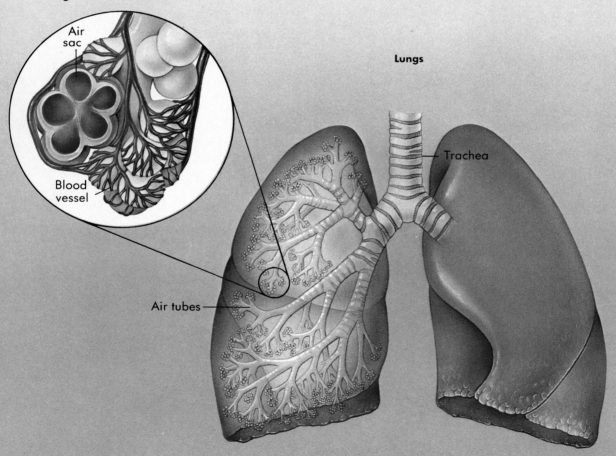

Air sac

Blood vessel

Lungs

Trachea

Air tubes

Bubbles of exhaled gases

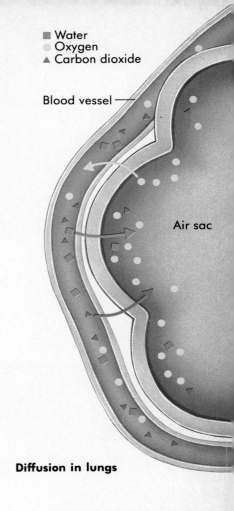

- Water
- Oxygen
- Carbon dioxide

Blood vessel

Air sac

Diffusion in lungs

Find the tiny blood vessels surrounding the air sacs in the lungs. The blood in these vessels contains little oxygen. The air in the air sacs contains much oxygen. Oxygen naturally moves from an area where there is more oxygen to an area where there is less oxygen. This kind of movement is called **diffusion.** Oxygen diffuses from your air sacs into the blood vessels in your lungs.

The drawing describes the movement of oxygen, carbon dioxide, and water particles in the air sacs of the lungs. As oxygen diffuses from the air sacs into the blood, carbon dioxide and water diffuse from the blood into the air sacs. When you exhale, you excrete carbon dioxide and water from your lungs.

When you go swimming, you can sometimes see the gases you exhale. Find the bubbles in the picture, rising from the swimmer's mouth. These bubbles contain the carbon dioxide gas the person exhales.

Think About It

1. How do your muscles work to move air in and out of your lungs?
2. Describe the passage of inhaled air through the respiratory system.
3. **Challenge** What happens in your trachea when food goes down the wrong pipe?

diffusion (di fyü′zhən), movement of particles from an area having more of those particles to an area having less of those particles.

3 What Does Your Circulatory System Do?

Long ago, people thought they could cure a sick person by causing the person to bleed. Doctors in the Middle Ages thought a sick person had bad blood. They thought when a person was bled, the bad blood was let out of the body. The man in the drawing is receiving this often-harmful treatment. Today, we realize that the blood, which circulates through the body, nourishes the body cells and keeps them healthy.

Blood consists of two parts. The blood in the test tube in the picture is separated into its two parts. The yellow fluid—**plasma**—is mostly water. Nutrients, some oxygen, and waste products are dissolved in the blood plasma. You might notice yellow fluid oozing out from a scab if you scrape yourself.

plasma (plaz′mə), the yellow, fluid part of blood.

Blood-drawing in the 1500s

Parts of the blood

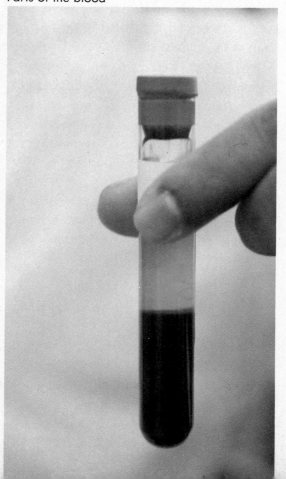

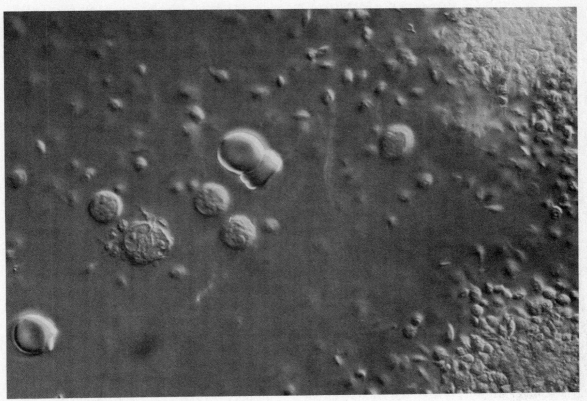
Blood cells and platelets

The thick, red mixture at the bottom of the test tube consists of the blood cells that make up the second part of your blood. The picture shows a close up view of blood cells. The smooth, disk-shaped cells are **red blood cells** that carry most of the oxygen in your blood.

Find the round, rough-surfaced cells in the picture. These **white blood cells** protect you from disease. White blood cells surround and destroy harmful organisms that might make you ill.

Notice the tiny specks in the picture of the blood cells. These specks—or **platelets**—form from pieces of cells. The platelets release a substance that helps a blood clot form if you cut yourself. The blood clot acts like a plug to keep your blood from draining out of your cut blood vessel.

red blood cell, a cell that carries oxygen in the blood.

white blood cell, a cell that protects you from disease.

platelets (plāt′lits), cell pieces that release a substance which helps form a blood clot.

Have You Heard?

When you look at the inner side of your arm, you can see the blood vessels near the surface of your skin. Some blood vessels look blue through your skin. The blood that these vessels carry, however, is a deep red color.

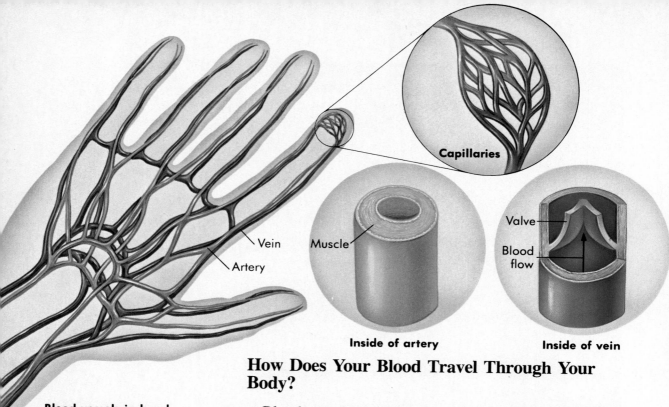

Capillaries

Muscle

Inside of artery

Valve

Blood flow

Inside of vein

Vein

Artery

Blood vessels in hand

artery (är′tər ē), a blood vessel that carries blood away from the heart.

capillary (kap′ə ler′ē), a tiny blood vessel that allows wastes, oxygen, and nutrients to pass between the blood and the cells.

vein (vān), a blood vessel that carries blood to the heart.

valve (valv), a structure in the veins or heart made of 2 flaps of tissue that prevent blood from flowing backwards.

How Does Your Blood Travel Through Your Body?

Blood vessels carry blood to and from all your cells. Notice the three kinds of blood vessels in the hand. The blood vessels that carry blood away from the heart are called **arteries.** Notice that the walls of the arteries are lined with muscles which contract to push the blood along. You feel the contraction of the artery walls when you take your pulse.

Arteries connect to tiny blood vessels—the **capillaries.** Red blood cells must flow through the capillaries in single file, since the capillaries are so narrow. Capillaries are present near all your cells. Thin capillary walls allow nutrients to move from the blood into the cells. The cells' wastes move through the capillary walls into the blood.

Veins connect to capillaries and return the blood to the heart. Blood moves slowly through the veins. Find the two flaps of tissue—or **valve**—in the vein picture. Valves keep blood moving toward the heart by preventing blood from flowing backwards.

The heart, shown in the picture, is a powerful, muscular organ. When the heart muscles contract, blood is pumped to the lungs and other parts of the body. Notice that the heart is divided down the middle into two pumps, a right pump and a left pump. Each pump has two chambers, separated by valves similar to the valves in the veins.

Two large veins enter the top, right chamber of the heart, bringing blood that has been used by the cells. This blood must be resupplied with oxygen. Locate the bottom chamber of the heart's right pump. This chamber pushes the blood through an artery that branches into capillaries in the lungs.

In the lungs, oxygen diffuses into the blood, and carbon dioxide and water diffuse out of the blood. The blood is ready to be used by the cells. Find the veins that bring the oxygen-rich blood back to the top, left chamber of the heart. Next, the blood flows into the bottom chamber of the left pump. From here, the heart pumps the blood into the main artery that divides and carries the blood throughout the body.

Have You Heard?

Place your hand over your heart. You probably placed your hand on the left side of your upper chest. However, the heart is in the very center of the chest, directly under the breastbone. The heart is tilted so that the strong, lower heart muscles stick out under your left ribs. This is why you feel your heart beating more strongly on the left side.

Human heart and lungs

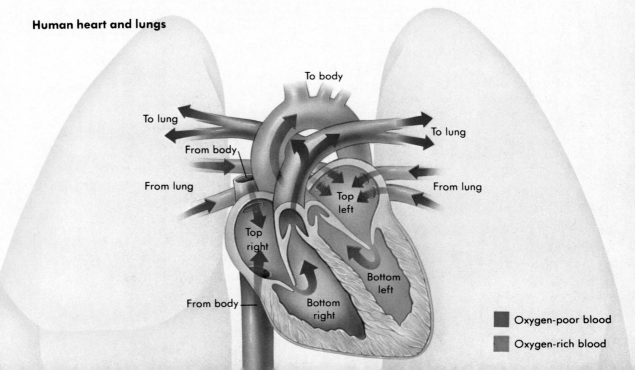

To body

To lung

From body

To lung

From lung

From lung

Top left

Top right

Bottom left

From body

Bottom right

Oxygen-poor blood

Oxygen-rich blood

Circulatory system

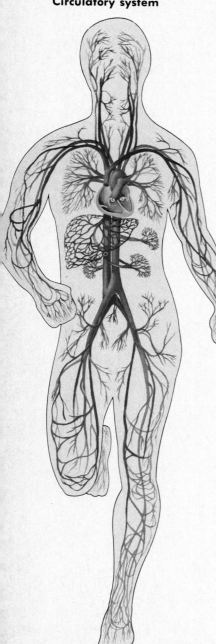

Where Does Your Blood Go?

Arteries carry oxygen-rich blood to all organs of your body. Different organs receive different amounts of blood. Find the organs in the chart that receive the most blood.

The digestive system receives one-fourth of the body's oxygen-rich blood. The blood in the capillaries of your small intestine pick up nutrients that are used by all your cells.

Your voluntary muscles need a lot of energy to help you move. One-fifth of your body's oxygen-rich blood flows to these muscles. The rest of the blood is pumped to your brain, skin, heart, kidneys, and other parts of the body.

The picture shows how arteries, capillaries, and veins form a network through your body. The blood continuously flows through your circulatory system to bring oxygen and nutrients to your cells and to carry away the cells' wastes.

Circulation of blood through the body

Body System	Approximate percentage of blood from heart
Digestive system	25%
Voluntary muscles	20%
Kidneys	20%
Brain	14%
Skin	9%
Heart	5%

Think About It

1. Describe the two parts of blood.
2. Describe arteries, veins, and capillaries and tell what each kind of blood vessel does.
3. Trace the path of blood through the heart and lungs.
4. **Challenge** How does moving your muscles help circulate your blood?

Activity

Examining the Effects of Exercise

Purpose
To measure heart rate and breathing rate before and after exercise.

You Will Need
• open area for free movement
• watch or clock with second hand

Directions
1. Work with 2 other students to observe and record the effects of exercise on your heart and breathing rates. One student will be the observer. The other student will be the recorder.
2. Make a chart so you can record your pulse and breathing rates per minute after resting, walking, and running.
3. Ask the observer to measure your resting heart rate by taking your pulse when you are relaxed. The observer will place 2 fingertips just under your jaw to find the pulse in your neck, as shown in the picture. The observer will count your pulse for 30 seconds, while the recorder keeps time. Multiply the pulse the observer counted by 2 to find your pulse rate for 1 minute. Write this rate on your chart.
4. Count the number of breaths you take during 30 seconds. The recorder will keep time. Multiply the number of breaths by 2 to get the breathing rate for 1 minute. Record this rate.
5. Walk around slowly for 2 minutes, as timed by the recorder. Then, record your pulse and breathing rate as before.
6. Run in place for 2 minutes. Ask the observer and recorder to take and record your pulse and breathing rate again.
7. Switch jobs, and repeat steps 1–6 for the other 2 students.

Think About It
1. Compare your resting pulse and breathing rate to your pulse and breathing rate after you walked.
2. How did these rates change after you ran?
3. **Challenge** How do a faster breathing and pulse rate help you when you exercise?

4 How Do Your Cells Get Energy?

Some days you wake up and jump out of bed. The sun shining outside your window makes you want to sing. You skip into the kitchen and greet your family with a smile. On days like these you feel as if you have extra energy.

However you feel, your body is always using energy. The living epidermis cells of your skin use energy to replace the dead cells that peel off. Marrow cells in your bones use energy to make some of your blood cells. Muscle cells need energy to contract. Besides needing energy for their special jobs, all cells need energy to grow and repair themselves.

The burning candles in the picture use oxygen to release heat and light energy. Your cells also use oxygen to release energy. The process that cells use to release energy is called cell respiration.

In cell respiration, oxygen and glucose undergo chemical changes to release certain products. Find the products of the reaction in the word equation. Energy is the useful product released by cell respiration. Carbon dioxide and water also result from this reaction.

Respiration

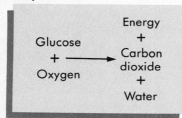

Glucose + Oxygen → Energy + Carbon dioxide + Water

Light energy from burning candles

The arrows in the picture show the movement of glucose, oxygen, carbon dioxide, and water in and out of the cell. Notice that the cell is next to a capillary. The blood carries glucose and oxygen to all the cells and removes the carbon dioxide and water the cells do not need.

The systems of the body must all work together to provide the cells with energy. The digestive system breaks down food. The respiratory system provides oxygen. The circulatory system carries nutrients and oxygen to the cells and removes wastes. The lungs, kidneys, and skin excrete the wastes from the body. Your body systems work together to keep your cells alive and healthy.

Think About It

1. Describe five ways your cells might use energy.
2. Write and explain the word equation that describes cell respiration.
3. **Challenge** How would a lack of food affect respiration in your cells?

Have You Heard?

Sometimes when you exercise, your muscle cells cannot get enough oxygen. The muscle cells must get extra energy from a process that does not require oxygen. A waste that results from this process builds up in your muscle cells and makes your muscles ache.

Cell respiration

Capillary

Oxygen

Glucose

Cell

Water

Carbon dioxide

Energy

131

Do You Know?

Donated Blood Can Save Lives

Emergency! A woman has cut herself and is losing blood rapidly! The bleeding must be stopped, and the lost blood must be replaced quickly.

A scene such as this one is not unusual in a hospital. Loss of blood is one of the most dangerous conditions an injured person faces. How does a hospital, such as the one in the picture, handle this kind of emergency?

Most hospitals can get blood from a blood bank. People donate a pint of their blood to the blood bank. Medical workers run tests on the donated blood to classify the blood into one of four groups: type A, type B, type AB, or type O.

Blood of some types cannot mix with other types without forming clumps of blood cells. When a medical worker gives a transfusion, he or she must use a type of blood that will not clump in the person receiving the transfusion.

But donated blood stays healthy for only several weeks unless the blood cells are separated from the liquid plasma. The plasma can be stored for long periods of time.

In the early 1940s, Dr. Charles Drew discovered how to store blood plasma. Dr. Drew also discovered that, for most transfusions, plasma works as well as blood that contains blood cells. Before Dr. Drew learned how to store plasma for transfusions, injured people often died simply because the right kind of blood was not in storage or immediately available to them. Dr. Drew's discoveries have saved many lives.

Surgery requires blood transfusion

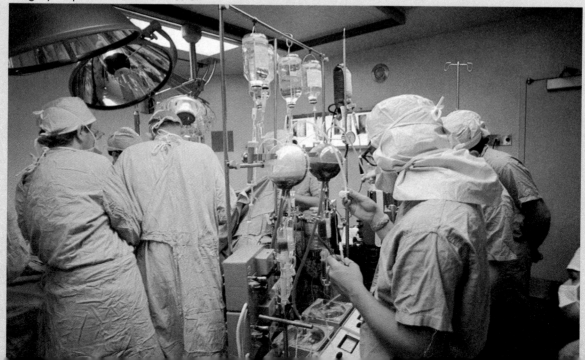

Tie It Together

Sum It Up

Number your paper from 1-9. Next to each number, unscramble the words to complete the sentences. Unscramble the bold letters to solve the riddle in the picture.

1. When you elihan the diaphragm muscle lowers and the srbi move up and out. The space densii your gunls enlarges. Air rushes in to fill the space.

2. The air enters the enso, where scuum removes dirt and bacteria and the air is warmed to body temperature.

3. Air and food pass together down the throat until the arectha and the esophagus split off. The stipoletig prevents food from entering the lungs.

4. The air passes through the nalrxy, which has two vocal cords that can vibrate when you lehexa.

5. The air flows into the lungs through tubes that end in ira scas. Plicarelais surround the air sacs.

6. Oegynx-orop blood is pumped from the heart to the lungs. In the lungs the blood picks up exongy.

7. The blood returns from the lungs to the heart through large inevs. The heart then pumps the blood through trearesi, which carry the blood to the rest of the body.

8. Cells use the untrenist transported in the laspam of the blood. Taplestel help form blood clots. Thewi dlobo sclel destroy harmful organisms in your body. Edr oblod clels carry oxygen in the blood.

9. Cells use oxygen and glucose carried in your blood to release energy. Carbon dioxide and water are excreted as swatse.

Challenge!

1. It is healthier for you to breathe through your nose than through your mouth. Explain why.

2. If someone were choking on a piece of food, why would the lack of voice be a sign that the person was not getting air into the lungs?

3. Why is it incorrect to say that all arteries carry oxygen-rich blood and all veins carry oxygen-poor blood?

4. Explain the difference between breathing and cell respiration.

Science Words

artery	platelets
capillary	red blood cell
diaphragm	trachea
diffusion	valve
epiglottis	vein
larynx	white blood cell
plasma	

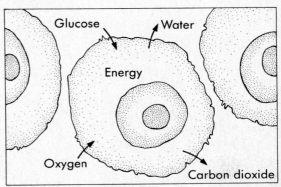

I give you energy for life.

Laboratory

Measuring the Carbon Dioxide That You Exhale

a

Purpose
To observe that exercise affects the amount of carbon dioxide which you exhale.

You Will Need
- limewater
- large clear jar
- tape
- 2 straws
- clock with second hand

Stating the Problem
The cells in your body release energy for all your activities. Water and carbon dioxide gas are produced as wastes. You can infer how much energy your body uses when you do different activities by measuring the amount of carbon dioxide that you exhale.

Predict how exercise would affect the amount of carbon dioxide that you exhale. Would the amount of carbon dioxide that you exhale increase or decrease after exercise? Write down your prediction and reasons for it.

Investigating the Problem
1. Half fill a clean jar with limewater. Mark the level of limewater with a piece of tape on the outside of the jar. Place a straw in the limewater, as shown in picture *a*.
2. Limewater turns milky when it mixes with carbon dioxide. Ask a partner to time how long it takes for the limewater to become milky as you blow through the straw. See picture *b*. Record the time. *CAUTION: Do not allow any limewater to get into your mouth. Swallowing limewater might make you ill.*

b

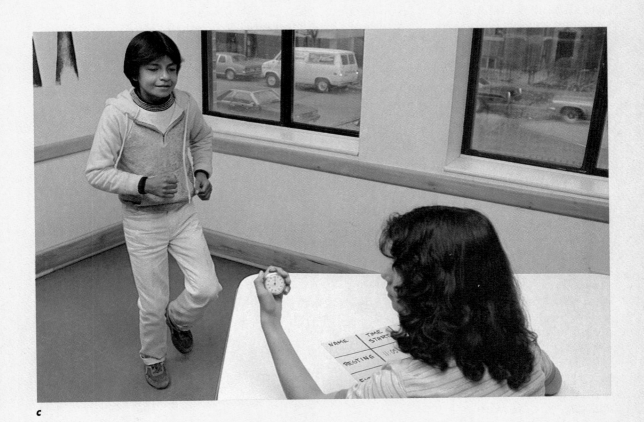

c

3. Discard the milky limewater. Wash and dry the jar. Refill the jar with fresh limewater, as in step 1. Place a clean straw in the jar.
4. Jump rope or run in place for 1 minute, as shown in picture c.
5. Ask your partner to keep track of the time as you exhale into the limewater. Stop exhaling when the limewater turns milky.

Record the time.
6. Keep track of time for your partner as he or she repeats the activity.

Making Conclusions
1. How did exercise change the amount of carbon dioxide that you exhaled? Was your prediction correct?
2. How long do you think

it would take for limewater to turn milky when you exhale into it after running for 3 minutes? Explain your answer.
3. Imagine that you could use a device that would allow you to exhale into limewater as you slept. Would it take longer for the limewater to turn milky than in step 2? Explain your answer.

135

Careers

Blood-Bank Technologist

"Gee, giving blood was easier than I thought."

"Most people say that the first time they donate blood," says Alicia. Alicia is a blood-bank technologist with the American Red Cross. "Blood banking is the collecting, testing, and storing of blood. Every time people donate blood, technologists test a sample. The tests help us classify the blood by its type. We also test blood for disease organisms and iron content.

"It takes about eight hours to do all the tests on the blood samples. We want to be sure of our results. We provide blood to hospitals all over the city. People who need blood depend on our careful work."

During an operation, a patient may lose some blood. This blood is replaced by blood from the blood bank that matches the patient's type. Many operations would be impossible without these extra blood supplies.

Alicia says her interest in science began in grade school. "The teacher brought in some lungs from a lamb. She explained how the lungs work and how the blood circulates. I became more and more interested in how the human body works. Later, I went to college to study medical technology and blood banking.

"Many exciting developments are taking place in blood banking. Blood must be refrigerated and can be stored for only a limited period of time. In 1970, blood could be kept for only 21 days. In 1982, it could be stored for 30 days. Soon, we will be able to keep blood for 45 days or longer.

"Scientists are also finding ways to change blood types of donated blood. So, a patient with a rare blood type has a better chance of getting blood.

"I think I have one of the best jobs in the world. I work to help people who are ill."

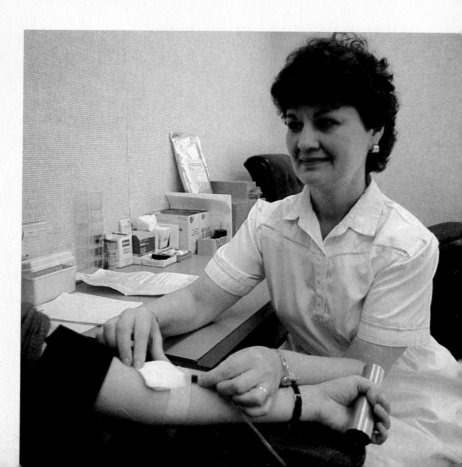

Many people work in hospitals to help make people well.

Nurses are usually responsible for the day-to-day care of a patient. A nurse gives medicine and supervises other treatments for a patient according to the doctor's orders. Some nurses assist doctors in surgery. A nurse maintains a patient's records and notifies the doctor of the patient's condition.

Hospital attendants help nurses perform many duties. Attendants are often called nursing aides and orderlies. Attendants care for the comfort and cleanliness of patients. They may also help patients move from place to place within the hospital.

People who want to become nurses usually go to a nursing school for two to four years. Hospital attendants can train on the job.

Many hospitals have dental departments. **Dental hygienists** clean and polish teeth. They also take tooth X rays. People who want to become dental hygienists go to a school of hygiene for two to four years.

Some hospital patients may not be able to fully use their arms or legs. A **physical therapist** works with patients to regain the use of their limbs. Because of a disease or accident, a patient may have to be taught how to walk again. Therapists use exercises, massages, and whirlpool baths to treat patients.

To become a physical therapist, a student goes to college for four years.

Sometimes a doctor needs to find certain information about a disease and its treatment. They go to the hospital's medical library. The **medical librarian** helps doctors and nurses find the information they need. Librarians go to college for five years. Medical librarians also have a good background in the field of medicine.

The librarian may need a **library technician** to help out in the library. The technician trains for two years in college.

Doctors, nurses, therapists, librarians, and attendants are all part of a medical team. Their goal is to help patients in the best possible way.

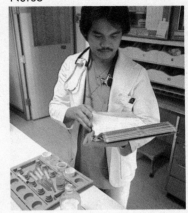
Nurse

Dental hygienist

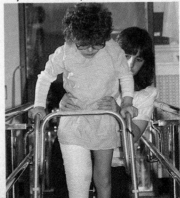
Physical therapist

On Your Own

Picture Clue

Look closely at the photograph on page 90. Compare the photograph to the picture on page 98. How do the circular rings help you? Notice the black spots in the picture. These black spots are cells that control the formation of the rings.

Projects

1. Examine a chicken leg. See if you can find the fibers of the muscles, and the cartilage and ligaments at the ends of the bone.

2. Some of the first modern scientific research on the stomach was done by William Beaumont in the early 1800s. Look in an encyclopedia to find out how Dr. Beaumont was able to perform his experiments on a living person.

3. Make your own stethoscope by attaching a funnel to a rubber tube. Place the funnel over your heart. Put the tube to your ear, and listen to your heart beat. Where does your heartbeat sound the loudest? Where is it weakest? Look in a medical encyclopedia to find which parts of the heart make the different sounds.

Books About Science

Blood and Guts by Linda Allison. Little, Brown, 1977. Fun experiments in this book will help you learn how your body works.

Facts About the Human Body by Marianne and Mary-Alice Tully. Watts, 1977. Do you have questions about your body? This book will help answer your questions.

What If You Couldn't . . . ? by Janet Kamien. Scribner's, 1979. Learn how handicapped people live healthy, active lives.

The World of Bionics by Alvin and Virginia Silverstein. Methuen, 1979. Can machines do what your body does? Find out!

Unit Test

Matching

Number your paper from 1–6. Read the description in Column I. Next to each number, write the letter of the word or phrase from Column II that best matches the description in Column I.

Column I

1. tough fiber that connects a muscle to a bone

2. the second layer of skin

3. tough, flexible material that forms part of the skeleton

4. muscle that you need not control

5. passageway between the throat and the stomach

6. narrow tube where digestion is completed

Column II

a. cartilage

b. dermis

c. involuntary muscle

d. tendon

e. ligament

f. small intestine

g. esophagus

Multiple Choice

Number your paper from 7–10. Next to each number, write the letter of the word or phrase that best completes the statement.

7. In the air sacs, oxygen moves into the bloodstream by
   a. excretion.
   b. diffusion.
   c. respiration.
   d. digestion.

8. The blood cells that carry oxygen to your cells are the
   a. red blood cells.
   b. white blood cells.
   c. platelets.
   d. all the above

9. Blood vessels that carry blood away from the heart are the
   a. veins.
   b. arteries.
   c. valves.
   d. capillaries.

10. In cell respiration, oxygen and glucose undergo chemical changes to release carbon dioxide, water, and
    a. nutrients.
    b. carbohydrates.
    c. energy.
    d. plasma.

UNIT FOUR
YOUR BODY: REGULATION AND RESPONSE

Computer
Giving information
About the man
Always working.

Brian Blanchard *age 10*

Chapter 9
The Nervous System

A hurdler has to be in good shape to compete in a race. But jumping hurdles takes more than just a strong heart and healthy lungs. A hurdler must have split-second timing. If the hurdler jumps a second too soon or a second too late, she will miss the hurdle. To clear the hurdle, she must jump at just the right time. Her eyes, arms, and legs must all work together as she races. The teamwork of her muscles and nerves allows her to clear the hurdles and perhaps win the race.

The lessons in this chapter will help you understand how your nervous system allows you to notice and respond to everything around you.

1 Measuring Reaction Time
2 How Do You Detect and Respond to Changes?
3 How Do Your Senses Gather Information?
4 How Do Your Nerves Send Messages?
5 What Do Your Spinal Cord and Brain Do?

1 Measuring Reaction Time

You step off the curb to cross the street. Suddenly a speeding car appears near you. How long does it take you to jump out of the way? Your reaction time is the period between your awareness of something and your response to it. You can measure the reaction time of your class.

Form a circle with your classmates, as shown in the picture. Ask one student in the circle to time the exercise with a stopwatch. The timekeeper holds the stopwatch in the right hand. As the timekeeper says "Go," and starts the stopwatch, the student to the right of the timekeeper starts to pass a signal of hand squeezes around the circle. As the hand signal reaches the timekeeper, the timekeeper immediately stops the stopwatch. Record the class's reaction time. Repeat the exercise three times.

Now, do the exercise while one person tells a joke or while the class sings a song.

Think About It

1. What changes in the exercise increased or decreased reaction time?
2. **Challenge** List ways you could vary the exercise to change the reaction time of the class.

2 How Do You Detect and Respond to Changes?

Buzzzzzz! That annoying sound rouses you from your peaceful sleep. At first, you might think the buzz is your alarm clock. Then, you realize your alarm clock is not ringing. It is the middle of the night. The buzzing continues close to your ear. You realize a mosquito is making the noise. You swat at the mosquito, but the mosquito flies away.

The sudden presence of a buzzing mosquito is a change that might occur in your immediate environment. Changes occur around you twenty-four hours a day. Changes also continually occur inside your body. For example, when you wake up, your cells need more oxygen. To stay healthy, you need to be able to respond to the changes both inside and outside your body.

Any change that you detect and can respond to is a **stimulus.** Find the stimulus in the picture. The person detects and responds to the stimulus to keep himself safe from harm. Like the person in the picture, you use your nervous system to detect and respond to stimuli.

stimulus (stim′yə ləs), any change that you detect and can respond to. [Plural: stimuli (stim′yə lī).]

Have You Heard?

Even the tiniest organisms must detect and respond to changes in their environments. Tiny worms that can fit on the head of a pin have nervous systems complete with tiny brains.

People respond to stimuli

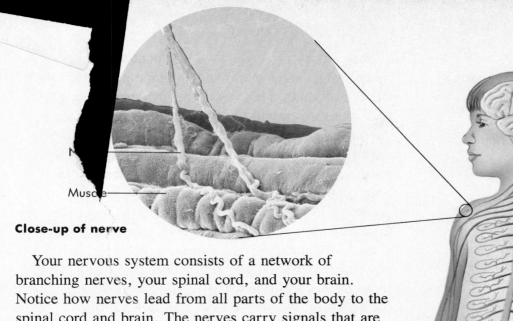

Muscle

Close-up of nerve

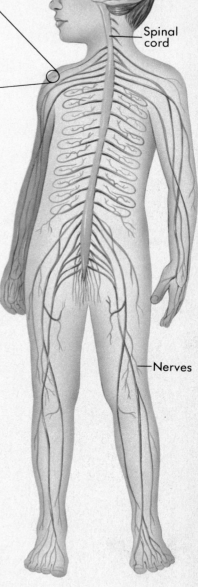

Brain

Spinal cord

Nerves

Nervous system

Your nervous system consists of a network of branching nerves, your spinal cord, and your brain. Notice how nerves lead from all parts of the body to the spinal cord and brain. The nerves carry signals that are interpreted in the brain. Messages from the brain are sent through the nerves in the spinal cord to other nerves that lead to the muscles, as shown in the picture.

Follow the path a nerve signal might take when a mosquito buzzes near your ear. The buzzing sound stimulates a nerve in your ear. The nerve carries a signal to your brain, where the signal is interpreted. At first, your brain might interpret the buzzing as a ringing alarm clock. As you wake up, your brain reinterprets the signal as the buzzing of a mosquito. Your brain sends a message down through the spinal cord to nerves that lead to your arm muscles. Your arm muscles contract as you try to swat the mosquito.

Think About It

1. Give examples of two kinds of changes to which your nervous system allows you to respond.
2. Trace the path a nerve signal travels through the nervous system.
3. **Challenge** What stimulus might nerves in your digestive system detect? Describe how your involuntary muscles respond to the stimulus.

3 How Do Your Senses Gather Information?

Your senses allow you to learn ab[   ]orld around you. Imagine all the stimuli t[   ]at the circus can sense. They taste crunchy [   ]smell fresh popcorn, watch the dancing ele[   ]hear the music of a band. You have other [   ]gather information about your body. Nerve e[nerve]your muscles, for example, send information [   ]your body's position and the activities of your internal organs. Your senses give you information about changes that are going on inside and outside your body.

Each of your senses allows you to gather specific kinds of information about your changing world. Your sense of vision, for example, detects light stimuli. Chemical information is picked up by your senses of smell and taste. Your sense of hearing lets you gather information carried by sound waves.

All your senses use **receptors**—or special cells that detect specific kinds of stimuli. Receptors are found at the ends of nerves.

receptor (ri sep′tər), a cell that detects a specific kind of stimulus.

Stimuli at the circus

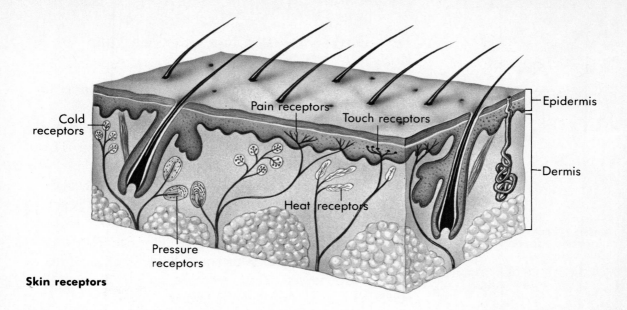

Cold receptors

Pain receptors

Touch receptors

Epidermis

Dermis

Heat receptors

Pressure receptors

Skin receptors

Your skin has five different kinds of receptors. Notice the small, round receptors in the epidermis. These receptors respond to the gentle pressure you know as touch. In contrast, the larger oval receptors, located deep in the dermis, detect stronger pressures. Find the branching nerve endings in the picture. When these receptors are stimulated you feel pain. Heat and cold are detected by two different receptors. Compare the number of heat and cold receptors in the picture. You have many more cold receptors than heat receptors.

You can feel many sensations besides heat, cold, touch, pressure, and pain. The fuzziness of a puppy, the wetness of ice water, and the roughness of sandpaper are other sensations you feel. All sensations are a combination of signals from the five types of skin receptors.

Receptors are distributed unevenly over your body. Lightly run the top of your pencil over your lip. Contrast this sensation to what you feel when you rub the top of your pencil over the back of your hand. You have many more touch receptors on your lips than on the back of your hand.

Find Out

When you are deprived of one of your senses, the other senses work to make up for the loss. Ask a partner to help you put on a blindfold and guide you in a walk outdoors. Note all the things you can recognize through only your senses of touch, hearing, and smell.

How Do You Detect Changes Inside Your Body?

Raise your arm above your head like the person in the picture. Without looking up, you know exactly how your hand is positioned. You can feel if your fingers are curved or if your palm is facing toward the ceiling. The drawing shows tiny nerves wrapped around muscle fibers. These nerves respond when the muscles change position. The information you get from nerves in your muscles tells you the position of all parts of your body.

You need many different kinds of information to regulate the systems of your body and to react to all the changes around you. Your receptors, deep inside the muscles of your organs and in your eyes, ears, nose, tongue, and skin, gather all the information you need to stay safe and healthy.

Muscle receptors give information about body position

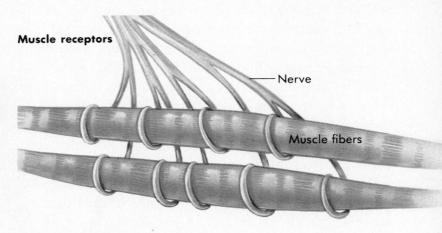

Muscle receptors

Nerve

Muscle fibers

Think About It

1. How does your nervous system detect changes?
2. What do your five kinds of skin receptors do?
3. What do receptors in your muscles do?
4. **Challenge** Nerves wrap around the bases of the tiny hairs in your skin. What stimuli do these nerves help you detect?

Activity

Mapping Your Touch Receptors

Purpose
To compare the distribution of touch receptors in the palm and back of the hand.

You Will Need
- paper
- 2 colored pens
- blindfold
- hairpin
- centimeter ruler

Directions
1. Trace your hand on paper, as shown in the picture. Label one of the tracings *palm* and the other *back*.
2. Make a key for your map as shown. One color will signify that a single point was felt. The second color will signify 2 points were felt.
3. Ask your partner to put on a blindfold. Spread the tips of a hairpin 1 cm apart, as shown in the picture. Press the hairpin gently on the palm of your partner's hand. Ask how many points were felt.

4. If a single point was felt, mark the corresponding location on your map with the first colored pen. If both points were felt, mark the location on your map with the second colored pen.
5. Move the points to different parts of the palm. Each time, ask your partner how many points he or she feels.
6. Repeat steps 3–5 for the back of your partner's hand.
7. When you are finished, reverse roles, and ask your partner to make a map of your hand.

Think About It
1. Explain why sometimes you felt only 1 point when 2 points touched your skin.
2. On which side of the hand was your sense of touch the most accurate?
3. How is the map of your hand different from the maps of your classmates? Explain why there might be differences in your senses of touch.
4. **Challenge** Explain why some areas of your hand are more sensitive to touch than other areas.

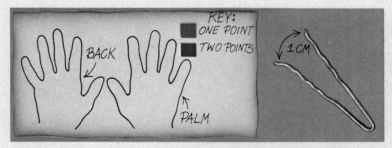

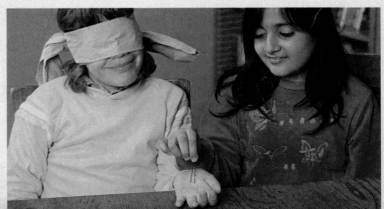

4 How Do Your Nerves Send Messages?

sensory (sen′sər ē) **nerve cell,** a nerve cell that passes signals from the sense receptors to the spinal cord or brain.

motor nerve cell, a nerve cell that passes signals from the brain or spinal cord to the muscles.

Imagine that you are in a relay race. You are waiting for your turn to run. Your teammate dashes up to you and hands you the baton. You run as fast as you can to hand the baton to the next runner. Then, you stop and wait until it is your turn to run again.

Just as relay racers pass a baton in a relay race, your nerve cells relay signals through your body. Your nerves are bundles of nerve cells.

Your nervous system is made of different kinds of nerve cells. Trace the **sensory nerve cell** in the picture that carries nerve signals from the receptor cell in the muscle to the spinal cord. Nerve cells in the spinal cord relay signals to and from the brain. In the brain the nerve signals are interpreted.

After the signals have been interpreted, the nerve cells in the spinal cord relay messages to the **motor nerve cells** that connect with muscle fibers. The message sent down the motor nerve cell in the picture caused the leg muscle to contract. The different nerve cells work together to allow the gymnast to perform on the horse.

Path of nerve signal

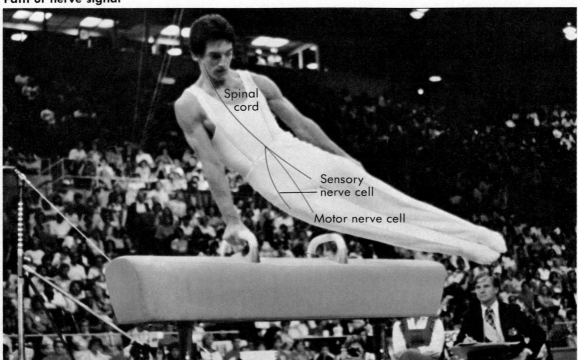

Spinal cord

Sensory nerve cell

Motor nerve cell

Find the three parts of the nerve cell in the drawing. The branching **dendrites** respond to stimuli. The dendrites trigger a change inside the nerve cell. This change carries a signal—or **nerve impulse**—down the dendrites.

At the end of the dendrites is the round **cell body** that keeps the nerve cell healthy and able to transmit nerve impulses. The long **axon** extends from the base of the cell body. The axon transmits nerve impulses down the length of the cell.

dendrite (den′drīt), the end of a nerve cell that responds to stimuli by triggering a nerve impulse.

nerve impulse (im′puls), a signal sent by a nerve cell.

cell body, part of a nerve cell that keeps the cell healthy and able to transmit nerve impulses.

axon (ak′son), the long part of a nerve cell that transmits nerve impulses away from the cell body.

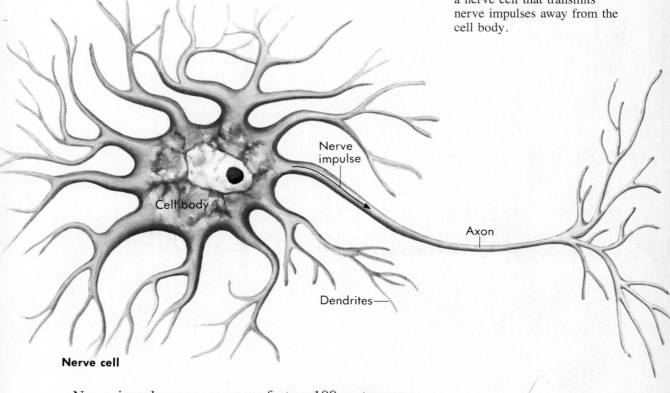

Nerve impulse

Cell body

Axon

Dendrites—

Nerve cell

Nerve impulses can move as fast as 100 meters per second. At that speed, a nerve impulse could travel from the tips of your fingers to your brain 150 times in just 1 second! The rapid-traveling nerve impulses help you react quickly to changes that occur continually inside and outside your body.

Have You Heard?

Most nerve cells are so small and delicate that scientists cannot experiment on them. However, one kind of sea animal—the squid—has long, thick nerve fibers. Its axons may be 1 mm wide and several meters long. The first scientific experiments on nerves were done on the axons of the squid.

How Do Nerves Relay Impulses?

Notice the space—or **synapse**—between the axon of one nerve cell and the dendrites of the next nerve cell. To relay information, nerve cells must pass impulses over synapses, much as racers pass a baton in a relay race. When a nerve impulse reaches the end of an axon, a special chemical is released. When enough of this chemical crosses the synapse to the receiving dendrites, the next nerve cell begins sending a nerve impulse.

If an axon does not release enough chemical, the nerve impulse will not cross the synapse. Synapses keep your nervous system from becoming overloaded with signals. Without synapses, the smallest stimulus would trigger nerve impulses, and your muscles would automatically respond. You do not respond to every stimulus your receptors detect because your synapses stop some nerve impulses from being transmitted.

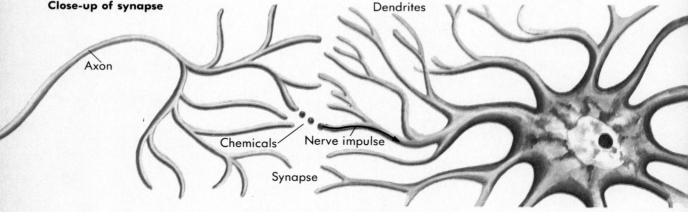

Close-up of synapse

Dendrites

Axon

Chemicals

Nerve impulse

Synapse

Think About It

1. How are spinal, sensory, and motor nerve cells different?
2. Describe the structure of a nerve cell.
3. How do nerve impulses travel from cell to cell?
4. **Challenge** How might some chemicals affect your nervous system?

Discover!

Antivenin Stops Cobra Poison from Working

Cobra

The cobra in the picture is one of the most dangerous animals in the world. If this snake bites an animal, the snake's poison can kill the animal in only a few minutes. How can a poison work so fast?

Some snake poisons work quickly by affecting an animal's nervous system. But a medicine, called antivenin, can stop the action of these snake poisons. It does so by combining with the snake poison in the body of the animal that was bitten. The drawings show how the snake poison affects the nervous system and how antivenin works against the poison.

Normally, messages that pass through an animal's nervous system tell its muscles what to do. The first drawing shows how messages are usually transmitted between nerves. When the message reaches the end of one nerve, it releases a chemical. This chemical travels across the synapse between *Nerve 1* and *Nerve 2*. When the chemical reaches the dendrites of *Nerve 2*, it starts the message going again.

Drawing *b* shows how the snake poison works. The poison contains a chemical that reacts with the nerve chemical. The poison stops the nerve chemical from carrying messages between the nerves. Then, the nerves cannot send messages to the animal's muscles, and the muscles stop working. The animal's lungs or heart stops working, and the animal dies.

Drawing *c* shows how antivenin stops the action of snake poison by combining with it. The snake poison is no longer free to stop the nerve chemical in the synapse from carrying messages between the nerves.

Antivenin for one kind of snake poison may not have any effect on another kind of snake poison. For that reason it is important to know what kind of snake bit an animal before giving that animal antivenin.

a
Nerve chemical crosses synapse

b
Nerve chemical stopped by snake poison

c
Antivenin combines with snake poison

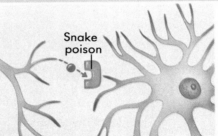

5 What Do Your Spinal Cord and Brain Do?

reflex (rē′fleks), automatic response of muscles to a certain stimulus.

Have You Heard?
Dogs have a reflex that you can easily observe. When you rub a dog's back, the dog will lift its hind leg and scratch.

"Now, please cross your leg," requests the doctor in the picture. Then, he taps the girl's crossed leg just below her kneecap with a small hammer. Her leg swings forward automatically. The automatic response of muscles to a certain stimulus is a **reflex.**

Follow the path a nerve impulse takes in the knee-jerk reflex in the drawing. Nerve cells in the spinal cord relay nerve impulses from sensory nerve cells directly to motor nerve cells.

The spinal cord at its widest part is only about 0.5 centimeters across. Nerve impulses can cross this small distance quickly on their way from the sensory to the motor nerve cells. You do not notice the tap of the doctor's hammer before your leg jerks. The nerve impulses do not have time to reach your brain before the motor nerve cells cause your leg muscles to contract.

Notice that other nerve cells in the spinal cord relay nerve impulses to the brain. When the nerve impulses reach your brain, you feel the tap the doctor gave your kneecap. Your spinal cord relays signals both to your muscles and to your brain.

Knee-jerk reflex

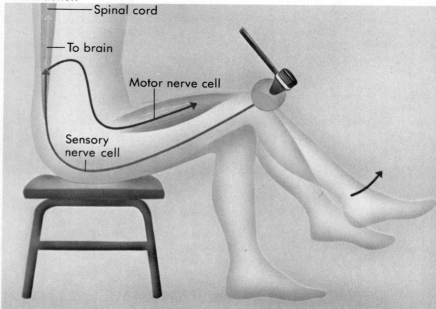

Reflex action

Spinal cord

To brain

Motor nerve cell

Sensory nerve cell

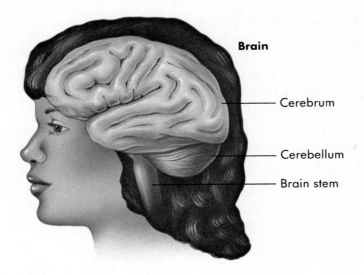

Brain

— Cerebrum

— Cerebellum

— Brain stem

The cerebellum aids balancing

Over ten billion nerve cells are packed into your brain. These nerve cells are organized into different structures. Find the wrinkled **cerebrum,** the largest structure in the brain. The smaller **cerebellum** fits below the cerebrum. Notice the column of tissue called the **brain stem** underneath the rest of the brain. Each of these structures does many different things.

Your brain stem controls your body's automatic activities. For example, when you breathe, your brain stem directs the movement of your diaphragm muscle. And when your body gets overheated, your brain stem sends messages to your sweat glands and to the blood vessels in your skin. Then, your sweat glands release sweat, and your blood vessels enlarge to help cool you.

The main job of your cerebellum is to help your voluntary muscles work together smoothly. If you lift your left leg like the person in the picture, the muscles in your right leg have to work to support your weight. Receptors in your leg muscles send signals through sensory nerve cells to your cerebellum. There, the signals are interpreted. The cerebellum then sends messages back to your leg muscles to make sure you keep your balance.

cerebrum (sə rē′brəm), the large, wrinkled top portion of the human brain that controls thinking and voluntary movements.

cerebellum (ser′ə bel′əm), the part of the brain beneath the cerebrum that regulates muscle movements.

brain stem, part of the brain that controls automatic body functions.

155

Have You Heard?
If one part of the brain is damaged, often another part of the brain can take over to make up for the loss. For example, someone injured in a serious accident might lose the ability to speak. After a while, the person might be able to talk again. Other areas of the brain might take over for the damaged area so that the person can relearn to talk.

What Does Your Cerebrum Do?

Your cerebrum gives you conscious control over your muscles and your thoughts. When you notice that your pencil point is dull and decide to sharpen it, your cerebrum is active.

Notice that different regions of the cerebrum control different parts of the body. Find the region that controls the hand. Compare the size of this region to the size of the brain region that controls the foot. The region of the cerebrum that controls the hand is much larger. You use your hands for a wider variety of activities than you use your feet. The areas of the cerebrum that control the hands must be large to give you that extra control.

The cerebrum not only directs your voluntary movements, it also determines what you feel. For example, cold receptors in your tongue send impulses when you lick an ice cube. Sensory nerve cells lead from your tongue to the area of the cerebrum for the sensation of coldness. When this part of the brain receives signals, you feel cold. If the signals from the cold receptors could be routed to the pain region of the brain, you would feel pain, not cold.

Control regions of cerebrum

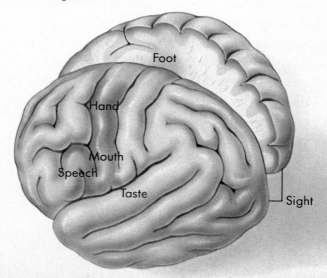

156

Girl looks at pear

Right eye's image

Left eye's image

Cerebrum combines images

The cerebrum organizes signals it receives from the sense receptors. As the girl in the picture looks at the pear in front of the fruit bowl, each of her eyes forms a different image of the pear. Notice that the pear appears to shift toward the grapes in the right eye's image and toward the banana in the left eye's image. The cerebrum combines these two images into the view that the girl actually sees. If your cerebrum did not organize information from your sense receptors, you could not respond to many stimuli in your environment.

Other regions of your cerebrum store information brought to you by your sense receptors. This information becomes your memories. When you recall the information, you might see a picture of a place you visited in the past. You might even be able to smell the odors and hear the sounds of that special place.

You also use your cerebrum when you solve a math problem, work on a puzzle, or explain your thoughts to your friends. Whenever you figure something out or express yourself, your cerebrum is active.

How Does Your Brain Regulate Your Activities?

Imagine the path the nerve impulses must follow when the person in the picture kicks the soccer ball. As he decides to kick the ball, his cerebrum sends a message through the nerves in his spinal cord. These nerves send impulses to motor nerve cells that lead to his leg muscles. As these leg muscles contract, receptors in the muscles of his other leg send signals that reach his cerebellum. The cerebellum relays messages to his muscles to help him balance. At the same time, the person's brain stem sends messages to his heart to beat faster.

Your brain stores much more information than is contained in your library's card catalog. Your brain uses this information to direct all your body's activities.

Think About It

1. Explain how a reflex works.
2. Describe the parts of your brain, and explain how each helps regulate your body's activities.
3. **Challenge** The region of the cerebrum that controls the mouth is larger in humans than in other mammals. Why is this control center especially important for us?

The nervous system helps a person control movements

Tie It Together

Sum It Up

Describe what is happening in this picture. Be sure to include all the science words in the chapter as well as the words *spinal cord* and *brain*.

Challenge!

1. List some changes in your environment that you detect and respond to every day.

2. People who play the guitar often develop callouses or thickened skin on their fingertips. How do callouses help the guitar players?

3. From which part of your body do sensory nerves lead directly to your brain? How does this help you?

4. If someone did not have good reflexes, where would a doctor look for the cause of the problem?

5. What would happen to a person's sight if the vision center of the brain were damaged?

Science Words

axon

brain stem

cell body

cerebellum

cerebrum

dendrite

motor nerve cell

nerve impulse

receptor

reflex

sensory nerve cell

stimulus

synapse

Chapter 10
Life Cycles and Hormones

All animals change as they grow. The tiny tadpoles in the pictures change from pond-bottom swimmers to land-dwelling frogs. You also change as you grow. Your glands produce special chemicals that maintain your body and direct your growth.

The lessons in this chapter discuss the changes you go through as you grow, and describe how your endocrine system directs your growth.

1 Observing Changes in Your Body
2 How Does Your Body Change?
3 How Do Hormones Affect Your Body?
4 How Do Hormones Maintain a Chemical Balance?

1 Observing Changes in Your Body

The man in the center of the picture has caught his leg in a tree branch under the water. The two other people are trying to help him release his trapped leg. They need extra strength to respond to this emergency. Chemical changes in their bodies help them react with extra energy.

Think of a time when you felt a strong emotion, such as fear or excitement. Write down the emotion and the changes that took place in your body when you felt that emotion. Consider your pulse rate, breathing rate, and skin temperature. Compare your experiences with those of your classmates.

On a separate piece of paper, write down changes that occur in your body as you grow.

Think About It

1. What body changes that were due to emotions did you have in common with your classmates?
2. How does your body change as you get older?
3. **Challenge** How do growth changes and changes due to emotions differ?

Emergency situation

2 How Does Your Body Change?

All living things change as they grow. Compare the maple seedling to the mature tree. The soft stem of the seedling will change color, harden, and thicken to become like the tree's trunk. As the seedling develops, it will grow more leaves. Branches will form. Over the years the young tree will grow taller and wider, like the tree in the picture. You also change as you grow.

Even before you were born, you grew and changed in some dramatic ways. You began as one tiny cell that divided into trillions of cells. These cells changed in different ways. Some cells became your skin. Other cells developed into your heart and blood vessels. All your organs were formed by cells that changed in different ways.

Maple tree

Maple seedling

From the day you were born, you have continued to grow and change. Your body proportions, for example, have changed. Compare the size of the baby's head to the length of the baby's body. A baby's head measures about one-fourth the length of its body. In an adult the head is only one-eighth the person's height.

A baby's bones become harder as the bones grow in length. As bones develop, the baby is able to support its own weight and sit up. Muscles also grow in size. The baby learns to use its muscles for many different activities. At first, a baby becomes able to use its muscles to support itself in a sitting position. Then, the baby learns how to use its muscles to crawl, stand, walk, and run.

As you grow, you are able to use your muscles to do more and more things. You might have had trouble riding a bicycle when you were five years old. Now, you probably hop on a bicycle and ride it without even thinking about moving your legs and keeping your balance.

Comparing head size to body length

Have You Heard?

A baby has a soft spot at the top of the head where the skull bones have not yet grown together. The soft spot is made of cartilage. After a baby's first year, bone replaces the cartilage at the top of the skull, and the soft spot disappears.

How Do You Change During Adolescence?

Sometime between the ages of 9 and 18 years, you will go through a period of growth and change known as **adolescence.** At the beginning of adolescence, you will probably grow between 10 and 20 centimeters. You might gain between 8 and 20 kilograms of weight. This growth spurt probably will last for 2 or 3 years.

During adolescence your body proportions will change. Some parts of your body will grow faster than others. For instance, your hands and feet will grow more quickly than the rest of your body. You might feel awkward until your arms and legs catch up in growth.

Your body's shape will change too. Compare the pictures of the people before and after adolescence. The boy's shoulders widened and arm muscles became thicker. The girl's waist became thinner, and her hips widened.

People change during adolescence

As you go through adolescence, coarse hair begins to grow on different parts of your body. Boys and girls start growing hair under their arms and around their lower pelvic region. In addition, hair grows on a boy's chest and face.

As your body is changing on the outside, changes also occur inside your body. Your vocal cords become longer, making your voice fuller and deeper. A boy especially notices the change in his voice.

Other changes occur inside your body. Girls' reproductive organs—**ovaries**—begin releasing female reproductive cells. The reproductive organs in boys—**testes**—begin producing male reproductive cells. Ovaries and testes also release chemicals that cause the many physical changes of adolescence.

Adolescence begins for some people when they are only nine years old. Other people do not begin adolescence until they are in their late teens. Compare the twelve-year-olds in the picture. Notice how people of the same age grow at different rates. Just as everyone has a different appearance and personality, everyone has a different rate of growth and development.

ovaries (ō′vər ēz), female organs that produce reproductive cells and chemicals which cause body changes during adolescence.

testes (tes′tēz), male organs that produce reproductive cells and chemicals which cause body changes during adolescence.

Height differences in twelve-year-olds

   Human beings, on the average, live to be over 70 years old. The giant tortoise lives to be twice that age. Some oak trees live to be 2,000 years old.

How Do Adults Change?

   When a person becomes an adult, the person stops growing in height. However, an adult's body continues to change in many ways. Most of these changes are due to cells changing over time.

   As people grow older, the wear and tear on their cells begins to show. People in their twenties might begin to see wrinkles in their skin. Thirty-year-olds might notice a decline in their eyesight. As people age, their joints might become weak and stiff. Their hair might change color.

   Aging affects different people in different ways. Pablo Picasso was in his seventies when the picture below was taken. He, like a number of older people, remained healthy and active well into his nineties.

Think About It

1. Give three examples of how your body changed when you were a child.
2. Describe five physical changes of adolescence.
3. **Challenge** Damaged nerve cells cannot replace themselves. How might this affect people as they age?

Pablo Picasso

Activity

Examining Growth Patterns

Purpose
To measure and graph the heights of people of various ages.

You Will Need
- masking tape
- meter stick
- colored pencils
- graph paper

Directions
1. Measure the heights of people of different ages. Ask each person you measure to stand against the wall, as shown in the picture. Use a piece of masking tape to mark where the top of the person's head touches the wall. Use a meter stick to measure the distance from the floor to the tape.
2. Try to measure several people in each of the age groups included on the graph shown. Record the age and sex of each person you measure.

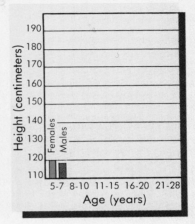

Height graph

3. Combine your information with that of your classmates. Organize the measurements into age groups shown on the graph. Then, separate measurements for males and females. Find the average height for males and females of each age group.
4. Draw a bar graph like the one in the picture to show the average heights of people in the age groups you measured. Choose a color to represent females and another color to represent males. Make a color key in the corner of your graph.

5. Graph the average height of the males and females in each age group.

Think About It
1. Which age group of males shows the greatest growth? Females?
2. Compare the growth pattern of females to the growth pattern of males.
3. At what age does growth stop in males? In females?
4. **Challenge** How might your height at a certain age differ from the average indicated on your graph?

3 How Do Hormones Affect Your Body?

Wilma Rudolph winning a race

The people in the pictures are great athletes. Wilma Rudolph's long legs helped her win gold medals in the Olympics. Jorge Velasquez's slight build helped make him an ideal jockey. He has won many races including the Kentucky Derby. How both of these athletes grew and developed was determined in part by the glands of their **endocrine systems.**

Endocrine glands make chemicals called **hormones** that act as messages for specific cells. The endocrine glands pass the hormones directly into the blood. Hormones flow through the blood vessels until they reach cells that can recognize and respond to the chemical messages of the hormones.

Endocrine glands are often located far away from the cells to which they send hormones. The tiny endocrine glands in front of your throat send hormones to all the bones in your body, even to your little toe. Your hormones pass through several meters of blood vessels. After a long journey the hormones reach your toes. The hormones' messages might take several seconds to be delivered.

Jorge Velasquez at Kentucky Derby

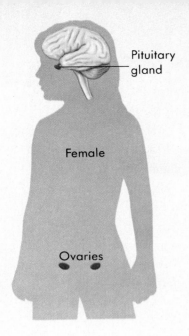

Female
Pituitary gland
Ovaries

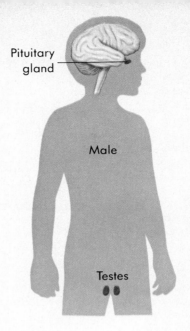

Pituitary gland
Male
Testes

Several seconds might not seem like a long time to wait for a message. But compared with the nervous system, which delivers messages in just a fraction of a second, the endocrine system sends messages extremely slowly. The nervous system sends messages that your cells must respond to quickly. Your endocrine system sends messages that your cells respond to more slowly.

The tiny **pituitary gland,** pictured below the brain, is one example of an endocrine gland. The pituitary gland releases growth hormone that tells your bone cells and muscle cells when to grow. Growth hormone controls many of the changes your body goes through during childhood and adolescence.

Your pituitary gland has another important role in determining your growth. The gland produces hormones that tell other endocrine glands when to start working. Find the ovaries and testes in the drawings. The ovaries release hormones that help a girl's body mature. The testes produce hormones that help a boy's body change during adolescence. The ovaries and testes do not produce these hormones until the pituitary gland sends the message.

pituitary (pə tü′ə ter′ē) **gland,** endocrine gland in the head that produces growth hormone and hormones that control other endocrine glands.

Find Out

If the pituitary gland continues to release high levels of growth hormone after adolescence is completed, an unusual condition results. Look in a medical encyclopedia to discover how excess growth hormone affects adults.

insulin (in′sə lən), hormone made and released by cells in the pancreas which regulates the amount of glucose that enters the cells.

adrenal (ə drē′nl) **gland,** endocrine gland on top of the kidney.

adrenaline (ə dren′l ən), hormone released by adrenal glands when the body needs extra energy.

Have You Heard?

When a person's pancreas does not release enough insulin, a disease called diabetes mellitus (dī′ə bē′tēz me lī′tus) results. The amount of glucose in a diabetic's blood can rise to levels that might make the person very ill. Many people with diabetes give themselves shots of insulin to control the amount of glucose in their blood.

How Do Hormones Control Cells' Activities?

Your endocrine system also helps regulate the daily activities of your cells. For example, pancreas cells, shown in the picture, produce a hormone—**insulin**—that increases the amount of glucose which enters the cells. After you digest your food, your pancreas releases insulin so your cells can use the glucose in your blood.

Find the **adrenal glands** on top of the kidneys. Your adrenal glands help you respond to changes in your environment. These glands produce the hormone **adrenaline** that causes the liver to release stored glucose. When you become excited or frightened, your adrenal glands release adrenaline. Your liver, in response to the adrenaline's message, releases glucose into the blood. Your cells take in glucose and produce extra energy. Then, you can respond quickly to whatever excited or frightened you.

Two endocrine glands

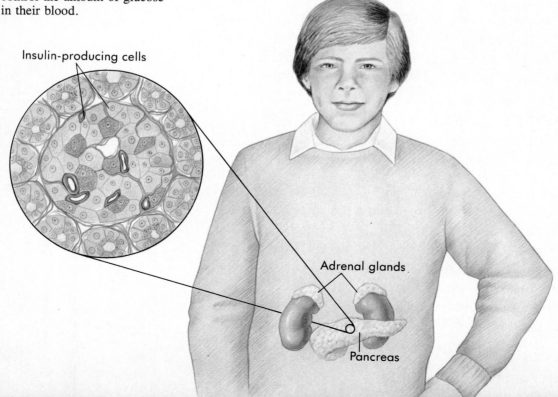

Insulin-producing cells

Adrenal glands

Pancreas

Adrenaline helps swimmers race

The swimmers in the picture are taking off from the starting blocks. Their adrenal glands are pumping adrenaline through their blood, so their muscle cells have extra energy. With the help of their adrenal glands, the racers will try to beat the pool record.

Your endocrine glands help you in many ways. Some glands help your body grow and change. Other glands regulate your cells' daily activities. Still other glands help you respond to changes in your environment. Your endocrine glands help keep you healthy and fit.

Think About It

1. What do hormones do?
2. Give examples of ways endocrine glands regulate changes in your body.
3. **Challenge** How might someone's adrenal glands help the person respond to an emergency?

171

4 How Do Hormones Maintain a Chemical Balance?

Plants with different amounts of hormone

Just as your hormones regulate your growth, plant hormones regulate the growth of plants. Compare the two plants in the picture. The taller plant has too much hormone, so its stem has grown unusually tall. The smaller plant has less hormone. The amounts of hormone controlled how the plants grew.

Feedback is the way plants and animals control the amounts of hormones released. By using feedback, endocrine glands control the effects of hormones on the body.

A thermostat in a house shows how feedback works to control the temperature in the house. The thermostat in the picture is set for 19° Celsius. The thermometer on the thermostat records the temperature in the house. When the temperature falls below 19° Celsius, the thermostat turns on the heater. When the thermostat's thermometer reads 19° Celsius, the thermostat shuts the heater off.

Feedback process to control house's temperature

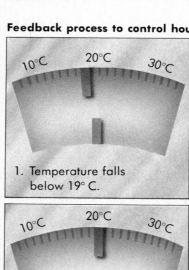

1. Temperature falls below 19° C.

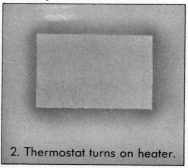

2. Thermostat turns on heater.

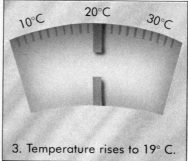

3. Temperature rises to 19° C.

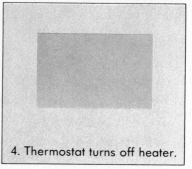

4. Thermostat turns off heater.

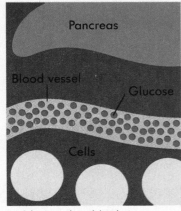
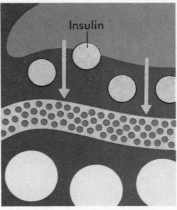
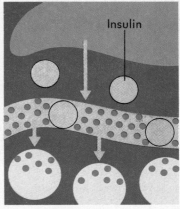

1. Glucose level high

2. Pancreas releases insulin

3. Cells absorb glucose

In much the same way that a thermostat controls the temperature in a house, endocrine glands control the effects of hormones. The pancreas in the pictures helps control the amount of glucose in the blood. When the amount of glucose increases above a certain amount, the pancreas releases insulin to help the cells take in the excess glucose. When the pancreas detects the lower glucose level in the blood, it stops releasing insulin. The pancreas's feedback process keeps the glucose in your blood at a safe level.

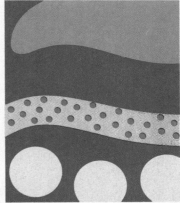

4. Glucose level drops and pancreas stops releasing insulin

Hormones are powerful chemicals. Your cells need only small amounts of hormones to function properly. Endocrine glands use the feedback process to ensure that the right amounts of hormones are released into your blood.

Think About It

1. What is feedback?
2. How does your pancreas use feedback to control the amount of glucose in your blood?
3. **Challenge** What might happen in the pancreas's feedback process when a person has diabetes?

Discover!

Scientists Found a Lifesaving Substance for Diabetics

The month was February. The year was 1922. Dr. Joseph Gilchrist trudged wearily up the stairs. He was a young man, but he was thin and frail. Gilchrist was a diabetic. And, though he was a doctor, he could not cure or control his deadly disease.

But Dr. Gilchrist had heard that a former classmate Dr. Fred Banting and his assistant Charles Best, shown in the picture, had found a way to control diabetes. Dr. Gilchrist decided to volunteer for his friend's experiments.

For many years scientists had known that diabetes had something to do with the pancreas. Dogs whose pancreases were removed developed diabetes. Their cells could not use the glucose in their blood. Scientists thought that the pancreas controlled the uptake of glucose by the cells. But they were not able to use that knowledge to cure diabetes.

Later, scientists learned that the pancreas has two kinds of cells. One kind of pancreas cell produces digestive enzymes. The other kind of pancreas cell controls the cells' uptake of glucose. Perhaps a substance from the glucose-controlling cells could be isolated. The substance could be given to diabetics to control the disease.

Dr. Banting and Charles Best set out to find that substance. They reasoned that the pancreas's strong digestive enzymes might destroy the glucose-controlling substance if the two were mixed. So they found a way to stop the pancreas cells in a dog from making digestive enzymes.

Then, they removed the dog's pancreas, mixed the pancreas cells with water, and injected the fluid into a dying diabetic dog. Soon the dog regained strength and was frisking around the laboratory. Banting and Best had isolated the glucose-controlling substance from the pancreas. The substance was named insulin.

With insulin, Dr. Gilchrist regained his health. He assisted Banting and Best in their research of diabetes. Banting and Best's discovery has allowed thousands of diabetics to live healthy lives.

Banting and Best

Tie It Together

Sum It Up

1. Imagine that you are searching through the attic of an old house. You find the photographs below in a book. Describe how the person changed as he got older. Be sure to include the words *child, growth hormone, pituitary gland, adolescence, testes,* and *adult.*

2. Imagine that the floorboards of the attic suddenly begin to creak, and a shadow falls across your book. Describe your reaction. Include the words *adrenal gland, endocrine system, adrenaline, hormone, bloodstream, pulse,* and *breathing rate.*

3. In what order should pictures *a, b, c,* and *d* appear? Describe what happens in each picture as the pancreas uses feedback to control the amount of glucose in the blood.

Challenge!

1. A baby's head is one-fourth the length of its body. An adult's head is only one-eighth his or her height. Give a reason for this difference in proportion.

2. How is a tree's growth pattern different from a person's growth pattern?

3. Explain how the pituitary gland controls when body hair begins to grow during adolescence.

4. What might happen if your adrenal glands released adrenaline all the time?

5. How does an air conditioner use feedback to control the temperature in a house?

Science Words

adolescence	hormone
adrenal gland	insulin
adrenaline	ovary
endocrine system	pituitary gland
feedback	testes

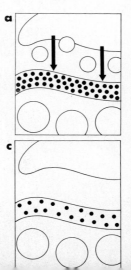
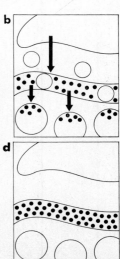

Chapter 11
Health and Fitness

After riding home on your bicycle, you are hot and thirsty. You open the refrigerator door to choose a snack. A cheese sandwich would taste good, but a sandwich will not quench your thirst. The sandwich also might spoil your appetite for dinner. You choose an apple as your snack. The cool, juicy apple gives you energy and quenches your thirst. After eating the apple, you run outside to meet your friends.

The lessons in this chapter will help you learn about many things you can do to stay healthy.

1 Examining Food Labels
2 How Do Foods Keep You Healthy?
3 How Do You Keep Your Body Healthy?
4 How Can Drugs Affect Your Body?

1 Examining Food Labels

Nutrients in foods give you energy and help your body grow and maintain itself. All foods contain some nutrients. You can find out about nutrients in some foods by examining labels like the one in the picture.

Find three different kinds of packaged foods in your home. Examine the labels to find information on the amounts of nutrients in each serving. Bring the packages or cans to class.

Combine your information with the information gathered by your classmates. Make a chart like the one shown to compare the amounts of some nutrients in one serving of each kind of food.

Nutrient chart

	Brand X Yogurt 1 Serving	Brand Y Peanut butter 1 Serving	Brand Z Bread 1 Slice
Carbohydrate	32 grams	4 grams	15 grams
Protein	7 grams	10 grams	3 grams
Fat	5 grams	16 grams	1.5 grams
Vitamin C	2%	0%	0%
Iron	2%	4%	10%

Nutritional information

NUTRITION INFORMATION PER SERVING		
SERVING SIZE	1 OZ. (½ CUP)	
SERVINGS PER CONTAINER:		15

	1 OZ.	WITH ½ CUP WHOLE MILK
CALORIES	110	190
PROTEIN	2 g	6 g
CARBOHYDRATE	20 g	26 g
FAT	1 g	5 g

PERCENTAGE OF U.S. RECOMMENDED DAILY ALLOWANCE (U.S. RDA)

PROTEIN	2	10
VITAMIN A	45	50
VITAMIN C	100	100
THIAMINE	30	30
RIBOFLAVIN	40	50
NIACIN	35	35
CALCIUM	2	15
IRON	60	60
VITAMIN D	100	100

INGREDIENTS: SUGAR, ROLLED OATS, MALTED BARLEY, SALT, YEAST, VITAMIN A, RIBOFLAVIN.

Think About It

1. Which foods contain the most proteins? Carbohydrates? Fats?
2. Which foods have a high vitamin C content? A high iron content?
3. **Challenge** Explain why different brands of the same food might have different amounts of nutrients.

2 How Do Foods Keep You Healthy?

dietary fiber (dī/ə ter/ē fī/bər), plant material in foods that helps remove wastes from the large intestine.

Foods high in carbohydrates

You wake up suddenly. It is eight o'clock in the morning! You turned off your alarm and overslept. You put on your clothes, grab your books, and leave the house without eating breakfast. Later, you feel tired and restless. Because you skipped breakfast, your body lacks some nutrients you need to feel healthy and to stay alert.

Foods contain six kinds of nutrients—carbohydrates, fats, proteins, vitamins, minerals, and water. Find the foods that contain carbohydrates in the picture. Most carbohydrates are sugars and starches that your body breaks down and uses for energy. Other carbohydrates are **dietary fiber**—or plant materials that your body cannot digest. Dietary fiber helps you flush wastes from your large intestine.

Fats in the butter, oil, nuts, meats, and other foods in the picture also give you energy. When you eat more fats and carbohydrates than your body can use, your body changes these excess nutrients into fat tissue. The fat tissue in your body holds in heat and cushions your organs. When your body cannot get enough energy from the foods you eat, some of this fat tissue is broken down by your cells. Digested fats also make up some hormones and cell parts.

Foods high in fats

178

Foods high in protein

The foods in the picture are high in protein. Like fats, proteins also make up hormones and cell parts and provide energy. Proteins, however, do not provide as much energy as fats. Proteins are very important for building cells. All proteins are made of chemical building blocks called **amino acids.** During digestion, proteins are broken down into their separate amino acids. Your body uses amino acids to make new proteins. The new proteins help repair old cells and make new ones.

Carbohydrates, fats, and proteins can provide energy for your cells. Food energy is measured in **Calories.** Most people of your age need over 1200 Calories of energy to keep their hearts beating, stomachs churning, nerves sending impulses, and to carry out other basic body activities. The more active you are, the more Calories your body uses.

To help stay healthy, you must balance the food energy you take in with the energy your body uses as you move, grow, and think.

amino (ə mē′nō) **acids,** chemical building blocks that make up protein.

Calorie (kal′ər ē), unit of energy provided by food.

Find Out

You need 22 kinds of amino acids as building blocks in your body. Your body can make 13 of these amino acids. The other 9 amino acids must be obtained from the foods you eat. Look in a book on nutrition for a list of foods that contain these 9 *essential* amino acids.

Foods high in vitamin A

Foods high in vitamin B

Foods high in niacin

How Do Vitamins, Minerals, and Water Help You?

Unlike the other nutrients, vitamins, minerals, and water do not supply you with energy. However, they play a very important role in keeping you healthy. Eleven different vitamins help keep your cells working properly. The foods shown that are high in vitamin A, for example, help your eyes work well. Vitamins are found in a variety of foods.

The foods pictured also supply you with minerals. You need eighteen different minerals to keep your body healthy. Some minerals allow your nerves to send impulses and your muscles to contract. Another mineral, the sodium in salt, helps control the amount of water in your cells.

Water is the most abundant substance in your body. Body fluids are made mainly of water. Without these fluids, cells could not receive or use other nutrients or get rid of wastes.

Think About It

1. What do carbohydrates, fats, and proteins do for your body?
2. What do vitamins and minerals do for your body?
3. **Challenge** Explain how body fat might be helpful to people who live in a cold climate.

Foods high in vitamin C

Foods high in vitamin K

Activity

Measuring the Calories You Need

Purpose
To compare your Calorie intake and your energy use.

You Will Need
• paper and pencil

Directions
1. On a piece of paper, record everything you eat for the next 24 hours. Be sure to record the amount of each food you eat. On a separate piece of paper, record all your activities during the next 24 hours. Include the amount of time you spend doing each activity.
2. Use the Calorie chart to calculate the number of Calories in the foods you ate.
3. Add up the Calories in the foods you ate. This total is your Calorie intake for that 24-hour period.

Calorie chart

Food	Calories	Food	Calories
Apple	70	Ham, slice	135
Banana	100	Lettuce, head	60
Bread, slice	68	Milk, cup	160
Butter or margarine, pat	100	Orange	65
Carrot	20	Peanut butter, spoonful	93
Cereal, bowl	100	Potato	155
Cheese, slice	115	Rice, serving	180
Chicken, leg	310	Roast beef, slice	260
Corn, serving	170	Tomato	40
Egg	110	Tuna fish, can	380
Green beans, serving	45	Yogurt, plain, serving	150

Activity chart

Activity	Calories/hr	Activity	Calories/hr
Baseball	280	Running	600
Basketball	450	Skating	500
Cycling	300	Skipping rope	500
Dancing	500	Sleeping	70
Exercising	240	Swimming	520
Piano playing	175	Tennis	480
Reading, sitting	125	Walking	300

4. Use the activity chart to calculate the number of Calories you used doing each of your activities. The chart does not include the 1200 Calories you need each day to keep your body functioning.
5. Add the Calories you needed for each activity and the Calories you needed to keep your body functioning. This sum is all the Calories you used during that 24-hour period.

Think About It

1. Which foods provided most of your Calories?
2. Which activity used most of your Calories?
3. Compare your total Calorie intake with the number of Calories you used. Did your activities use up the Calories from the foods you ate?
4. **Challenge** Suppose you begin to practice a new sport. How might your Calorie needs change?

3 How Do You Keep Your Body Healthy?

Imagine that you are the ruler of a rich and beautiful country. One day, a stranger comes to your palace and asks, "Of all your possessions, great ruler, which is the most valuable?" You think of your jewels, gold, land, horses, and crown. None is your most valuable possession. You smile and answer, "My health is my most valuable possession."

Health is everyone's most valuable possession. You do many things to maintain your health. For example, you probably floss your teeth once a day, and brush them after each meal.

Healthy teeth and gums

Enlargement of bacteria on teeth

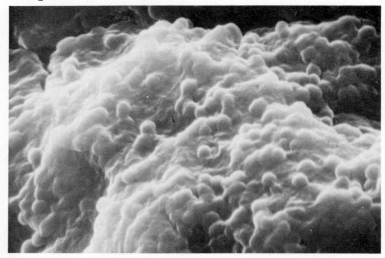

When you eat, bacteria such as those in the picture feed off the sugars in the food that gets on your teeth. The bacteria's waste products are strong acids that dissolve the minerals which make up your teeth. The acids can make holes, or cavities, in the teeth's surface. Other bacteria get between your teeth and gums and weaken the gums. Brushing and flossing your teeth gets rid of many of these bacteria and their harmful acid wastes. Your teeth and gums stay healthy like the white, shiny teeth and pink gums in the picture.

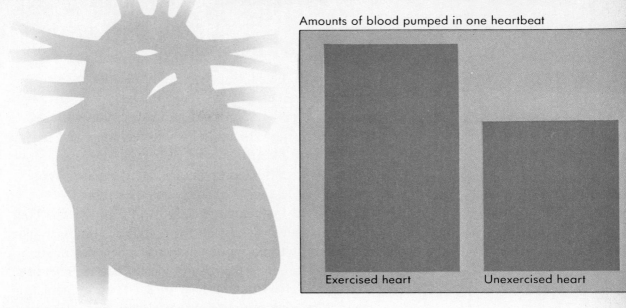

Amounts of blood pumped in one heartbeat

Exercised heart   Unexercised heart

Comparing exercised and unexercised heart

Exercise is another way you keep your body healthy. Any physical activity, even a quick dash to first base, strengthens your muscles and stretches your tendons. When you exercise continuously for fifteen minutes or longer, capillaries in your muscles open up to bring more oxygen to your muscle cells. Then, your muscles can work more efficiently.

By exercising every day, for example, by riding a bicycle to school, you strengthen your heart muscle. Compare the amount of blood pumped by the exercised heart to the amount of blood pumped by the unexercised heart. The exercised heart pumps more blood with each heartbeat. So, a strong heart can beat slower than an unexercised heart but still deliver the same amount of blood to the cells. A strong, exercised heart does not need to work hard to keep you healthy.

Regular, continuous exercise also increases the amount of air you can inhale at one time. Then, more oxygen enters your bloodstream and moves throughout your body. As a result, your muscles can get more energy, and you do not tire easily.

Have You Heard?

Members of the Tarahumara (tar ə hü′mä rə) tribe in northern Mexico are very strong runners. Their favorite sport is a game that goes on for several days. The players run between villages, kicking a wooden ball. Some players run 300 km over rugged mountains without stopping.

183

Why Is Sleep Important?

Sleep also helps keep your body healthy. Scientists cannot explain exactly how sleep helps your body. If you do not get enough sleep, however, you will feel tired and restless. Sleep helps you feel alert and healthy.

When you sleep, many of your body processes slow down. Your pulse and breathing rate decrease. Your temperature lowers. Voluntary muscles relax.

Other body systems are active while you sleep. Your digestive system breaks down food. Your pituitary gland releases growth hormone while you sleep. Brain stem cells send impulses that cause you to dream. Scientists are studying the brain activity of the sleeping person in the picture. The scientists hope to learn how sleep helps the body function at its best.

Think About It

1. How do brushing and flossing keep your teeth and gums healthy?
2. Describe three ways exercise helps your body.
3. **Challenge** How could eating a large meal just before going to bed each night affect your body?

Studying sleep

Do You Know?

What Are the Stages of Sleep?

A scientist who has spent many years studying sleep was asked this question: "Why do we need sleep?" His answer: "If we do not sleep, we get very sleepy."

No one knows exactly why we sleep. But scientists have learned a lot about *how* we sleep. The person in the picture is taking part in a sleep experiment. From sleep experiments, scientists have learned that there are four different stages of sleep.

When you first fall asleep, your heart starts to beat more slowly. Your breathing slows down. If something wakes you, you might not think that you had been asleep. Some people call this kind of sleep dozing. Scientists call it stage 1 sleep.

Next, if you are not awakened, you drift into a deeper sleep. Your pulse and breathing become even slower than they were during stage 1 sleep. But you can still be awakened quite easily. If you take a catnap, you probably will not get any further than this stage of sleep, which is called stage 2.

If you sleep longer than about twenty minutes, you go into the third stage of sleep. Your body is very relaxed. It would take a loud noise to wake you up.

You have probably heard of people who walk in their sleep. No one knows what makes people sleepwalk. But a person can sleepwalk only during stage 4 sleep. This is the deepest kind of sleep. If someone wakes you up during stage 4, you might feel very confused. It might take you a few minutes to get used to being awake.

After about ten minutes of stage 4 sleep, you go back to stage 3 and then to stage 2. Then, something quite different begins to happen. Your heartbeat becomes rapid. Your eyelids flutter, and your eyes move. This stage of sleep is called REM (rapid eye movement) sleep.

Most dreams happen during REM sleep. Scientists who study dreams often make noises or talk to sleeping people in the REM stage. They are trying to find out what effects noises can have on dreams. As sleep research continues, scientists might also learn what causes dreams and how dreams might be helpful to people.

Sleep research

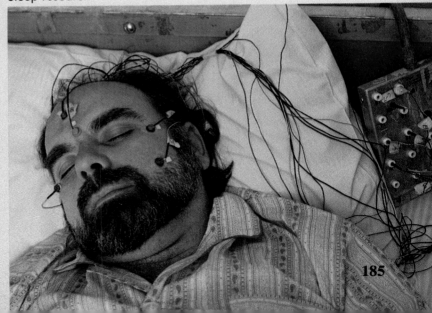

185

4 How Can Drugs Affect Your Body?

antibiotic (an´ti bī ot´ik), a prescription drug that kills bacteria.

Have You Heard?

The antibiotic penicillin was discovered by Sir Alexander Fleming in 1928. Fleming was growing bacteria in a dish for an experiment. When mold accidentally got into the dish and grew, all the bacteria around the mold died. Fleming discovered that the mold produced a substance that killed his bacteria. He named the substance *penicillin* after the name of the mold that produced it.

When you see green mold on food, you throw the food away. You may think because mold spoils food, mold can only harm you. One green mold, however, produces a substance that is used in medicine. A doctor might prescribe the medicine when you have a bad sore throat. The substance helps you get well.

This substance, called penicillin (pen´ə sil´ən), is an **antibiotic.** Doctors prescribe antibiotics when bacteria in your body make you ill. Antibiotics kill bacteria. A doctor might prescribe other medicines when you have the flu. You also might take medicine that does not have to be prescribed. For example, if you have a bad stomach ache, an adult in your family might give you medicine to help you feel better.

All these medicines are drugs that change the way cells in your body work. For medicines to help you, you must follow the directions on the label. Find the directions on the back of the medicine bottle. Notice that people of different ages are given different directions. If you do not follow the right directions, medicines can make you very sick. Used correctly, however, medicinal drugs can help you get well and stay healthy.

Directions on medicine bottles

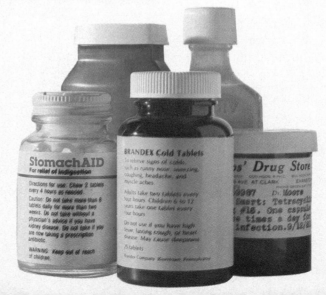

Food and drinks containing caffeine

Drugs are found in substances besides medicines. Drugs affect the body in different ways. **Stimulants** increase the rate that nerve impulses cross synapses. The food and drinks shown have small amounts of the stimulant caffeine. Such foods and drinks can keep a person awake when the body needs sleep.

Other stimulants stronger than caffeine in foods and drinks can be harmful to a person's health. These stimulants can damage the heart, for example.

In contrast to stimulants, **depressants** decrease the rate that nerve impulses cross synapses. Alcohol in liquor is a depressant. Some body processes slow down when a person takes a depressant. Breathing rate, pulse rate, and blood pressure can decrease. Because of such effects, depressants, like stimulants, can harm the body.

Hallucinogens are drugs that may interfere with the nerve chemicals that carry messages across synapses. Hallucinogens can cause a person to see, hear, and feel things that exist only in the person's mind.

Marijuana (mar ə wa′nə) is a drug that can be hallucinogenic. Marijuana can cause confusion, slow reaction time, and weaken a person's memory. Scientists are studying marijuana to find out if the drug damages brain cells. It is known that smoking marijuana can damage the lungs.

stimulant (stim′yə lənt), a drug that increases the rate that nerve impulses cross synapses.

depressant (di pres′nt), a drug that decreases the rate that nerve impulses cross synapses.

hallucinogen (hə lu′sn ə jen), a drug which changes the way that the brain works. Hallucinogens might interfere with nerve chemicals in the brain.

How Can Drugs Affect the Body Over Time?

Many drugs can be even more harmful if used for a long period of time. Compare the smoker's lungs with the lungs of a nonsmoker. When a person smokes, tar from the smoke gets into the person's lungs. Tar formed the black spots in the lungs of the smoker. This tar damages the lungs. As a result of lung damage, a smoker might have trouble breathing. Smoking can also lead to fatal lung and heart diseases.

Frequent use of some drugs over a long period of time can cause physical dependence on such drugs. Physical dependence means that a person needs to take a certain drug to keep from feeling ill. The stronger the drug, the stronger the effects the person might feel when drug use is stopped. A person who is physically dependent on a strong depressant might die if suddenly deprived of the drug. A doctor's guidance can help a person overcome drug dependence.

Think About It

1. What are two ways medicines can help the body?
2. Describe five ways drugs can harm the body.
3. **Challenge** How might taking a depressant affect someone driving a car?

Nonsmoker's lung

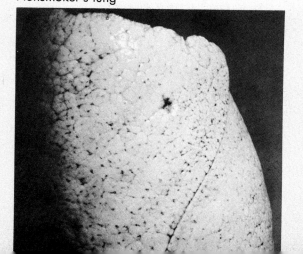

Smoker's lung

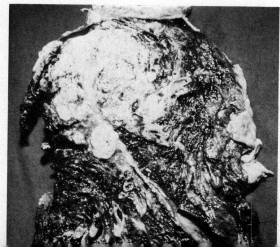

Tie It Together

Sum It Up

1. Imagine that you are the coach for a gymnast who is training for the Olympics. Plan her activities and diet for one school day. Include the number of Calories she uses doing each activity. Describe how exercise helps her body. Plan a menu for all her meals. Be sure to include the nutrients she gets from each food. Describe what happens to her body as she sleeps.

2. Unscramble the underlined words to complete the sentences.
   a. A clughanoline is a drug that causes a person to see, hear, or feel things that exist only in the person's mind.
   b. A stimulant escanires the rate that nerve impulses cross synapses, while a prestansed decreases that rate.
   c. A prescription medicine that kills bacteria is an ictiobiant.
   d. All drugs change the way that body lecls work. If drugs are not used as directed, they can marh the body.

Challenge!

1. Describe the nutrients in a bowl of vegetable beef soup.

2. If a person wanted to gain weight, how should the person change his or her diet and activities?

3. How does regular exercise help your heart and lungs work together well?

4. Some bacteria in your body make vitamins for you. How could taking some antibiotics affect your nutrition?

5. How might taking hallucinogens affect a person's driving?

Science Words

amino acid

antibiotic

Calorie

depressant

dietary fiber

hallucinogen

stimulant

Laboratory

Stress

Purpose
To observe how stress affects memory and pulse rate.

You Will Need
- plastic margarine tub with lid
- construction paper
- scissors
- glue or tape
- 15 assorted small items
- clock with second hand

Stating the Problem

Have you ever been in a hurry and forgotten to do something important? Have you ever been nervous before a test and made mistakes on questions to which you knew the answers? If so, you know how it feels to be under stress. You know from experience that stress can affect your memory.

Stress can also cause changes in your body. When you are under stress, you might begin to sweat, or your stomach might hurt. Your pulse and breathing rates might change. You can find out

a

how stress can affect you as you take a simple memory test. Predict how increased stress might affect your memory and your pulse rate. Record your predictions.

Investigating the Problem
1. On a piece of construction paper, trace a circle the size of the lid of a margarine tub. Cut out the circle. Glue or tape the circle to the top of the lid.
2. Choose 15 small items, and put them in the

margarine tub. See picture a. Cover the margarine tub, and set it aside.
3. Count and record your pulse as shown in picture b.

b

4. Exchange margarine tubs with a classmate. When your teacher gives a signal, remove the lid from the margarine tub, and look at the contents for 30 seconds. Try to notice something about each item that will help you remember each one. Do not move the objects in the margarine tub.

5. After 30 seconds put the lid back on the margarine tub. Before you write down the items that you remember, take your pulse as you did in step 3. Record your pulse rate on a chart like the one shown in c.

6. When your teacher gives the signal, list the names of all the items that you remember seeing in the margarine tub. You will have 30 seconds to write the list.

7. Open your margarine tub, and correct your list. Cross off the items that were not in the margarine tub. Record on your chart the number of items that you remembered correctly.

Resting pulse _____ beats per minute

Test 1 (30 seconds) _____ beats per minute
_____ number of items remembered

Test 2 (15 seconds) _____ beats per minute
_____ number of items remembered

Test 3 (8 seconds) _____ beats per minute
_____ number of items remembered

c

8. Exchange tubs with another classmate. Repeat steps 4–7 twice. The first time you repeat the exercise, you will have 15 seconds to observe the contents. The second time you repeat the exercise, you will have 8 seconds.

Making Conclusions
1. What caused you to feel stress while memorizing the contents of the margarine tubs?
2. How did having less time affect your scores on the memory tests? How do you think stress affected your performance on the memory tests?
3. How can stress affect a person's pulse rate?
4. Are the body changes that are due to stress permanent? Explain your answer.

Careers

Orthopedic Technician

Leroy has some advice for people who would like a career in medicine. "Remember that doctors and nurses are not the only ones who work in hospitals. Many different jobs are available in a hospital."

Leroy works in a hospital as an orthopedic technician. It is his job to apply and remove casts.

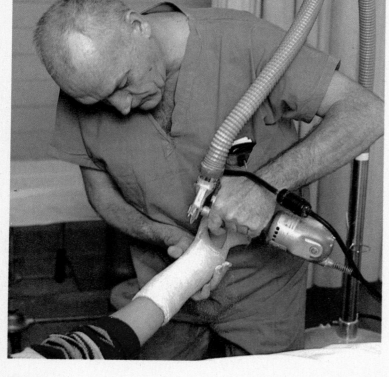

He also fits patients for back braces, crutches, and canes.

"The whole idea of a cast or brace is to keep the injured part of the body in one position. This way, the injury will heal properly.

"To make a cast, I wrap wet plaster bandages around the area where a bone is broken. The wet bandages must be molded carefully. Then, after the bandages dry, the arm, leg, or other body part will stay in the right position."

Leroy often works with patients who have just had surgery. "Many times after an operation, part of a patient's body needs to remain completely still. I set up different lines, weights, and pulleys around the patient's bed to keep the body still. I also try to keep the patient comfortable."

Leroy remembers becoming interested in a medical career in high school. He worked as an orderly in a hospital while going to college.

"I like this job because I am working with people. But some people can present a real challenge. I may put a cast on a three-year-old child. But thirty minutes later, the child might find a way to take the cast off. I explain to the child that the broken bone will heal only if the cast stays on.

"The best part of my job is seeing a patient after being healed. It is rewarding to know I helped someone regain the use of an arm, leg, or back."

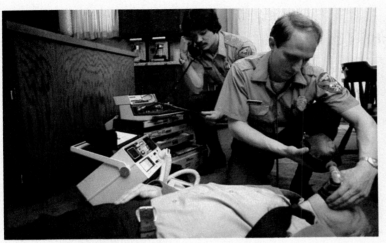
Emergency medical technicians

Pharmacist

Many people who have jobs in medicine do not work in hospitals.

When an accident occurs, the first medical workers on the scene may be **emergency medical technicians** (EMTs). EMTs drive emergency vehicles. They give emergency medical care to victims of car accidents, heart attacks, near drownings, and other emergencies. The EMTs can use a radio to contact a doctor at the hospital. The doctor advises the EMTs of what to do until the patient reaches the hospital.

You can become an emergency medical technician after taking a training course.

If a doctor wants you to take medicine, he or she usually gives you a prescription. The prescription is a written description of the medicine. You take the prescription to a **pharmacist.** A pharmacist usually works in a drugstore. The pharmacist looks at the prescription and prepares the correct medicine. Pharmacists sometimes mix and weigh certain substances to make the medicine. Pharmacists go to college for four to six years.

Many schools have cafeterias that provide lunches for the students. A **dietician** plans the meals and supervises the cooking to be sure the meals are nutritious.

Dieticians also plan menus for hospitals, nursing homes, and companies.

To become a dietician, you must study food science in college for four years.

In your classroom, you might have a chart showing the skeleton or muscles of the human body. That detailed drawing was done by a **medical illustrator.** These artists go to college to develop their skills. They make drawings, paintings, and charts that doctors study in books and magazines. Medical illustrators also make models of body parts that you may find in a museum.

193

On Your Own

Picture Clue

Look at the picture on page 140. This person is trying to control his heartbeat while sitting in a chair. How do you think the wires and the instruments help the person do this? Compare this picture to the picture of the sleeping person on page 184. How are these pictures similar?

Projects

1. You can measure your reaction time. Ask a partner to hold the end of a meter stick. Hold your thumb and forefinger near the bottom of the meter stick, but do not touch the meter stick. When your partner drops the meter stick, catch it between your thumb and forefinger. The smaller the distance the meter stick falls, the faster your reaction time. Practice the exercise to see if you can improve your reaction time.

2. Make a collage illustrating the changes your body goes through as you get older. Cut out magazine pictures of people of different ages who are doing different activities.

3. Compare foods that are sold in supermarkets in different communities. How do the foods differ from the foods you eat? What are different sources of proteins eaten by people of different ethnic backgrounds?

Books About Science

Aging by Virginia Alvin and Glen Silverstein. Watts, 1979. Learn about the aging process and society's changing attitudes toward older people.

Bodyworks: The Kids' Guide to Food and Physical Fitness by Carol Bershad and Deborah Bernick. Random House, 1979. Discover the hows and whys of keeping fit.

Is the Cat Dreaming Your Dream? by Margaret Hyde. McGraw-Hill, 1980. Find out about your dreams and their meanings.

The Mind and Body by Christopher Pick. Warwick, 1980. How do the body and mind work together? This book can tell you.

Unit Test

Matching

Number your paper from 1–10. Read the description in Column I. Next to each number, write the letter of the word or phrase from Column II that best matches the description in Column I.

Column I

1. a change to which you can respond
2. a nerve cell that carries impulses from the brain and spinal cord to the muscles
3. a chemical that endocrine glands release into the bloodstream to regulate cells' activities
4. the period of growth and change in a person between the ages of nine and eighteen years
5. a gap between the axon of one nerve cell and the dendrite of the next nerve cell
6. a cell that detects a specific kind of stimulus
7. the gland that produces growth hormone and other hormones which control some endocrine glands
8. the large, wrinkled top part of the brain that controls thinking and voluntary movements
9. a hormone that is released when the body needs sudden energy
10. the process endocrine glands use to regulate the amount of hormone they release

Column II

a. adolescence

b. cerebrum

c. feedback

d. hormone

e. motor nerve cell

f. pituitary

g. receptor

h. sensory nerve cell

i. adrenaline

j. stimulus

k. synapse

Multiple Choice

Number your paper from 11–13. Next to each number, write the letter of the word or phrase that best answers the question.

11. Which is *not* a nutrient?
    a. Calorie
    b. fat
    c. mineral
    d. carbohydrate

12. Which is a drug that kills bacteria?
    a. stimulant
    b. amino acid
    c. antibiotic
    d. hallucinogen

13. What happens when you sleep?
    a. Your pulse and breathing rate decrease.
    b. Your digestive system breaks down your food.
    c. Nerve cells in your brain stem are active.
    d. all the above

UNIT FIVE
ENERGY AND ITS USE

Magnetized
All running to the center
All wanting to be there
All attracted
All together.

Heather Hindman *age 12*

Chapter 12
Force, Work, and Energy

The ant in the picture is carrying food to her colony. The leaf looks tiny to us. However, the leaf is both larger and much heavier than the ant. Imagine yourself trying to pick up a load of bricks weighing more than twice as much as you do. The ant needs a lot of energy to do all that work. You need energy to do work such as cleaning your room or hitting a ball.

The lessons in this chapter will help you recognize the many ways you use energy.

1 Using Energy to Do Work
2 How Do Forces Affect Objects?
3 What Is Work?
4 What Is Energy?
5 How Do People Use Energy for Power?

1 Using Energy to Do Work

Taking out the trash, raking leaves, playing ball, and swimming are work. Your muscles need energy to do all these activities. The more work you do, the more energy you need.

Notice when your muscles make you feel that you are doing work as you do each of the following movements. Stretch out your arm, and hold a book. Then, raise the book as shown in the picture. Hold the book steady. Walk a few steps, still holding the book. Then, lower the book to a desk, and leave the book there.

Rest one hand on a chair or desk to balance yourself. Raise and lower your body by bending your knees slowly. Now, hold yourself in the lower position for a few seconds. Notice how your muscles feel.

Think About It

1. When did you feel that your muscles were working the hardest?
2. In which activity did you need the most energy?
3. **Challenge** Against what force did you have to work in order to lift the book?

2 How Do Forces Affect Objects?

The men moving furniture in the picture have a difficult job. They lift heavy furniture from the floor of a house. They carry the furniture out of the house and down the stairs. Then, they lift the furniture onto a truck. Finally, they put the furniture down in the truck.

The motion of the furniture changes when the men lift, carry, or lower it. If the men let go of the furniture, gravity will pull it down. Gravity changes the furniture's motion. Anything that could change the motion of an object is a **force**. A force can be a push or pull.

force, anything that could cause a change in an object's motion.

A force can change an object's motion in several ways. First, a force can make an object at rest start moving. Second, it can stop a moving object. Third, it can speed up or slow down a moving object. Last, it can change the direction of an object's motion.

The motion of the furniture changes only because the men use force on it. The motion of any object changes only because a force or forces act on it.

Using forces on an object

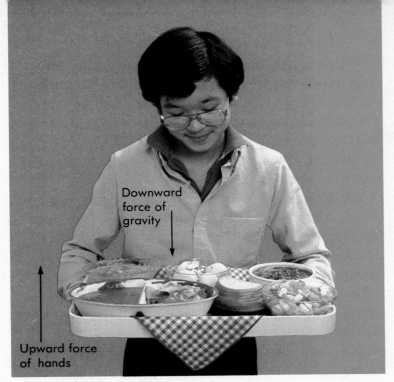

Downward force of gravity

Upward force of hands

Some forces acting on an object

Find Out

Look in a book of world records to find out the greatest weight a person has ever lifted.

Have You Heard?

The strength of an organism depends on the surface area of the organism and on the size of the organism. An ant is strong because the amount of surface on its body is large compared to the ant's size.

A force does not always change an object's motion. You can pull on a heavy chair without making it move. The chair remains at rest because gravity is stronger than you are. In this case two forces—gravity and your force—act on an object.

Usually, many forces act on an object. The picture shows some of the forces acting on a tray of food. Gravity pulls down on the tray. But you hold the tray up with just enough force to balance gravity. If you put the tray down on a table, the table, instead of you, holds the tray up.

Think About It

1. What can a force do to an object?
2. Explain when a force might not change an object's motion.
3. **Challenge** Describe some of the forces acting on you as you walk.

3 What Is Work?

work, the result of a force moving an object through a distance along the same line as the force's direction.

When movers lift a heavy chair, they use force to raise it some distance above the floor. The directions of the force and of the chair's motion are both upward. The swimmer in the picture also uses a force. His hands and feet push back on the water to make him go forward. His pushes and the water both go in the same direction—backward.

You probably think that the movers and the swimmer "work hard." A scientist would agree with you. In science, **work** is done only when a force moves an object through a distance. The directions of both the force and the distance must be along the same line.

Now, think about movers trying to push a piano across a room. They cannot push hard enough to move it. Their muscles are "working hard." But they do no work because they cannot make the piano move. They do not use their force to move the piano any distance across the floor. You also do no work on a book when you hold it steady. You use a force to hold the book up. But you do not use that force to make the book move up or down. You do work on the book only when you use force to make the book move.

Using force to do work

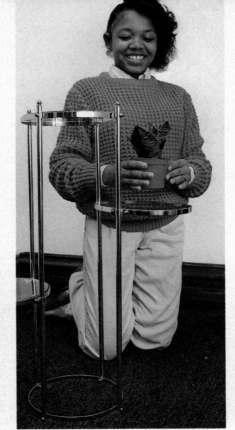

Doing different amounts of work

You do a lot of work every day. Imagine that you are the student in the pictures. When you put a plant on a shelf, you lift the plant up a certain distance. If you put the plant on a higher or lower shelf, you change the distance you lift the plant. If you lift a heavier plant up to the original shelf, you must use more force. You change the amount of work you do by changing the amount of force, the amount of distance, or both.

Think About It

1. When does a force do work on an object?
2. You push on a stuck door but cannot open it. Have you done any work? Explain.
3. **Challenge** You climb a ladder, stopping on each step. When are you doing any work? Explain.

4 What Is Energy?

energy, the ability to do work.

kinetic (ki net′ik) energy, the energy an object has because it moves.

Objects doing work

All the pictures on this page show work being done. The girl swings her legs out. The engines of the rocket push the rocket up. The bowling ball hits and pushes the pins back.

Any object can do work if it has energy. For example, you eat food to give you energy to live, run, study, and clean your room. Rocket engines get their energy by burning fuel. In science, energy means being able to do work.

When you do work on an object, you give that object some of your energy. By throwing a ball, you do work on the ball. You give energy from your moving arm to the ball. Now, the ball has the energy to move. In doing work, you transfer energy from yourself to the ball.

From many observations, scientists have learned that energy does not just appear and disappear. Energy has to come from somewhere and go somewhere. This observation led scientists to separate energy into two kinds. One kind is the energy of motion—kinetic energy. All moving objects have kinetic energy. A moving ball, a runner, and a flying airplane have kinetic energy.

Girl doing work

The bow will have stored energy

Different amounts of potential energy

Think about the motions of the archer and the bow and arrow shown. The archer will do work on the bow when he pulls back on the string of the bow. As he pulls, he will give the string kinetic energy. But the energy does not remain as kinetic energy. When the string stops moving, the energy is stored in the bow. This kind of energy is **potential energy.** The bow now has the energy to do work on the arrow. When the archer lets go of the string, the bow gives its energy to the arrow. When the arrow is in motion, it has kinetic energy.

Each of the cheerleaders shown did a different amount of work to lift herself to a different height. So each person gained a different amount of potential energy. The cheerleaders will eventually jump down. Each person's amount of potential energy will become an equal amount of kinetic energy.

potential (pə ten′shəl) **energy,** stored energy.

205

How Is Energy Wasted?

Energy changes from kinetic to potential and back again many times in your daily life. No matter how many changes happen, the total amount of energy always stays the same.

Often, however, the energy changes into a form we cannot use. This kind of change happened when the cheerleaders hit the floor. Some of their kinetic energy went into the floor, and some of it made a sound. They could not use that energy to do any work.

The force of friction wastes much energy. When two surfaces rub each other, friction between them causes heat. The picture shows sparks from great friction between two surfaces. Friction wasted energy that could have run the machine. We use oil or grease to reduce friction and energy waste.

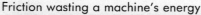
Friction wasting a machine's energy

Think About It

1. How does an object's energy change when work is done on that object?
2. What is kinetic energy? Potential energy?
3. **Challenge** Explain why a bouncing ball rises to a lower and lower height after each bounce.

Activity

Using Energy in Racing Cars

Purpose
To observe changes in an object's energy.

You Will Need
• 4 meter sticks
• tape
• scissors
• balloon
• small toy car

Directions
1. Tape the meter sticks onto a table or the floor. The meter sticks should make an alley just wide enough for the car to move through, as shown.
2. Put a piece of tape between the meter sticks at the 5-cm mark. This tape marks the starting line for your car.
3. Blow up your balloon. Hold it closed as your partner attaches it to your car with tape. Your car should look like the one in the picture.
4. Still holding the balloon closed, put your car at the starting line. Your partner should stand near the end of the meter sticks.
5. Let go of the balloon, and watch your car move down the alley.
6. Write down the distance your car moves by subtracting 5 cm from the centimeter mark where the car stops.
7. Repeat steps 3–6 twice.

Think About It
1. Which kind of energy did your car have as it stood at the starting line? During the race?
2. How did friction waste the car's energy as the car moved down the track?
3. How would the distance the car traveled have been different without friction?
4. **Challenge** How could you change your car or the alley to make the car go faster and farther?

5 How Do People Use Energy for Power?

power, the rate at which work is done.

energy source, the original material or place from which energy can be produced.

Think about all the things you and your family do during a usual day. Many of these activities need electricity. Years ago, people did most of these jobs by hand and took more time to do them. For example, suppose you have to whip egg whites. You will spend about five times more time whipping the eggs by hand than an electric mixer will. You and the mixer use about the same amount of energy, but the mixer uses less time. In science, how quickly you do work is **power.** The mixer is more powerful than you are because it does the same work in less time.

We must produce electric power to help us do daily tasks. The drawing shows an electric power plant. To make electricity, some power companies use falling water. Other power companies use heat from inside the earth, from burning coal, or from some other **energy source** to heat water. The falling water, hot water, or steam turns fanlike blades. The blades turn a machine that produces electricity. Eventually, the electricity flows through wires to homes, businesses, and factories.

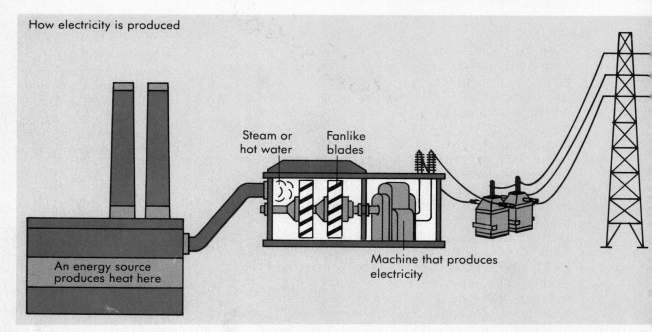

How electricity is produced

Steam or hot water

Fanlike blades

An energy source produces heat here

Machine that produces electricity

Electric companies spend billions of dollars every year to make electricity. People pay to get electricity from these companies.

The electric company in your community puts a meter in your home. This meter records how much electricity your family uses. The meter probably looks something like the one in the picture. The dials show the amount of electricity you use. Your electric bill tells you this amount and the charge for the energy.

Think About It

2. Explain how electric power is produced.
3. **Challenge** A baker kneads dough for eight minutes. A machine does the same job in two minutes. Both the baker and the machine do the same amount of work. Which one is more powerful?

Find Out

Ask an adult in your family to help you locate your electric meter. Then, read it to find out how much electricity your family has used since your last bill.

An electric meter

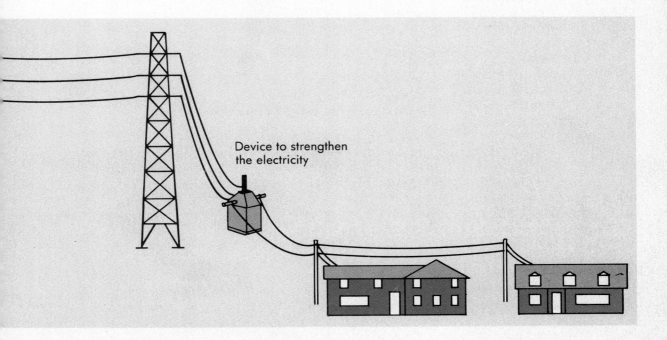

Device to strengthen the electricity

Do You Know?

How Does a Diver Gain Energy?

The diver leaps into the air. For a moment, he seems to hang suspended. Then, he slowly begins a graceful turn. He completes his dive, entering the water, hardly making a splash.

The diver needs energy to make the twists and turns of a fancy dive. The diver gains potential energy as he climbs the ladder to the top of the diving board.

He gains more potential energy when he jumps high into the air just before he dives. The diver's potential energy is changed into kinetic energy as he falls toward the water.

Since kinetic energy is the energy of motion, the greater the diver's speed, the more kinetic energy he has. A diver diving from a 3-meter board is traveling at a speed of about 28 kilometers per hour before entering the water.

The diver's potential energy becomes kinetic energy

To dive gracefully, a diver needs to learn how to control his or her body movements while falling through the air. Most divers learn to dive first from a low diving board. Since the diver has little potential energy at the top of a low dive, the diver has little kinetic energy when hitting the water. Because the diver is not moving quickly, it is easier to learn to control body movements.

As the diver gains control, he or she advances to a higher diving board. The diver can learn to perform complicated and graceful dives, such as the one shown in the picture.

Tie It Together

Sum It Up

Look at the picture of the ball, and answer the questions.

1. When was force used on the ball? When is any work done on the ball? Explain your answers.

2. The ball is moving fastest just before it hits the ground. What kind of energy does it have there?

3. How can the student change the power with which he throws the ball?

Challenge!

1. You push and push on a brick wall, but nothing happens. What can you say about the forces acting on the wall?

2. You pick up a game and carry it across a room. When is work done on the game? Explain.

3. Compare the meaning most people use for the word *work* with its scientific meaning.

4. You press the coils of a spring together and then let them spring apart. Explain when work is done and what kind of energy the spring has in both conditions.

5. Explain how two machines can do the same amount of work but have different amounts of power.

Science Words

energy

energy source

force

kinetic energy

potential energy

power

work

Chapter 13
Electricity

In the picture a flash of lightning appears during a summer thunderstorm. Lightning is electricity that can be dangerous to people. Even though electricity can be useful, you must be careful whenever you use it.

People have been interested in electricity for thousands of years. Today, people have many ways of using and controlling electricity.

The lessons in this chapter describe the part electricity plays in the study of matter.

1 Observing Electricity

2 How Do Electric Charges Act?

3 What Is Electric Current?

4 How Does Current Move in a Circuit?

1 Observing Electricity

Perhaps you know what happens when you rub together certain objects, such as balloons and wool cloth. These objects have extra electricity after you rub them together.

Place five or six pieces of puffed rice cereal in a balloon. Then, blow up the balloon and tie its neck closed with string. Rub the balloon with wool cloth about twenty times as shown in the first picture. Move the cloth in only one direction. Notice what happens between the cloth and the balloon.

Next, rub a plastic comb with the cloth as you did the balloon. Then, hold the balloon, and bring the comb near it, as shown in the second picture. Notice what happens between them. Make the cereal "dance" inside the balloon by moving the comb around.

Think About It

1. How did you give the balloon and the comb extra electricity?
2. Compare the way the balloon and the comb acted with the way the balloon and the cloth acted.
3. **Challenge** What caused the objects to change their motion?

2 How Do Electric Charges Act?

You might get a shock when you walk across a rug and touch some metal. Perhaps you even notice a spark. You might have to pull apart a shirt and a sock after you take them out of the clothes dryer. Maybe you hear or see a spark and feel its shock.

Sparks often happen after two objects are rubbed together. The rubbing gives an electric charge to both objects. For example, if you rub a balloon with wool cloth, both objects become electrically charged. When you bring them near each other, they pull on—or attract—each other. The pictures show how this motion might look.

Giving two objects an electric charge

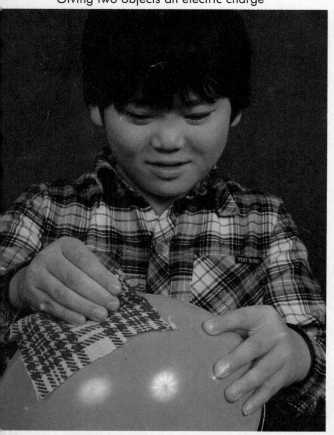

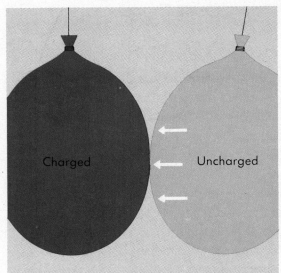

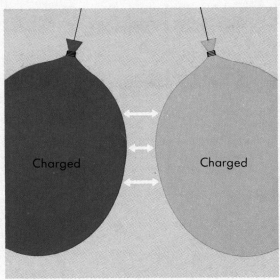

Charged balloon attracts uncharged balloon

Charged balloons repel each other

You can also give an object a charge by bringing it near a charged object. In the drawing, a charged balloon is near an uncharged balloon. At first, the charged balloon pulls the uncharged balloon toward it. The uncharged balloon picks up some charge from the charged balloon. Suddenly, the charged balloons push away from—or repel—each other and do not come back together.

By observing charged objects, people have learned that charge comes in only two kinds. One kind is positive. The other kind is the opposite—negative. Two objects with a positive charge repel each other. So do two objects with a negative charge. Like charges repel each other. But an object with a positive charge and an object with a negative charge attract each other. Unlike charges attract each other.

Whenever the motion of an object changes, a force or forces must be acting on the object. The attracting and repelling between the balloons are signs of a force acting on the balloons. Charged objects have an electric force between them.

Find Out

The study of electricity is a very old part of science. Learn more about the history of electricity by reading about it in an encyclopedia. Be sure to check into the work of the scientists Volta, Galvani, and Ampère.

215

Where Do Charges Come From?

atom (at′əm), a particle that makes up matter.

proton (prō′ton), a particle with a positive charge that is in the center of an atom.

neutron (nü′tron), a particle with no charge that is in the center of an atom.

electron (i lek′tron), a particle with a negative charge that moves around in an atom.

You can cut a piece of paper into smaller and smaller pieces. Finally, you reach a piece too small to be cut. Matter comes in even smaller pieces that are too tiny to be seen. These particles of matter are **atoms.** Inside every atom are even smaller particles that carry positive and negative charges.

Study the model of an atom shown. Notice that most of an atom is empty space. The center has two kinds of particles. Each particle with a positive charge is a **proton.** Each particle with no charge is a **neutron.** Moving about are particles of matter with negative charges—the **electrons.** A proton has the same amount of charge as an electron. But the charges are opposites.

Most of the time, objects have the same number of protons as electrons. So the positive charges balance the negative charges, and the object is uncharged.

The electric force attracts the electrons and protons to each other. This force holds all matter together.

An oxygen atom

Proton

Neutron

Electron

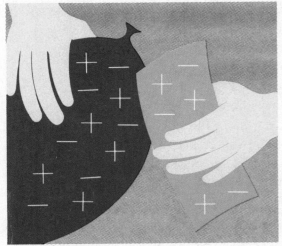

Before rubbing

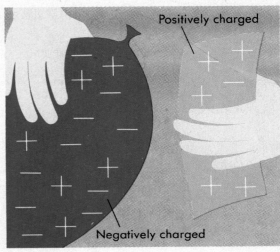

Positively charged

Negatively charged

After rubbing

Electrons can move about more freely than protons or neutrons. Rubbing two objects together takes electrons away from one object and moves them to the other. The drawings show what happens. The object with extra electrons now has a negative charge. The object left with more protons than electrons has a positive charge.

Sometimes many extra electrons build up on an object. The electrons repel each other because they have the same kind of charge. They move as far from each other on the object as they can.

If charge keeps building up on an object, the electrons become crowded. All at once, some of them jump to a nearby object, and you see a spark. All sparks happen in this way. Lightning, which is just a big spark, results from charge building up on clouds.

Have You Heard?

Around 400 B.C. the Greek thinker Democritus was the first person to say that matter could be divided into particles. He named these particles *atomos,* the Greek word meaning "cannot be cut."

Think About It

1. How will two objects with negative charges act?
2. How are the particles in an atom charged?
3. **Challenge** What do you think happens to two oppositely charged balloons after they touch each other for a while?

217

3 What Is Electric Current?

electric current, a flow of charges.

Sparks show that charges move. A flow of charged particles is an **electric current.** Just as air has wind currents, matter can have electric currents. A spark is really a burst of electric current in the air.

In a wire an electric current is a flow of electrons. The drawing shows how a current passes through a copper wire. Every atom has one or two electrons which wander about in the spaces between the atoms. When you turn on a light, the electrons in between move in one main direction as a current. These motions happen very quickly. The light shines almost immediately. But if you had to wait for one electron to make its way along the wire, you would wait several hours for the light to shine!

Electric current passes through different materials differently. For example, current passes easily through many metals. It is much harder for current to pass through air, rubber, glass, and plastic.

How current moves through a metal

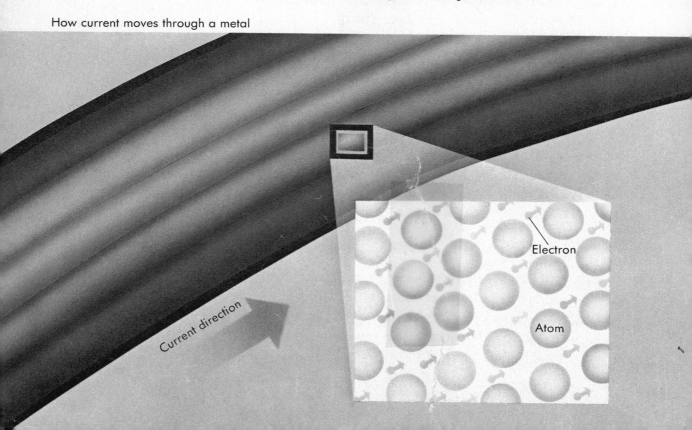

Current direction

Electron

Atom

Some conductors

resistance (ri zis/təns), a measure of how well electric current passes through a material.

conductor (kən duk/tər), a material through which electric current passes easily.

insulator (in/sə lā/tər), a material through which electric current passes with difficulty or not at all.

Have You Heard?

Tires of trucks that carry gasoline are made to conduct electric current. Instead of letting charge build up on the metal truck, the tires conduct the charge to the ground. In this way, not enough charge builds up to spark a fire on the truck.

Some insulators

Resistance is a measure of how well an electric current passes through a material. Current passes easily through materials with low resistance. These materials are **conductors.** Most metals, especially gold, silver, copper, and aluminum, are good conductors.

Current moves with more difficulty or not at all through materials with high resistance. These materials are **insulators.** Rubber, glass, and plastic are good insulators. The pictures show some good conductors and some good insulators.

How Do People Put Resistance to Good Use?

People use both conductors and insulators. In your home, electric current moves through metal wires to reach many appliances. Insulators cover the wires to keep the current away from you and your home. Notice how the insulator covers the wire in the picture.

Current reaches the light bulb in the picture through copper wires. But, inside the bulb, the current must pass through very thin wires. They are made of another metal that has a higher resistance than copper. Current makes these wires heat up because it is harder for the current to pass through them. The wires become so hot they give off light.

Inside an electrical cord

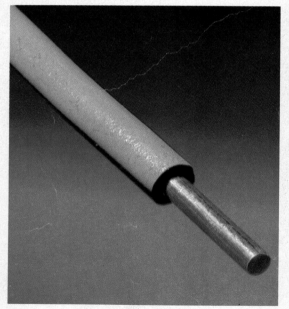

Heated wires inside a light bulb

Think About It

1. What is electrical resistance?
2. Compare a conductor with an insulator.
3. **Challenge** Use the idea of resistance to explain how the wires in a toaster toast bread.

Discover!

Electricity Can Help Heal Injuries

The discovery of electricity in the 1700s was an exciting event. At the time people suggested many uses for electricity. Some people thought that electric current could be used to cure people who were ill. Those dreams took a long time to come true.

In the last few years doctors have been experimenting with electric current to solve some medical problems. Probably the most successful of these experiments has been the treatment of broken bones with electricity. The pictures show a broken bone before and after treatment. The broken arm or leg is placed within an electrically charged region. A weak electric current flows inside the broken bone. This electric current helps the broken bone grow together. No one understands exactly how the electric current helps heal broken bones. But doctors are carefully studying the results of their experiments to learn how this treatment works.

Doctors are also testing the effect of electric current on wounds. Doctors place a small cloth over the wound and soak the cloth in a solution. Then, an electric current passes through the cloth. Wounds treated in this way sometimes heal twice as fast as those that were not treated with electric current.

It seems that we are finally on our way to using electricity in ways that were suggested two centuries ago!

Broken bone before treatment

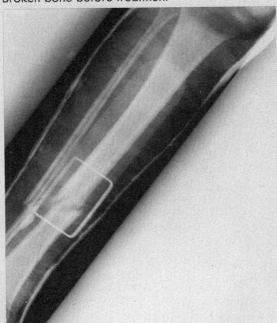

Broken bone after treatment

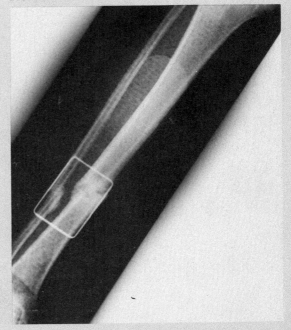

4 How Does Current Move in a Circuit?

The electricity we get from electric power plants is very easy to use. At the flip of a switch, electric current reaches your lamp or toaster. But, to be used, electric current must follow a closed path called a **circuit.**

The picture shows a dry cell. A dry cell or a battery is a source of electrical energy. One pole of the dry cell has a positive charge. The other pole has a negative charge. The dry cell "pushes" current from the negative pole through a circuit and back to the positive pole. This electrical "push" is like the push of the water pump shown. The pump does work on the water to send the water back up the pipe. The dry cell does work on the electrons to send current through the circuit.

circuit (sèr′kit), a path for current to follow from a source of electrical energy and back again.

The dry cell and the water pump do work

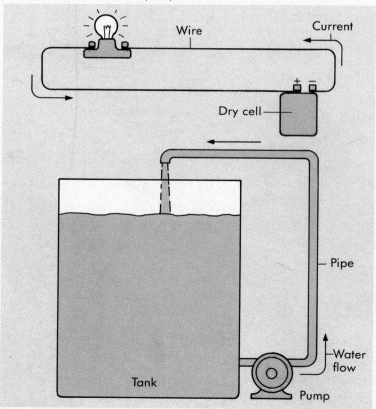

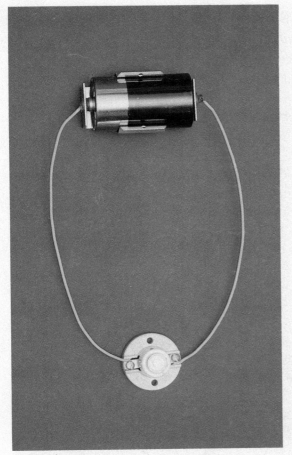

A closed circuit

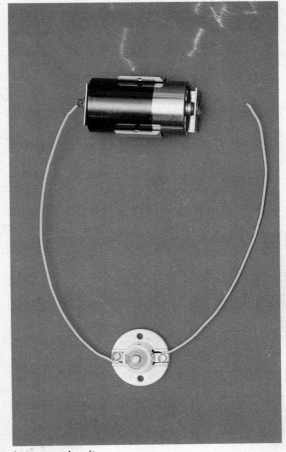

An open circuit

Notice in the first picture how each part of the circuit is connected. A wire leads from the dry cell to the bulb. Another wire connects the bulb back to the dry cell. Current follows the path from the dry cell through the bulb and back to the dry cell.

The lighted bulb shows that current is flowing. The circuit is closed because the path for current to follow is unbroken.

Notice that the bulb in the other picture is not lighted. One of the wires is not connected. Current cannot flow in this open circuit because the path has been broken. Current can flow only in a closed circuit.

Find Out

Ask an adult in your family to help you trace the circuit in a flashlight.

Find Out

Find out what an electric "ground" is. A book on electricity or an encyclopedia will have the answer.

How Do We Use Electricity Safely?

Electrical energy can provide heat and light for our homes and energy to run appliances. People use so much electrical energy that they often take it for granted. However, you must never take for granted the safe use of electrical energy.

The picture shows wiring in a house. The wiring is kept out of the way because electric current can be dangerous to people. The wiring is insulated to keep the current in the circuit. A small amount of current can shock or burn you. Current that gets into paper or wood can start a fire by heating that material.

People must be able to control electric current so they use it only when needed. Switches serve this purpose. A switch opens and closes the circuit to let current reach a certain appliance.

Wiring inside a house

Circuit breakers

Fuses

Your home is wired with several circuits. Plugging in a lamp or flipping a wall switch connects the lamp into one of these circuits. Too many appliances on one circuit allow too much current to flow. Since heat from too much current can start a fire, you should not use too many appliances at once.

Most homes have devices that stop too much current from flowing through circuits. The **circuit breakers** shown are switches. A metal piece in a **fuse,** also shown, melts apart when too much current passes through it. Both devices open the circuit when too much current flows through them. When this happens, some of the appliances must be unplugged. Only an adult should reset the circuit breaker or replace the fuse to close the circuit. Then, fewer appliances should be used at the same time.

circuit (sėr′kit) **breaker,** a switch that opens a circuit when too much current flows through it.

fuse, a device that opens a circuit when too much current melts a piece of metal inside it.

Think About It

1. What is a closed circuit? An open circuit?
2. What is a fuse? A circuit breaker?
3. **Challenge** Why do you think an electrician should be called if a fuse blows a few times in a row?

Activity

Using Switches to Control Current

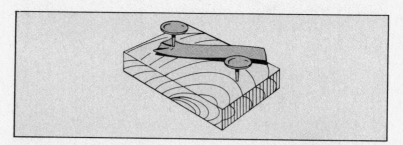

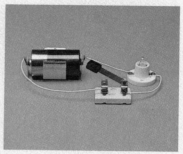

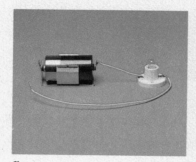

Purpose
To infer how a switch controls current in a circuit.

You Will Need

- either a switch or 2 thumbtacks, aluminum foil, and a flat piece of cork, wood, or cardboard
- 3 pieces of insulated wire with stripped ends
- 1.5-volt dry cell
- flashlight bulb
- socket for the bulb

Directions
1. If you are making a switch, make it like the one shown. Do not press the tacks all the way down into the cork, wood, or cardboard you are using.
2. Place the bulb into the socket, but do not completely screw the bulb into the socket. Connect a wire between the dry cell

a

and the socket. Connect a second wire to the socket, but do not connect it to the dry cell. Your circuit should look like the one shown in *a*. Ask your teacher to check your circuit.
3. Connect the second wire to the dry cell. Then screw the bulb into the socket. Observe what happens.
4. Partly unscrew the bulb. Disconnect a wire from the socket and connect it to one end of the open switch. Connect a third wire from the other end of the switch to the socket. Screw the

b

bulb into the socket. Your circuit should look like the one shown in *b*. Ask your teacher to check your circuit.
5. Close the switch. Observe what happens.
6. Open the switch and disconnect the circuit.

Think About It

1. What does a switch do to a circuit?
2. How do switches make it easy to control electricity?
3. **Challenge** If you made your own switch and used a smaller piece of foil and a stronger current, how could your switch act as a fuse?

Tie It Together

Sum It Up

1. Copy in your notebook the drawing of the atom. Label the protons, electrons, and neutrons in your drawing.

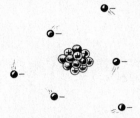

2. Write sentences about the pictures, using the words given.

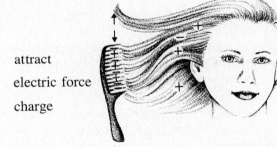

attract
electric force
charge

high
low
resistance
conductor
insulator

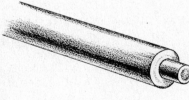

current
dry cell
closed circuit
bulb
switch

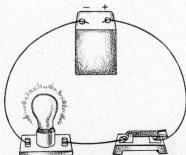

Challenge!

1. Describe how you can put a charge on an object and how the charged object might then act.

2. Describe what happens to some of the atoms on a balloon and on a wool cloth when you rub the balloon and cloth together.

3. Some electric heaters have wires that heat up and glow when current passes through them. Use the idea of resistance to explain how the wires heat up.

4. You connect a dry cell, a bulb in a socket, and a switch with wires in a circuit. The bulb does not light, however. Explain what the problem(s) could be.

5. Explain how fuses and circuit breakers help protect your home from fire.

Science Words

atom
circuit
circuit breaker
conductor
electric current
electron
fuse
insulator
neutron
proton
resistance

Chapter 14
Magnetism and Electricity

The student in the picture is hiking in the woods. The hike is part of an outdoor training program. She is not lost because her map and compass help her keep on course. The map helps her identify landmarks. The compass has a magnet that tells her the direction.

The lessons in this chapter will show how closely related magnetic effects and electricity are.

1 Predicting How Magnets Will Act

2 What Is a Magnetic Field?

3 How Does Electricity Cause Magnetism?

4 How Does Magnetism Cause Electricity?

1 Predicting How Magnets Will Act

Magnets are fun to play with because of the way they act. To learn about magnets, tie some string around the middle of a small bar magnet, as shown. Do the same for another bar magnet. Notice whether the ends marked *N* point in the same direction. Then, predict what will happen when two ends marked *N* come near each other. Now, notice what happens between these ends when you bring the magnets together. Do the same with the ends marked *S*. Then do the same with an end marked *N* and an end marked *S*.

Start again with the ends marked *N*, but this time bring the magnets together very slowly. Repeat with the ends marked *S* and then with one *N* and one *S*. Notice when the magnets start affecting each other.

Think About It

1. How do two like ends of a magnet affect each other? Unlike ends? Was your prediction correct?
2. Do magnets have to touch to affect each other? Explain.
3. **Challenge** What seems to be acting between two magnets brought near each other?

2 What Is a Magnetic Field?

magnetic field, the region around a magnet where the magnet's force acts.

magnetic pole, the place on a magnet where the force is strongest.

Perhaps you know how to make a paper clip chain using a magnet. Not only does the magnet attract the first clip, but each clip also attracts the next one. When you take the magnet away, the clips no longer attract each other. The chain falls apart. The magnet has something that the paper clips do not.

A magnet has a force that acts between the magnet and certain other objects, such as steel paper clips. The force of a magnet can act on these objects without touching them. In the picture the bar magnet attracts some iron filings and makes others line up around it. The force acts all around the magnet. The region around a magnet where the force acts is the **magnetic field.**

The iron filings are densest where the magnetic field is strongest—at a magnet's **poles.** If you let a magnet hang by a piece of string, the magnet will turn so that one pole always points north. This pole is the north-seeking pole, or north pole. The other pole of the magnet is the south-seeking pole, or south pole. No matter what its shape, every magnet has at least one of each kind of pole.

The magnetic field around a bar magnet

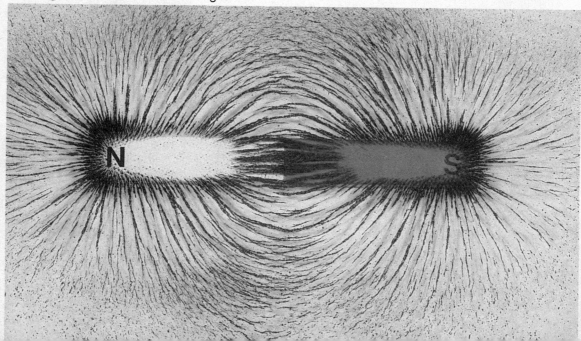

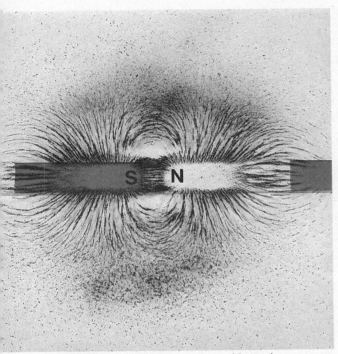

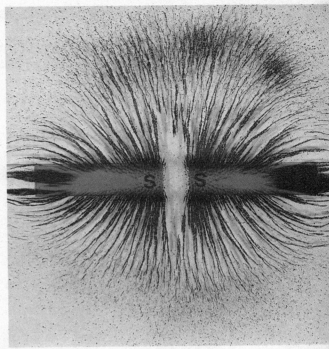

The magnetic field between unlike poles   The magnetic field between like poles

Look at the space between the magnets in the pictures. In one picture the iron filings come together because unlike poles attract each other. The filings do not appear between the two poles in the other picture. Like poles repel each other.

Usually, magnets and magnetic objects are made of the metal iron. The difference between magnets and magnetic objects is that magnets keep their force. Magnetic objects, such as iron filings, are attracted by a magnet. But when you take the magnet away, the force goes with it. No force remains with the magnetic objects.

You can make a magnetic object become a magnet. You can leave an iron or steel nail next to a magnet for a long time. You can also rub the nail with the magnet many times in one direction. The nail will become a magnet by picking up the magnetic field of the magnet.

231

Sunspots are cooler areas on the sun's surface where the sun's magnetic field is noticeable. Sunspots always occur in pairs. One spot is a north pole, and the other spot is a south pole.

How Is the Earth Like a Magnet?

People have known for thousands of years that the earth is magnetic. The ancient Greeks knew of hard black stones that attracted iron. Later, people used this kind of stone to make compasses to tell them which way was north.

Magnets point north because the earth has a magnetic field and magnetic poles. The drawing shows the magnetic field of our earth. This magnetic field looks something like the magnetic field of a bar magnet.

Scientists think the earth has a magnetic field because the earth's center is mainly iron and nickel. They also think the spinning of the earth helps cause the magnetic field.

Mercury, Jupiter, and Saturn also spin and have magnetic fields. Venus spins, but very slowly—once in 244 days. It does not have a magnetic field.

Earth's magnetic field

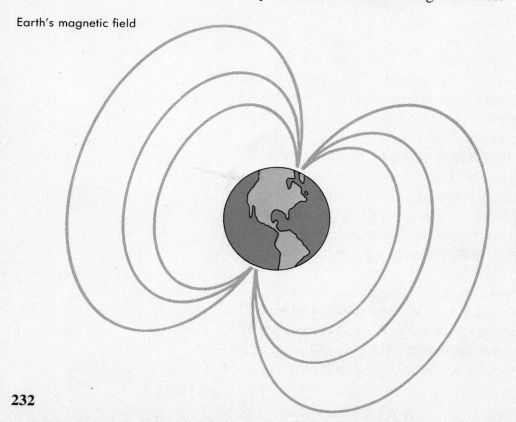

The drawing shows Jupiter's magnetic field. Jupiter is much larger than Earth and spins much faster—once every nine hours and fifty minutes. Jupiter's magnetic field is much larger and stronger than the magnetic field around Earth.

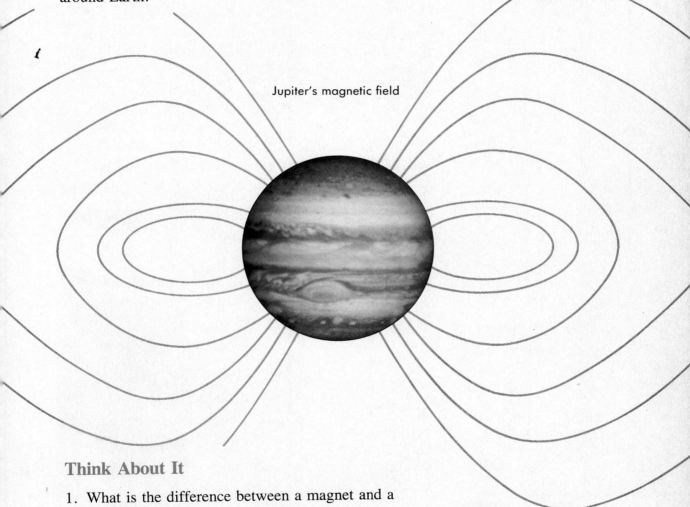

Jupiter's magnetic field

Think About It

1. What is the difference between a magnet and a magnetic object?
2. What is a magnetic field?
3. Name some objects that have magnetic poles.
4. How do we take advantage of earth's magnetism?
5. **Challenge** What tests can you do to find out about any magnetism an object might have?

233

3 How Does Electricity Cause Magnetism?

Magnets are made of certain materials. Iron is the most magnetic material in nature. Nickel and cobalt are magnetic, but less so than iron. Magnets and magnetic objects contain at least one of these materials.

How objects become magnets was discovered by accident about 160 years ago. One day, a teacher named Hans Christian Oersted was talking to his science class. He set up a kind of battery and some wires. A compass happened to be near a coil in the wires. The picture shows a setup similar to the one Oersted used.

Before Oersted connected his circuit, he noticed that the compass needle pointed north. When he connected the circuit, however, he noticed that the compass needle pointed toward the coil. He realized that the electric current in the circuit had a magnetic field of its own.

How current produces a magnetic field

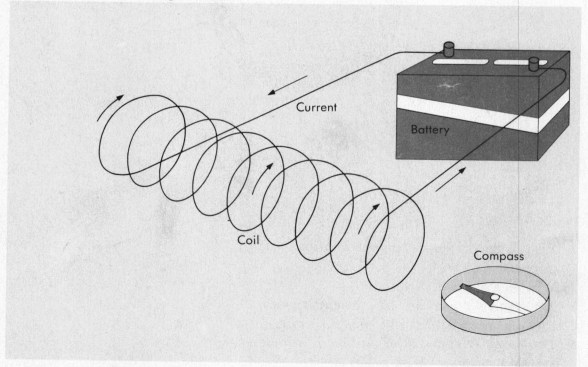

Current

Battery

Coil

Compass

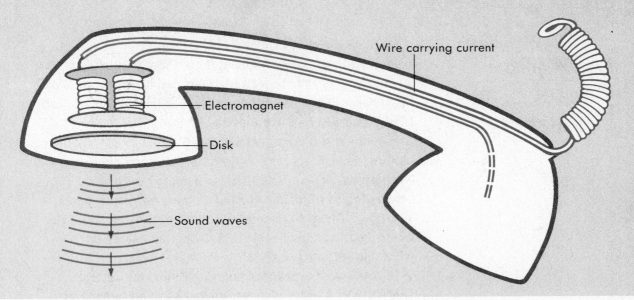

Wire carrying current

Electromagnet

Disk

Sound waves

An electromagnet in a telephone

This discovery pointed out two ideas. One idea was that **magnetism** is produced by the motion of electrons. Iron is magnetic because the motion of its electrons can be made to make a magnetic field. The electrons of most other materials cannot act this way.

The other idea was that magnetism can be turned on and off, just like electricity. We use this idea to make many devices, including motors, doorbells, and telephones. Each device has an **electromagnet**—a wire coil that becomes a magnet when a current flows through it. Notice the electromagnet in the telephone shown. Turning the current on and off very quickly makes the electromagnet attract and then release the metal disk. The movement of the disk sends out sound waves that you hear as a person's voice.

magnetism (mag′nə tizm), effects, such as a magnetic field, that result from the motion of electrons.

electromagnet (i lek′trō mag′nit), a wire coil that becomes a magnet when an electric current flows through it.

Think About It

1. What do electrons have to do with magnetism?
2. Name some devices that use an electromagnet.
3. **Challenge** What is the difference between the electrons in a magnet and those in plastic?

4 How Does Magnetism Cause Electricity?

After Oersted discovered how electricity causes magnetism, scientists realized that magnetism and electricity are closely related. They wondered if magnetism might be able to cause electricity too. Joseph Henry and Michael Faraday tested this idea.

Faraday's setup was something like the one in the picture. First he put the magnet in the metal ring. Nothing happened. The meter connected to the ring showed that no current flowed in the ring or the wires. Then he moved the magnet into and out of the ring. He found that current flowed in the ring and wires only when the magnet moved.

If you hold the magnet and move the ring instead, you still get a current in the wires. Moving either object changes the amount of magnetic field acting on the wires. So, a changing magnetic field can cause an electric current.

How a magnetic field produces current

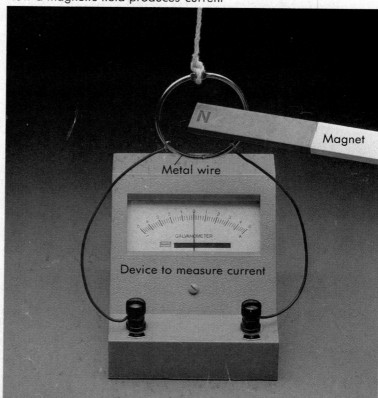

Magnet

Metal wire

Device to measure current

Generators in a power plant

At first, people were not certain how to use this discovery. Some people thought the idea would never be of any use. Today, the electric power companies use magnetism to make electricity. Every power plant has at least one machine that produces electricity by moving many magnets through wire coils. Such machines are **generators.** The picture shows generators in an electric power plant.

Some buildings have their own generators in addition to having electricity from a power company. Most hospitals have their own generators. If the power company cannot produce electricity, the hospital can use its generator. In this way the hospital still has electricity for lights and equipment during an emergency.

generator (jen′ə rā′tər), a device that produces electricity from the motion of magnets.

Have You Heard?

About 60 years passed before anyone was able to use the discovery made by Henry and Faraday. Then, in 1892, Nicola Tesla and George Westinghouse separately built the first industrial generators.

How Are Electricity and Magnetism Alike?

Electricity causes magnetism, and magnetism causes electricity. Both are caused by motion—either the motion of electrons or of magnetic fields. It is hard to separate one from the other. So scientists think electricity and magnetism are two parts of the same thing.

Many of our devices use electricity, magnetism, or both. Some of these devices are shown in the pictures. Electromagnets and generators are examples of ways people use electricity and magnetism.

Think About It

1. How can you use a magnet and a wire coil to produce an electric current in the wire?
2. How are generators important to us?
3. Why do scientists today think electricity and magnetism are part of the same thing?
4. **Challenge** Can a current result when both a magnet and a wire coil move? Explain.

Bicycle light generator

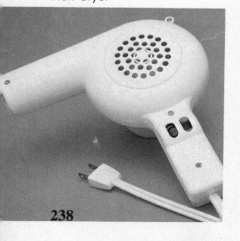

Hair dryer

Radio

Activity

Producing Electricity and Magnetism

Purpose
To observe how electricity and magnetism affect each other.

You Will Need
- about 8m of insulated bell wire
- small compass
- 2 magnets, one stronger than the other, either bar or horseshoe shaped

Directions
1. Wrap one end of the wire in a coil large enough for the magnet to enter. Put about 40 turns in your coil.
2. Wrap 10 turns of the other end of the wire around the compass. Connect the two ends of the wire. Your coils should look like those in the picture.
3. Pass the stronger magnet back and forth through the large coil. Notice any movement of the compass needle.
4. Repeat step 3 more slowly.

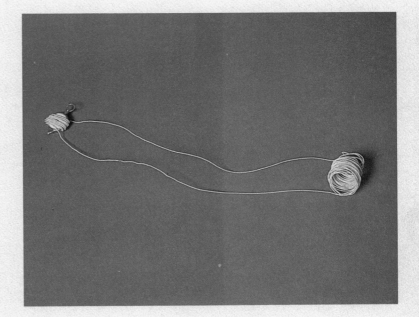

5. Repeat steps 3–4 using the weaker magnet.
6. Unwind half the turns in the large coil.
7. Repeat steps 3–5.

Think About It

1. What did you do that affected the movement of the compass needle?
2. How did decreasing the number of turns of wire affect the magnetic field produced?
3. **Challenge** What do you think happened to the current when you moved the magnet in a different direction?

Do You Know?

Magnets Can Record Your Voice

You turn on the tape recorder. A smooth voice says, "This is a recording. Magnets allow you to hear every word on this tape." How? To find out, follow the steps in the diagram.

When a person speaks into the tape recorder's microphone, sound energy from the person's voice is changed into electrical energy. Next, the electrical energy sets up a current.

The amount of current changes when the microphone picks up different sounds.

Find the recording head in the tape recorder shown in the picture. Inside the recording head is a small electromagnet. The changing electric current from the microphone produces a changing magnetic field around the recording head's electromagnet.

This magnetic field magnetizes flakes of powder made of iron and oxygen. These flakes of powder arrange themselves in patterns, much as iron filings arrange themselves in patterns around a bar magnet. The patterns change as the magnetic field changes.

But where is this powder? It is in the tape. As the tape rolls by the recording head, the powder becomes magnetized in patterns.

In order for you to hear the tape, these magnetic patterns must be changed into sound. The tape passes by a small electromagnet in the tape recorder's playback head. The magnetic patterns on the tape cause a changing current in this electromagnet. The current powers a speaker which plays the same sounds that were recorded on the tape.

Magnetic flakes of powder in tape or in discs also record information for computers. In fact, such magnets once stored all the words on this page in a space smaller than your pencil point!

Magnetic tape records and plays back sound

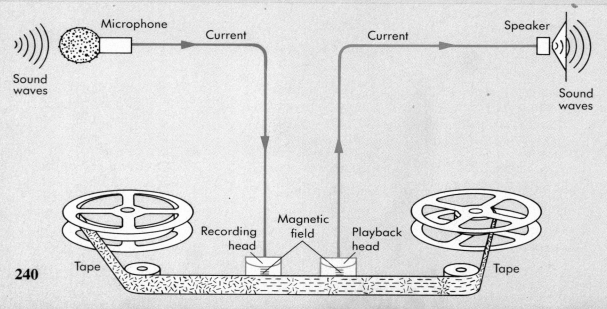

Sound waves — Microphone — Current — Recording head — Magnetic field — Playback head — Current — Speaker — Sound waves — Tape — Tape

Tie It Together

Sum It Up

1. Identify the kinds of magnetic poles that can cause iron filings to line up as shown in the pictures.

2. How is the earth similar to a bar magnet?

3. Draw a picture showing how you would set up equipment to make an electromagnet.

4. Compare electricity and magnetism by listing their characteristics. Be sure to include the words *charges, attract, repel, force, poles, magnetic fields, currents,* and *electrons* in your list.

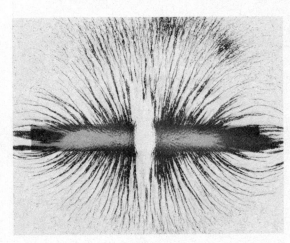

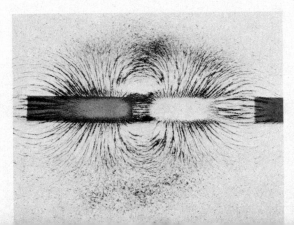

Challenge!

1. Describe how you can use a bar magnet as a compass.

2. Explain why you can use a magnet to make paper clips cling to each other in a chain.

3. What happens in a wire coil to make it become an electromagnet?

4. Explain how the motion of a magnet is important in causing an electric current in a wire coil.

Science Words

electromagnet

generator

magnetic field

magnetic pole

magnetism

241

Laboratory

Making Circuits

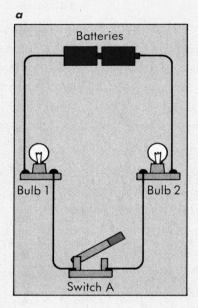

Batteries

Bulb 1   Bulb 2

Switch A

Purpose
To build and observe two kinds of electric circuits.

You Will Need
• masking tape
• marking pen
• 4 flashlight bulbs
• 4 sockets for the bulbs
• 2 switches
• bell wire
• 2 1.5-volt dry-cell batteries

Stating the Problem
You turn on many electric appliances by flipping a switch. The closed switch completes an electric circuit, so you can use an electric appliance that is plugged into the circuit.

There are two kinds of circuits. With a battery, wire, light bulbs, and switches, you can build both kinds of circuits. These circuits allow electricity to pass through different pathways.

Investigating the Problem
1. Use a marking pen and pieces of masking tape to label the switches and light bulbs. Label the switches *A* and *B*. Label the light bulbs *1, 2, 3,* and *4*.
2. Study the circuit in diagram *a*. Use 4 pieces of wire, 2 batteries, a switch, and bulbs *1* and *2* to construct the circuit shown in diagram *a*. Your circuit will look similar to the one in picture *b*. Close the switch. Observe and record what happens.

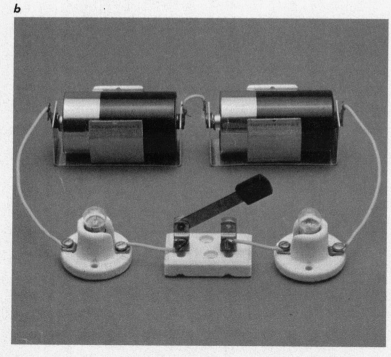

3. Open the switch. Unscrew bulb *1*. Close the switch. Record your observations.
4. Open the switch. Screw in bulb *1*. Unscrew bulb *2*. Close the switch. Record your observations.
5. Study the circuit in diagram *c*. Use 8 pieces of wire, 2 batteries, 2 switches, and 4 bulbs to construct the circuit. Your circuit will look similar to the circuit in picture *d*.
6. Close both switches. Record your observations.
7. Close switch *A*, and open switch *B*. Record your observations.
8. Open switch *A*, and close switch *B*. Record your observations.
9. Repeat steps 3 and 4 twice. The first time you repeat these steps, start by opening switch *A*. The second time you repeat these steps, close switch *A*, open switch *B*, and unscrew first bulb *3* and then bulb *4*. Record your observations.

c

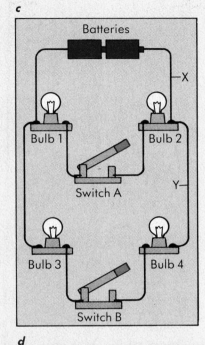

Batteries

—X

Bulb 1   Bulb 2

Switch A

Y—

Bulb 3   Bulb 4

Switch B

Making Conclusions
1. What effect does unscrewing a light bulb have on a circuit? How are the light bulb and the switch similar?
2. How are circuits *a* and *c* similar? How are they different?
3. Which type of circuit, *a* or *c*, do you think is wired into homes so people can use appliances one at a time?
4. Imagine additional switches at points *X* and *Y* in diagram *c*. Infer how they would affect the circuit.

d

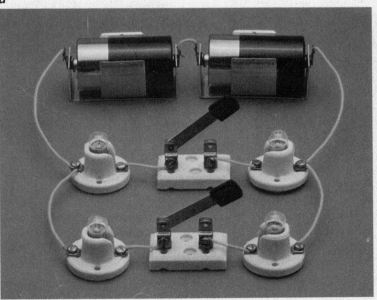

Careers

Electrical Engineer

Have you ever seen the inside of a radio or a computer game? It may just look like a jumbled pile of machinery. "But every piece of machinery is there for a reason," says Linda. "Each piece helps the radio or computer work."

Linda knows what she is talking about. She is an electrical engineer. Electrical engineers design and build radios, computers, motors, and other electrical equipment.

"My first engineering job was at a power generating station, where electricity is made. I designed some of the equipment and showed the construction workers how to put it together.

"Another job I had was working on transformers. A transformer is a large piece of equipment that changes the strength of electricity so people can use it. When a transformer broke down, an entire neighborhood might have been without electricity. It was my job to inspect the transformer and figure out how it could be fixed."

Today, Linda supervises other workers, including engineers. She meets with some of these workers every day to discuss problems that might come up.

"Electrical engineering is one of the best areas for jobs. People want all kinds of electrical equipment improved. We are also trying to improve ways of making electricity. These tasks require well-trained engineers.

"Engineers learn their basic skills in college. But a good engineer should also be creative and enjoy solving problems."

Electronics assembler

Almost every day you probably use something that works because of electricity. The school-bus engine cannot start without electricity. Televisions and telephones use electricity. Since electricity is a big part of our lives, people can find many jobs in this field.

Electronics assemblers put together all kinds of equipment, including radios, televisions, and calculators. Thousands of separate parts may go into a machine. Each assembler works on just one part. Assemblers must do their jobs accurately, or an entire machine might not work properly. Assemblers learn their skills on the job.

When a machine such as a television or a refrigerator breaks down, a **service technician** tries to fix it. This person knows every part of the machine and how it works. The technician often uses instruments to find the damage. He or she might then repair it in the home or take it to the workshop.

Students who want to be service technicians go to a special school for one or two years after high school.

One of the most exciting jobs in electronics may be that of the **special effects specialists.** These people create the special effects for movies and plays. A scene in a movie may call for a lightning storm. Perhaps two dinosaurs have to fight each other. A spacecraft may have to land on a planet. All of these special effects require the skills of specialists. Many of these people are **electricians** and **electrical engineers.**

Special effects specialists design and build models, such as dinosaurs and space ships, to use in the movie. They have to make sure the models look realistic. In some science-fiction movies, half of the movie is made in an electronics workshop! Many special effects specialists have at least two years of college training in electronics.

Service technician

On Your Own

Picture Clue

The object on page 196 seems very hairy. But notice how the "hairs" line up around the object. What can cause them to act in this way? You can find the answer on page 230.

Projects

1. Rub a plastic comb with wool cloth. Then, bring the charged comb near a very narrow, smooth stream of water from a faucet. Explain what happens to the stream of water.

2. Read in an encyclopedia how a dry cell in a flashlight is different from a car battery made of wet cells. With the help of an adult, build a wet cell.

3. Buzzers, locks, and telegraphs use electromagnets and are easy to make. Build one of these objects yourself. A book that describes how things work will show you how.

Books About Science

Computers by Linda O'Brien. Franklin Watts Inc., 1978. Explore the history, construction, and use of these amazing devices.

How Did We Find Out About Atoms? by Isaac Asimov. Walker and Co., 1976. Discover how the work of many people has changed our understanding of the atom.

Collins Young Scientist's Book of Power byMichal Kentzer. Silver Burdett Co., 1979. Read about what electric power is and how it affects our lives.

Unit Test

True or False

Number your paper from 1–5. Next to each number, write
true if the sentence is correct and *false* if the sentence is
incorrect. Make each false statement true by changing the
underlined word or phrase and writing the correct word or
phrase on your paper.

1. A force is a push or pull that might change the motion of an object.
2. Electricity and magnetism are parts of the same thing.
3. Insulators have low resistance.
4. Energy is done when a force moves an object through a distance.
5. A machine that does a job more slowly than a second machine has more power than the second machine.

Matching

Number your paper from 6–10. Read the description in
Column I. Next to each number, write the letter of the word
or phrase from Column II that best matches the description in
Column I.

Column I

6. a particle with a positive charge in the center of an atom
7. particles that make up all matter
8. force that wastes energy
9. a flow of electrons
10. opens a circuit when too much current flows through it

Column II

a. atoms
b. electric current
c. friction
d. fuse
e. neutron
f. proton

Multiple Choice

Number your paper from 11–14. Next to each number, write
the letter of the phrase that best completes the statement.

11. The cause of magnetism is
    a. the motion of electrons.
    b. the motion of neutrons.
    c. magnetic poles.
    d. magnetic fields.

12. Like electric charges
    a. attract each other.
    b. repel each other.
    c. first attract, then repel each other.
    d. do not attract or repel each other.

13. The magnetic field of a magnet
    a. stays with the magnet for a very short time.
    b. does not stay with the magnet.
    c. is weakest at the poles.
    d. is strongest at the poles.

14. People use generators to
    a. change electricity into magnetism.
    b. produce electricity.
    c. open or close a circuit.
    d. all the above

UNIT SIX
ENERGY SOURCES TODAY AND TOMORROW

Chapter 15 Energy Sources Today

Chapter 16 Energy Sources Tomorrow

It used the natural rays of the sun,
    But is shelter with
        conveniences
Like an apple tree
    absorbing the light
To make something good
    for humankind.

Brent Murray *age 10*

Chapter 15
Energy Sources Today

The waterfall in the picture shows the tremendous energy of falling water. Some communities use falling water as an energy source to make electricity. Other communities use other energy sources, such as coal or the atom. Without these energy sources, we would not have the many appliances and machines that we use every day.

The lessons in this chapter will help you identify important energy sources we use today to meet our energy needs.

1 Estimating How Much Energy We Use
2 In What Ways Do We Use More Energy Today?
3 What Are Fossil Fuels?
4 How Do We Get Energy from Falling Water?
5 How Do We Get Energy from Atoms?

1 Estimating How Much Energy We Use

Every time you turn on a television, radio, or record player, you use energy. You can estimate how much electrical energy you and your classmates use while watching television. Then, you can estimate how much coal power plants must burn to make that much electricity.

The amount of electrical power—or the number of watts—that a television uses is shown below the picture. Multiply this number of watts by the average number of hours you watch television each day. The number of watt-hours is the amount of electrical energy you use. Now, estimate the total number of watt-hours the students in your classroom use each day by watching television.

Electric power plants need about 1 kilogram of coal to produce about two thousand watt-hours of electrical energy. How much coal do the students in your classroom use each day just by watching television?

A color television uses about 100 watts of electrical power

Think About It

1. About how much coal would the students in your classroom use in a year if they continue watching television as much as they do now?
2. About 75 million homes in the United States have a television. Suppose these families watch television as much as you do. Approximately how much coal would be used to watch television in the United States each day? Each year?
3. **Challenge** What could cause an energy crisis?

2 In What Ways Do We Use More Energy Today?

You can see in the pictures that life today is very different from life in the 1800s. Not only do we dress differently, we also use many machines that save us time. Most machines use energy, such as electricity, to do work. We also use energy to make these machines and to get rid of them when they wear out.

Think of how much energy goes into making a car. First, people who make cars must eat food. Growing and transporting their food uses energy. Many of the workers drive to and from the factory. Their cars use the energy from gasoline. In the factory, electricity lights up the rooms and moves the assembly lines. Furnaces burn coal or oil to heat the factory. The factory workers use electric tools to put the cars together. Finally, when the cars are finished, they are transported to many parts of the world by trucks, trains, and ships that use fuels.

Modern kitchen

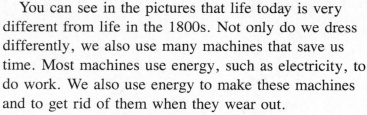

Kitchen in the 1800s

Worker in a car factory

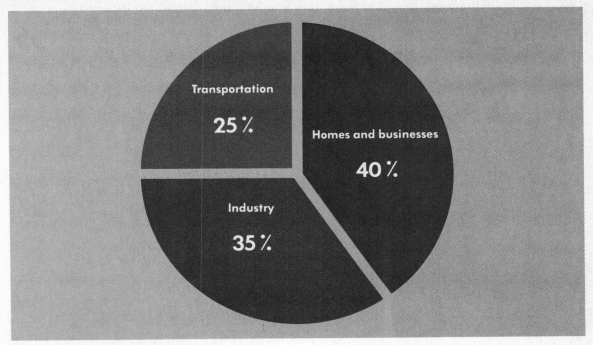

Energy use in the United States

The diagram shows how much energy people in the United States use for different activities. But each year we use more and more energy. Increasing numbers of people in the world have increased the amount of energy used. More and more people travel by cars, trains, and airplanes. Farmers use machines to grow food. Factories manufacture more products that use energy. Since the year 1900, the amount of energy people use has doubled about every twenty years.

To avoid running out of energy, we must plan our uses of energy wisely. For example, we can make cars that use less gasoline. We can also search for sources of energy that will last a long time.

Think About It

1. In what ways do we use energy today?
2. How are we using more energy every year?
3. **Challenge** How has using energy improved our lives?

3 What Are Fossil Fuels?

peat, a spongy mass of dead plant matter that changes into coal under heat and pressure.

coal, a solid fuel formed by pressure and heat acting on partly decayed plant matter.

Millions of years ago, large swamps covered many parts of the earth. The plants that lived in the swamps captured the sun's energy and stored it in their leaves, stems, and roots. When the plants died, the stored energy became trapped in their remains. The plants formed thick layers of dead matter on the swamp floor. After millions of years, the layers of dead plant matter became the coal we use today.

The diagrams show how this change happened. The dead plants started decaying as decomposers broke them down into simpler materials. But when more dead plants fell on top of the decaying plants, the decomposers' oxygen supply was cut off. As a result, the plants decayed only partly. The layers of dead matter eventually formed a wet, spongy mass called **peat.** Later, some of the peat was flooded by seas. The floods covered the peat with thick layers of mud and rock. The peat was packed into a hard material as more layers pressed down on it over many years. Eventually, the pressure produced heat in the lower layers. The heat and pressure chemically changed the peat into **coal.**

How coal forms

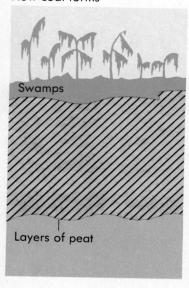

Swamps

Layers of peat

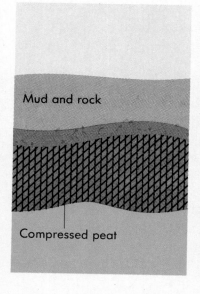

Mud and rock

Compressed peat

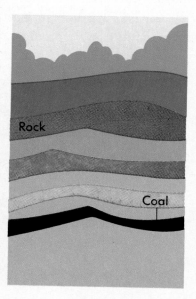

Rock

Coal

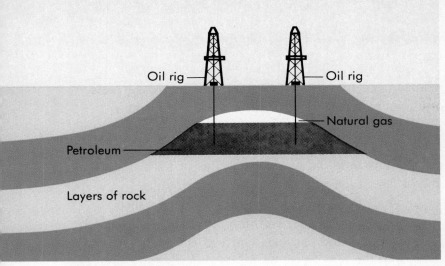

Drilling for petroleum

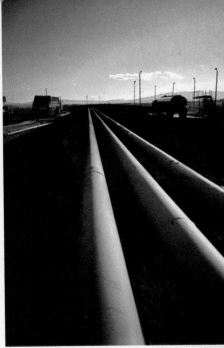

Natural gas pipeline

Petroleum is a liquid fuel formed from the remains of tiny ocean organisms that lived millions of years ago. Layers of sand and rock covered the partly decayed organisms on the ocean floor. Pressure and heat from the rock layers squeezed the dead matter into a thick liquid. After some time, this petroleum moved upward and became trapped between layers of rocks. Oil rigs, such as those in the drawing, drill wells into the rocks and pump out the petroleum. Oil companies clean the petroleum and separate it into gasoline, kerosene, oils, and waxes.

Some petroleum traps also have **natural gas.** The decaying organisms on the ocean floor released gases that became trapped in the rock layers that covered the organisms.

Natural gas is an odorless, poisonous gas that burns easily. Large pipes, such as those in the picture, carry natural gas from petroleum deposits to cities and towns. Gas appliances and furnaces burn natural gas for cooking food and heating homes.

Coal, petroleum, and natural gas are called **fossil fuels** because the energy in these fuels comes from the remains of dead organisms.

petroleum (pə trō′lē əm), a liquid fuel formed by heat and pressure acting on partly decayed organisms on the ocean floor.

natural gas, a gaseous fuel formed from gases released by decaying organisms on the ocean floor.

fossil fuel, any fuel formed from the remains of dead organisms.

255

nonrenewable energy source, a source of energy that we are using faster than it can be replaced.

Find Out

Besides producing energy, coal also is used to make various products. Use an encyclopedia to find out what some of these products are.

How Long Will Fossil Fuels Last?

Today, more than 90 percent of the energy we use comes from fossil fuels. People are using fossil fuels millions of times faster than the fuels are forming. Fossil fuels are **nonrenewable energy sources** because we cannot replace them as fast as we use them. The chart shows how long the world's supplies of fossil fuels might last at the rate we are using them today.

Another problem with using fossil fuels is the pollution they produce. Burning fossil fuels releases harmful gases and particles, such as sulfur dioxide and soot, into the air. These harmful products can cause health problems, kill wildlife, and damage buildings.

Fossil fuels probably will not meet our growing energy needs. We should use fossil fuels wisely so our supplies last longer. In the meantime we need to look for other energy sources.

Fossil fuel supplies

Type of fossil fuel	Number of years supplies are expected to last at present rate of use
Petroleum	Less than 100 years
Natural gas	Less than 100 years
Coal	Less than 500 years

Think About It

1. Name three fossil fuels and explain how they form.
2. Why are fossil fuels nonrenewable energy sources?
3. **Challenge** How can fossil fuels be helpful and harmful?

Do You Know?

Some Oil Rigs Are in the Ocean

Offshore oil rig

Welcome home! For some people the oil-rig platform in the picture *is* home for much of the year. The people living on this platform search for petroleum from the ocean bottom.

Some oil-rig platforms are as large as football fields. The towers of the oil rigs are sometimes 60 meters high, or as tall as 20-story buildings.

Some people living on the oil-rig platform are drillers. They operate the drill that digs the well into the underwater rock. Their job is much like drilling an oil well on land. But the drillers on the rig have 100 meters of water beneath them!

A team of geologists also works on the platform. The geologists study rock samples from the ocean bottom. They try to figure out how far underground petroleum can be found.

Cooks work on the oil-rig platform, making the food that is served in the rig cafeteria. Radio operators keep the people on the rig in touch with people on land. But everything the workers need must be on the rig, since they do not leave it during the weeks that they work there.

Most workers spend three weeks on the rig. Then, they return to land for three weeks before coming back to the oil rig.

Living on an offshore oil-rig is very different from living on land. The platform has no shopping centers, museums, or baseball parks. There is not much to do on the oil rig but work. So, for many people, a twelve-hour workday is common. The workers spend the free time that they do have reading, watching television and taped movies, or fishing.

Life on the oil rig can be difficult. Storms are sometimes dangerous. But for some people, the life is very rewarding.

Inside an oil-rig platform

4 How Do We Get Energy from Falling Water?

Using water to do work

For hundreds of years, people used the energy of moving water to do work. Fast-flowing rivers or waterfalls were used to power water wheels such as those in the pictures. The moving water pushed against the blades of the water wheel, causing it to turn.

The drawing shows a water wheel in the 1600s that was connected to gears which were connected to a grindstone. The turning water wheel caused the gears to move which made the grindstone turn. The turning grindstone crushed the grain that was placed under it into a flour. In more recent times people have used water wheels for powering pumps and other machines in factories.

Water wheel

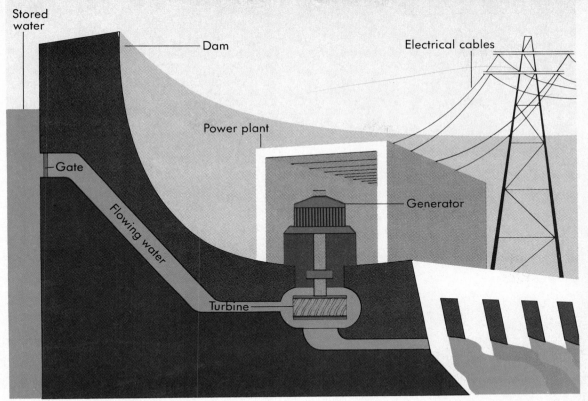

Stored water

Dam

Electrical cables

Power plant

Gate

Flowing water

Generator

Turbine

Producing hydroelectric power

The energy of moving water also is used to produce electricity. Some power plants use falling water to turn generators that produce electricity. Electricity produced by water power is called **hydroelectric power.**

Hydroelectric power plants are often built next to dams, where water flows from a high place to a low place. Dams hold the water in a storage area until the water is needed to produce electricity. The drawing shows how a dam and a power plant work together to produce electricity. When electricity is needed, the dam gates are opened to release the stored water. The water rushes through the gates and flows many meters downward. The rapidly flowing water is piped into the power plant where it turns the fanlike blades of machines—or **turbines.** The moving blades of the turbines turn a generator that produces electricity. Large cables carry the electricity to nearby towns and cities.

hydroelectric
(hī′drō i lek′trik) **power,** electricity produced by water power.

turbine (tėr′bən), a machine with fanlike blades.

259

renewable energy source, a source of energy that can be replaced a short time after we use it.

Have You Heard?

One of the largest hydroelectric power plants in the world is located in the United States. It uses water that flows into the Niagara Falls shown in the picture.

Niagara Falls

Is Falling Water a Good Energy Source to Use?

We do not have to worry about running out of water, as we do with fossil fuels. Falling water is a **renewable energy source** because the water we use is replaced in a short time. Water also is a good energy source because it does not pollute the air as fossil fuels do.

But energy from falling water can be used only in areas with rivers or waterfalls. In countries with many rivers, such as New Zealand, power plants use falling water to produce most of the electricity used. In the United States, hydroelectric power plants produce about one-seventh of the electricity we use. Areas that are dry or have few rivers cannot rely on falling water as an energy source.

Think About It

1. How can water wheels do work?
2. What is hydroelectric power?
3. How do dams and power plants work together to produce electricity?
4. **Challenge** How is a water wheel similar to a turbine in a hydroelectric power plant?

Robert Moses power plant near Niagara Falls

Activity

Making a Water Wheel

Purpose
To make a water wheel model that shows how falling water can do work.

You Will Need
- compass
- centimeter ruler
- cardboard
- scissors
- 15-cm-long wire
- tape
- string
- small paper box or other lightweight container
- 2 paper cups
- 2 small, heavy objects that will fit into the cups
- large pan
- container with a spout
- water

Directions
1. Using a compass, draw a 4-cm-radius circle on stiff cardboard. Cut out the circle.
2. Draw 5 lines about 3 cm long from the edge to the center of the circle, as shown. Cut the lines to form 5 blades.

3. Bend inward one side of each blade to make a wheel, such as the one shown.
4. Insert the wire into the center of the wheel. Tape both sides of the wheel to the wire that will form the shaft of the wheel.
5. Tie one end of a 15-cm-long string to the shaft. Tie the other end of the string to a lightweight container, such as a small paper box.
6. Cut a small rectangle from the tops of the 2 cups.
7. Place both cups in the pan. Place a small, heavy object in each cup to hold it down. Rest the shaft of the water wheel across both cups as shown.
8. Use a container with a spout to slowly pour water over the wheel from a height of about 10 cm. Observe the water wheel, and record your observations.

Think About It
1. What powered the wheel?
2. What kind of work did the water wheel do?
3. **Challenge** How could you increase the energy of the water pushing the wheel?

5 How Do We Get Energy from Atoms?

nucleus (nü′klē əs), the central part of an atom. [Plural: nuclei (nü′klē ī).]

nuclear (nü′klē ər) **energy,** energy released from the nucleus of an atom.

nuclear fission (nü′klē ər fish′ən), the splitting of a nucleus of an atom.

Model of an atom

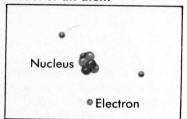

Nucleus

Electron

We can get energy from an atom by shooting particles at the central part—or **nucleus**—of the atom. The nucleus splits and releases large amounts of energy. Power plants can use this energy to produce electricity.

The diagram below shows the process used to release energy from the nucleus of an atom—or **nuclear energy.** A moving neutron particle hits an atomic nucleus, causing it to split into two smaller nuclei. The splitting nucleus releases neutrons and huge amounts of energy. Some of these neutrons hit other nuclei that also split. More neutrons and energy are released. The collisions between the neutrons and nuclei continue on and on in a chain reaction. Huge amounts of energy are released at each collision.

The splitting of atomic nuclei—or **nuclear fission**—can be harmful or helpful. In an uncontrolled reaction, so many collisions occur that the energy is released in an explosion. An atom bomb explosion results from an uncontrolled chain reaction. But scientists can decrease the collisions in a chain reaction by removing some of the neutron particles released by the splitting atoms. The nuclear energy released is controlled and used to produce electricity.

Nuclear fission

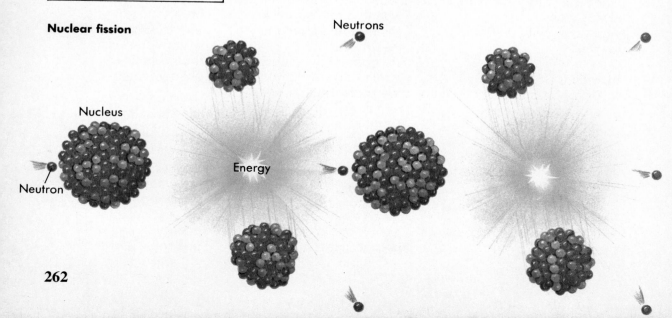

Neutrons

Nucleus

Energy

Neutron

Nuclear fission container in nuclear power plant

Nuclear power plants usually split uranium atoms to produce nuclear energy. This nuclear fission takes place in a container, such as the one in the picture. The container is made so that the nuclear fission is controlled and does not produce an explosion.

The nuclear energy produced in a nuclear power plant is used to heat large amounts of water to a high temperature. The hot water heats pipes carrying cooler water that boils into steam. The steam turns a turbine that turns an electrical generator. The electricity produced is used by homes, businesses, and factories.

A single gram of uranium can produce as much heat as 3 million grams of coal. The nuclear fission of uranium atoms provides enough energy to last a long time. Submarines and spacecraft can travel for months, using small amounts of nuclear fuel.

Today, many communities get their electricity from nuclear power plants. Some people prefer using nuclear energy to produce electricity because it does not pollute the air as fossil fuels do.

Storage container for radioactive wastes

Have You Heard?
Combining atoms at
temperatures millions of
degrees Celsius also releases
huge amounts of nuclear
energy. This process does not
produce as much radioactivity
as nuclear fission does.

Can Using Nuclear Energy Be Dangerous?

Nuclear fission produces **radioactive wastes** that give
off harmful particles and rays. In large amounts these
particles and rays can make people ill. Hundreds or
thousands of years must pass before some radioactive
wastes change into harmless substances. As a result,
nuclear power plants have to store the radioactive wastes
they produce. They store some wastes in large
containers, such as the one in the picture. The
containers have thick walls that help stop the radioactive
wastes from leaking through.

Some people think radioactive wastes eventually will
leak through the storage containers. Other people are
afraid that accidents might happen in the nuclear power
plants, which would release large amounts of radioactive
wastes into the environment. Today, scientists are trying
to find ways to make nuclear energy safer.

Think About It

1. How do we use nuclear fission to produce
   electricity?
2. How can radioactive wastes be harmful to people for
   hundreds of years?
3. **Challenge** How can nuclear energy be both helpful
   and harmful?

Tie It Together

Sum It Up

1. Draw pictures of a city street during the 1800s and today. List the energy-using devices that are included in your picture of today's city street but that are not included in your picture of a city street from the 1800s.

2. Explain what happens during coal formation at steps *a, b,* and *c* of the diagram.

3. Use an encyclopedia to find out what different hydroelectric power plants built near dams look like. Make a sketch of one of these power plants. Use labels and arrows to show how falling water is used to produce electricity. Include the dam, the direction of the moving water, turbines, a generator, and electrical cables in your sketch.

4. Draw a diagram showing the process of nuclear fission and the products released. Label all parts of your diagram.

Challenge!

1. List ten energy-using machines or appliances that save people time.

2. If petroleum forms from the remains of ocean organisms, why is it sometimes found under dry land?

3. Why are industrial cities often located near fast-flowing rivers or waterfalls?

4. How are fossil fuels and nuclear fuels alike? How are they different?

5. Would you prefer using coal or nuclear energy to make electricity? Why?

Science Words

coal	nucleus
fossil fuel	peat
hydroelectric power	petroleum
natural gas	radioactive wastes
nonrenewable energy source	renewable energy source
nuclear energy	turbine
nuclear fission	

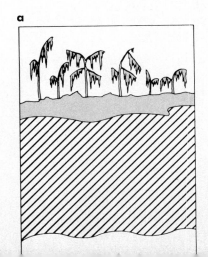

a

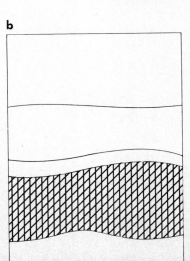

b

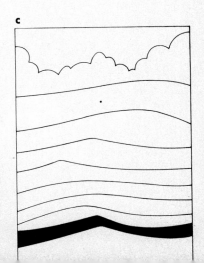

c

Chapter 16
Energy Sources Tomorrow

On a November evening in 1965, all the lights stopped glowing in parts of the United States and Canada. The picture shows what New York City looked like that night. The power failure that caused the blackout lasted about twelve hours. It created much confusion. Workers were stranded in elevators and subway tunnels. Radio and television stations went off the air. Stores closed. The blackout showed people what life would be like if we ran out of energy.

The lessons in this chapter describe energy sources that you may be using more frequently in the future. By using energy wisely, you can help our energy supplies last longer.

1 Predicting Temperature Change

If you ever walked barefoot outside, did you notice if sidewalks felt as hot as blacktop roads? What do you think caused the difference? You can use your observations to predict changes in water temperature.

Half fill two clear jars with cool water. Using a medicine dropper, add a few drops of black ink to one of the jars, as shown in the picture. Measure and record the water temperature in each jar. Place both jars in the sunlight. Predict which jar of water will become warmer. Measure and record the water temperature in each jar after fifteen, thirty, and forty-five minutes. Graph your temperature measurements for each jar of water.

Think About It

1. What information did you use to predict which jar of water would become warmer? Was your prediction correct?
2. **Challenge** Why is it a good idea to paint a doghouse white in the summer?

2 How Can We Use Energy from the Sun?

solar (sō′lər) energy, energy from the sun.

In about forty minutes the sun sends to the earth's surface about as much energy as people use in a year. We use energy from the sun without being aware of it. The sun's energy melts snow, warms your body, and dries the laundry on a clothesline. On some days the sun makes the streets seem "hot enough to fry an egg."

We can use the sun's energy—or **solar energy**—to heat homes and make electricity. To use solar energy, we must first find a way to collect it. The solar house in the picture uses a metal solar collector. Dark-colored sheets of metal are placed on the roof of the house. The metal heats quickly, and the dark color helps absorb energy from the sun. The solar collector faces the direction that gets the most sunlight. In the Northern Hemisphere, you would have a solar collector face south.

Solar house

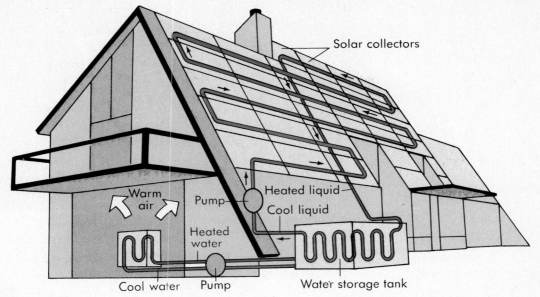

Solar collectors

Warm air

Pump

Heated liquid

Cool liquid

Heated water

Cool water

Pump

Water storage tank

Inside a solar house

You can see in the picture that a liquid circulates through pipes in a solar house. Solar energy heats the liquid as it moves through the solar collectors. The heated liquid then circulates to a water tank. There, the heat from the liquid is used to heat the water in the tank. Then, the cooled liquid returns to the solar collectors to absorb more solar energy. The heated water from the water tank is used to warm the air that moves through the house.

We can collect solar energy only when the sun shines. At night and on cloudy days, solar houses must use stored solar energy. You know that in the summer, rocks and stones get hot quickly and stay warm even when the sun sets. These materials store heat from the sun. A solar house has cement walls and floors that store heat. Also, the water tank stores water heated by solar energy. In these ways, stored solar energy can help keep the house warm even on a cloudy day. But after a few days of cool, cloudy weather, other energy sources must be used to keep the solar house warm.

Have You Heard?

People used solar energy many years ago. The French chemist Antoine Lavoisier built a solar furnace in the 1700s. He used 2 large lenses to focus the sun's rays. His furnace got as hot as 1000°C.

Airplane powered by solar cells

Solar cell

solar cell, a device that changes solar energy into electricity.

How Can Solar Energy Make Electricity?

We can use solar energy to make electricity. The **solar cell** in the picture is a device that uses the element silicon to change sunlight into electricity. Forty connected solar cells make enough electricity to charge a car battery. Large groups of solar cells can power a radio or an airplane, such as the *Solar Challenger* in the picture. In 1981 this airplane used about 16,000 solar cells to fly 35 kilometers across the English Channel.

Materials used for collecting solar energy can cost a lot of money. But solar energy does not pollute and is safe to use. The sun is also a renewable energy source because it constantly provides us with energy. Some scientists think we can find ways to capture enough solar energy to produce about one-fifth of our electricity and to heat most of our homes.

Think About It

1. How does a solar house collect and store solar energy?
2. Why is solar energy a good energy source to use?
3. **Challenge** What might happen to the water in a garden hose if the hose lies in the sun all day?

Activity

Making Fresh Water with Solar Energy

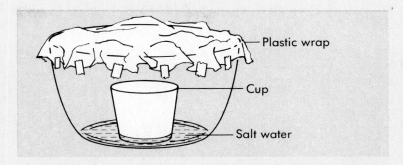

Plastic wrap

Cup

Salt water

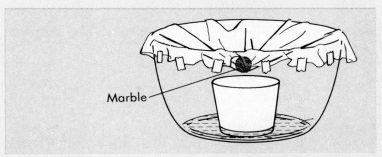

Marble

Purpose
To observe how solar energy can be used to make fresh water from salt water.

You Will Need
- large spoon
- salt
- water
- 2 cups
- large bowl that is deeper than the cups
- clear-plastic food wrap
- tape
- marble

Directions
1. Add 1 large spoonful of salt to a small cup of water. Mix well.
2. Pour a thin layer of salt water into the bowl.
3. Place a clean cup right side up in the middle of the bowl.
4. Cover the bowl with a sheet of clear plastic. Tape the plastic securely to the bowl, as shown.
5. Place a marble over the center of the cup, as shown. Do not let the plastic touch the cup.
6. Leave the bowl in sunlight until water collects in the cup. Lightly tap the marble on the plastic wrap to collect more water.
7. Remove the plastic wrap, and let the water in the cup and bowl evaporate completely.
8. Rub the bottom of the bowl and cup with your finger. Record what you feel in each container.

Think About It
1. What did you find remaining in the bowl or in the cup after the water evaporated?
2. What kind of water collected in the cup? How do you know?
3. How did solar energy help make fresh water?
4. **Challenge** How do you think solar energy is used in some parts of the world to increase the supply of drinking water?

3 What Are Other Energy Sources?

The wind helps move sailboats. Heat from inside the earth makes geysers erupt. Tides on seacoasts move on and off the shore. Winds, underground heat, and tides have energy. They are renewable energy sources that will last a long time.

The wind can do work. A windmill uses wind energy to pump water, grind grain, or make electricity. The blades of the modern windmill in the picture use wind energy to move gears that turn an electrical generator.

Some scientists think windmills can someday produce almost one-tenth of our electricity. They are studying ways we can use windmills to meet more of our energy needs.

The wind is clean and free, but it is not a perfect energy source. When the wind is calm, windmills cannot produce electricity. Windmills are sometimes noisy and take up a lot of space that can be used for homes or farms. People living in different places will have to decide whether the wind is a good energy source for them to use.

Modern windmill

Windmills on a farm

geothermal (jē′ō thėr′məl) energy; underground energy that is produced when atoms in the earth's core break down.

Steam from inside the earth

What Are Geothermal and Tidal Energy?

The steam in the picture coming from cracks in the earth's surface shows the energy beneath the ground. **Geothermal energy** is energy from inside the earth. The energy comes from atoms inside the earth's core. These atoms, such as uranium, continuously break down and release energy. Geothermal energy is like a furnace that heats the inside of the earth. It can heat underground water to a temperature of 300° Celsius!

The diagram shows how some places in the world use geothermal energy to produce electricity. Geothermal power plants use wells drilled deep into the ground. The wells let underground steam and hot water move up to the earth's surface. Then, pipes carry the steam to turbines and electrical generators in the power plants.

The Geysers Plant, in California, is the largest geothermal power plant in the world. It produces about half the electricity used in the city of San Francisco. But geothermal power plants can also pollute the environment by releasing harmful chemicals from underground.

Using geothermal energy to make electricity

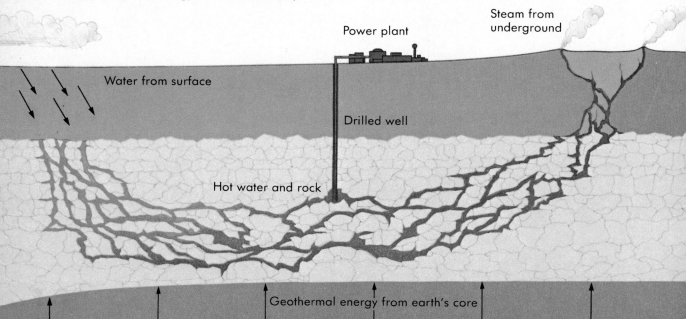

Power plant

Steam from underground

Water from surface

Drilled well

Hot water and rock

Geothermal energy from earth's core

Tidal power plant

Tides along the seacoast might be a useful energy source. **Tidal energy** comes from the movement of tides. The dam in the picture has a row of turbines and electrical generators set into its wall under the water. When the tide moves toward the shore, it flows through the dam and pushes the blades of the turbines. The turbines then turn the generators that produce electricity. As the tide goes out, water flows over the turbines in the other direction and produces more electricity.

Tidal energy is clean and safe to use. But only people living near seacoasts with high and low tides can use this energy source. Also, tidal power plants can disturb the habitats of organisms living near the seashore.

The sun, the wind, underground heat, and tides are a few of the renewable energy sources that are useful to us. Most scientists do not think that any one of these sources can provide all our energy needs. But if we find more ways to use these energy sources, we might not have to depend so much on fossil fuels.

tidal energy, energy from the movement of tides.

Have You Heard?

People in Iceland live in a cold environment. But they use hot underground water to heat outdoor swimming pools and grow bananas in greenhouses.

Think About It

1. How is geothermal energy produced?
2. What are the advantages and disadvantages of using wind, geothermal, and tidal energy?
3. **Challenge** How can some people use hot underground water to heat homes?

4 How Can We Save Energy?

For a long time we did not plan our energy use carefully. We used gasoline without thinking about how much petroleum the world had. Now, we know that fossil fuels are in limited supply. Many people are beginning to use energy sources more wisely.

Conservation is using energy more wisely. When we conserve energy, we try not to waste nonrenewable energy sources, so our supplies will last longer.

You can conserve energy by following the examples of the people in the pictures. Walk or ride your bicycle whenever possible. Turn down the heat in your home at night. Turn off lights and other electrical appliances when they are not in use.

conservation
(kon′sər vā′shən), using a substance or energy more wisely by not wasting it.

Ways to conserve energy

You can also save energy by using materials more than once. **Recycling** is changing a material to its original form so it can be used again. Making products from recycled materials uses less energy than making products from new materials. For example, we use aluminum metal to make cans. We have to mine and clean the aluminum before making the cans. Each step uses energy. When we recycle aluminum, we save about 95 percent of the energy that would have to be used to mine and clean new aluminum metal. The machine in the picture is used in recycling aluminum cans. The cans are chopped into small pieces that are melted and rolled into sheets. The recycled aluminum sheets are used to make new cans.

We also can recyle other materials such as glass, steel, and paper. The person in the picture is collecting old newspapers. Recycled paper can be used for making greeting cards, newspaper, grocery bags, and other products.

You may not think the small amount of energy you save can make a difference. But if everyone uses less energy, our energy supplies will last longer.

Think About It

1. How can we conserve energy?
2. How does recycling materials save energy?
3. **Challenge** How can conserving energy today help us tomorrow?

recycling (rē sī′kling), changing a material to its original form so it can be reused.

Find Out

Use a telephone book to find recycling centers near your home.

Recycling aluminum

Collecting paper for recycling

Do You Know?

One Person's Garbage Is Another Person's Energy Source

Garbage-burning power plant

How can we get rid of garbage? Do we have enough energy sources to meet our future energy needs?

These are two important questions that many people are asking today. Some people think that we might be able to solve both problems at the same time. They suggest using garbage as an energy source.

For a long time people buried garbage or dumped it on empty land. Now, empty land is scarce. But more and more garbage is produced each year.

In 1978, people in the United States threw away about 140 million metric tons of garbage from their homes. That means each person threw out about 2.5 kilograms of garbage every day. Industries and businesses add to the amount of garbage on the earth by producing billions of metric tons of wastes.

But garbage can be a good fuel to use. The things in garbage do not look like coal, petroleum, or natural gas; but they are chemically similar to these fossil fuels. As we use up our fossil-fuel supplies, we might be able to use garbage as an energy source.

Burning garbage is not a new idea. Some cities in Europe and the United States have been burning garbage for years. The heat that is produced by burning garbage is used to boil water. The steam that is produced is used to make electricity or to heat nearby buildings.

In Paris, France, some power plants burn almost 2 million metric tons of the city's garbage each year. The amount of energy produced is about the same as would be produced by burning almost a half million barrels of oil!

But there are problems in using garbage as a fuel. Garbage that burns easily, such as food scraps and paper, must be separated from metals, glass, and other materials that do not burn easily. This separation process can be costly. Another problem is that burning garbage can pollute the air.

Our fossil fuel supplies are limited. Burning garbage might be one kind of energy source that we can use to help meet our energy needs. This method could also reduce the amount of garbage piling up on the earth.

Tie It Together

Sum It Up

Write the following paragraphs in your notebook. Unscramble the underlined words and include them in the paragraphs.

We must look for new ngyere cossrue to avoid running out of energy in the future. In about forty minutes the nsu sends as much energy to earth as people use in a year. We can use rlsoa yergne to heat homes and make electricity. Solar houses use aolsr llecotcors to capture the sun's yreneg. A liquid circulates through the solar collectors and is theead. The liquid then heats the air that circulates through the house, to keep it warm.

Solar energy is a erwnelabe geeynr cousre because the sun constantly replaces the solar energy we use.

ndiw eergyn also is a renewable energy source. It turns the blades of windmills that connect to electrical trgroaense. Heat energy from under the earth is tmagoehlre yeergn. Power plants drill wells that carry tmesa from underground to the surface of the earth. The steam is used to make iycteelcrit. daitl egyren can be used to run electrical generators on smda. As the water moves through the wall of the dam, it moves the blades of turbines connected to electrical generators.

We svconere energy by using it wisely, so our supplies will last longer. Using ycreecld materials also saves energy. When we reuse the aluminum from aluminum cans, we save the yeenrg used to nmei and clean the aluminum. We will have more energy for the reuuft if we conserve energy now and look for new energy sources.

Challenge!

1. How could mirrors be used to help solar collectors capture more sunlight?

2. How does our geographic location determine whether we can use wind or tidal energy?

3. How are geothermal and nuclear energy alike?

4. Describe what you think would be an ideal energy source.

5. How do we save energy by using returnable bottles?

Science Words

conservation

geothermal energy

recycling

solar cell

solar energy

tidal energy

Laboratory

Storing Heat from Solar Energy

Purpose
To compare how well different materials can store heat from solar energy.

You Will Need
• 3 small metal cans
• black construction paper
• scissors
• masking tape
• balance
• vegetable oil
• water
• sand
• 3 thermometers

a

Stating the Problem
Do some materials store heat from the sun better than others? Some solar houses use water to store heat from solar energy. Do other materials store heat as well as water? Test oil, water, and sand to find out which material best stores heat from solar energy.

Investigating the Problem
1. As shown in picture *a*, cover all 3 metal cans with black construction paper.
2. Weigh out equal amounts of oil, water, and sand, as shown in picture *b*. Place each material in a separate can. Label the cans.
3. Place the cans in direct sunlight for 1 hour.

b

4. Place a thermometer in the material in each can, as shown in picture c. Record the temperature of each material.

5. Remove the cans from the sunlight. Continue recording the temperature of the materials every 2 minutes for the next 12 minutes. Make a chart such as the one shown. Fill in the chart with the temperatures of the materials.

c

	Sand	Water	Oil
Temperature in sunlight			
Temperature after 2 min			
Temperature after 4 min			
Temperature after 6 min			
Temperature after 8 min			
Temperature after 10 min			
Temperature after 12 min			

Making Conclusions

1. Would the temperature of the materials be different if the cans were not covered with black paper? Explain.
2. Why did you add the same amount of material to all the cans?
3. How did the materials differ in how well they stored heat from solar energy?

Careers

Mechanical Technician

During cold, winter days, one of the most important uses of energy is to provide heat. This heat is usually produced in a furnace. What would a person do if the furnace broke down on a cold, windy night in January? That person might call someone like Kim.

Kim is a mechanical technician who cleans and repairs furnaces. "I go out right away for emergency calls," says Kim. When people are without heat or hot water, some safety problems could develop. Fumes from the furnace could cause a fire. Or water pipes might freeze."

To fix a furnace properly, Kim has to know how the whole heating system works. "I studied architecture for a few years in college. I learned how plumbing, electrical, and heating systems are designed. Many mechanical technicians learn their skills by just training on the job. But those who also have college training seem to get better jobs."

In the last couple of years, Kim's son, Adam, has become interested in how furnaces work. "He enjoys using tools, so I am teaching him about furnaces. One of his most important lessons is how to be careful when working with heating systems. Part of doing a job is doing it safely."

Did you use a light switch today? Does someone drive you to school? Lights, cars, and other machines need energy to work. Many people use their skills to make sure we get this energy.

Petroleum engineers work to get petroleum out of the ground. Along with **geologists,** they help decide where to drill the wells. After the well reaches the petroleum, it does not come gushing up. The engineer must plan ways to force the petroleum out of the earth.

Petroleum engineers spend four years in college. Geologists also go to college for at least four years. In college, geology students learn about the inside and the surface of the earth. They also learn how and where petroleum forms.

At the supermarket, you buy eggs marked A, B, and C. These grades tell you the quality of the eggs. At coal mines, coal is graded too.

A **coal inspector** tests the coal. It must be a certain quality before the mining company can sell the coal. The inspector takes samples of the coal when it is loaded onto train cars. The inspector performs tests on the coal samples that point out any impurities. The inspector then reports the quality of the coal to the mine owners and coal buyers.

Coal inspectors learn their skills at a special school after high school.

More and more people are using solar energy in their homes and other buildings. **Solar mechanics** install the large collectors on the roofs. Most solar mechanics attend a special school for two years after high school.

Geologists

Petroleum engineers

On Your Own

Picture Clue

The picture on page 248 shows unusual houses built in Arizona where the days are mostly sunny. What do you see on the roofs? Why do the houses have cement walls? Can you identify the kind of houses these are?

Books About Science

Alternate Energy Sources by Jane Werner Watson. Watts, 1979. Read about energy sources that are renewable and nonpolluting.

Coal in the Energy Crisis by Charles Coomb. Morrow, 1979. Learn how coal is mined and used to make many products.

Energy for America by Irene Keifer. Atheneum, 1979. Explore ways in which we use fossil fuels for energy.

Nuclear Energy by Nigel Hawkes. Watts, 1981. Learn how nuclear power plants use nuclear energy to produce electricity.

Solar Energy for Tomorrow's World by Reed Millard. Julian Messner, 1980. Discover ways we can use solar energy to meet our energy needs today and in the future.

Projects

1. Find information in the library about solar houses. Use this information to make a model of a solar house. Show all the parts of the house.

2. Fill two glass jars with water. Use a mirror to collect solar energy. Focus the solar energy on one of the jars. Find out whether the water in the two jars heats up differently.

3. You and your classmates can start a recycling project by collecting aluminum cans. Bring the cans to a recycling center near your school. Recycling centers usually pay for the aluminum you bring. Have a class discussion to decide how to spend the money.

Unit Test

Multiple Choice

Number your paper from 1–4. Next to each number write the letter of the word or phrase that best completes the statement or answers the question.

1. Which of the following are examples of energy use?
   a. A gas furnace heats a home.
   b. A bus takes people to work.
   c. Workers use electric tools.
   d. all the above

2. Which is *not* involved in making electricity from nuclear energy?
   a. burning oil
   b. splitting atoms
   c. heating water
   d. making steam

3. Conservation
   a. can be practiced by only a few people.
   b. can help our energy supplies last longer.
   c. is similar to geothermal energy.
   d. all the above

4. An advantage of using geothermal, tidal, and wind energy is that they
   a. are nonrenewable energy sources.
   b. can be used anywhere in the world.
   c. are renewable energy sources.
   d. can be used to produce nuclear energy.

Matching

Number your paper from 5–12. Read the description in Column I. Next to each number write the letter of the word or phrase from Column II that best matches the description in Column I.

Column I

5. the process of splitting an atom

6. changing materials to their original form so they can be reused

7. produced by nuclear fission

8. machine with fanlike blades

9. energy from underground

10. a device that uses sunlight to make electricity

11. formed from the remains of dead organisms

12. electricity produced by water power

Column II

a. turbine

b. recycling

c. fossil fuels

d. radioactive wastes

e. hydroelectric power

f. solar cell

g. wind energy

h. nuclear fission

i. geothermal energy

UNIT SEVEN
WATER ON THE EARTH

Down, down in the deep dark sea
    Made of metal or steel, I see.
Could be a treasure chest
    Or it could *not* be.
It's just sitting there
    In the deep dark sea.

Chris Smith *age 12*

Chapter 17

Pathways of Fresh Water on the Earth

Can you guess what this substance is? It is necessary for life. But it has no calories, no vitamins, no proteins, and no carbohydrates. It can be visible, invisible, hot, cold, hard, or soft. The answer, of course, is water. Unlike other planets in the solar system, the earth is almost covered by water. In fact, the earth is often called the "Water Planet."

The lessons in this chapter explain where fresh water is found and how it moves on earth. You will learn where people get most of their drinking water.

1 Identifying Pathways of Water

2 Where Do Rivers Run?

3 What Causes Lakes to Disappear?

4 What Is Groundwater?

5 How Do Glaciers Change the Land?

1 Identifying Pathways of Water

The picture was taken from a satellite orbiting the earth. This picture shows how water circulates over the earth's surface. Fresh water, such as the water you drink, moves in rivers, in lakes, through the ground, and through the air.

Rivers carry fresh water to the ocean. Find the largest river in the picture. On a sheet of paper, sketch this river and other rivers that join it. Find lakes and an ocean or a large body of water. Add them to your drawing. Identify places on the map that you think might have been changed by moving water. Mark the places on your drawing with Xs.

Think About It

1. Describe the pattern formed where rivers join.
2. **Challenge** Does the photograph show any evidence of how water moves through the air? Explain.

Photograph taken from a satellite orbiting earth

2 Where Do Rivers Run?

Rain or snow that falls on hills, mountains, or fields flows into low places because water runs downhill. Rivers are low places into which the water flows. Rivers carry part of the rainfall into the oceans.

All rivers begin as tiny streams that carry away—or drain—rainfall from the surrounding land. The land drained by a stream is the stream's **drainage basin.** As a stream flows, it is joined by other small streams. Eventually, the stream becomes large enough to be called a river. The drainage basin of a river is all the land drained by the river and the land drained by each small stream that joins the river.

The picture shows the largest drainage basins in the United States. Notice how much land the Mississippi River drains. The Mississippi River is about 4,000 kilometers long. It begins as a narrow stream in Minnesota. It is nearly 1 kilometer wide where it empties into the Gulf of Mexico.

Drainage basins in the United States

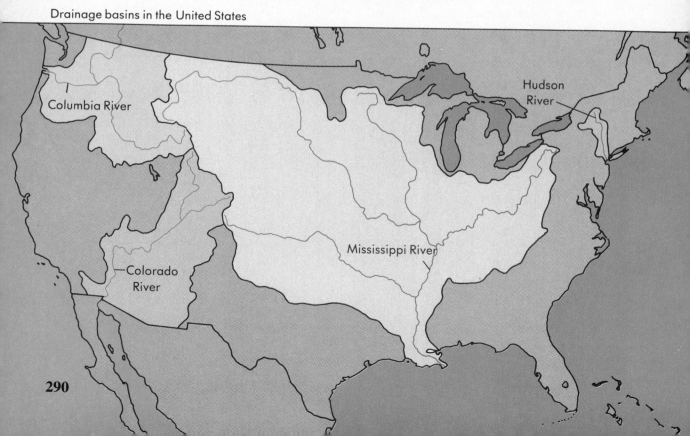

290

A mountain stream

A fan-shaped mound of earth

Most rivers start in mountains or on land that is higher than the level of the sea. The river in the picture starts in the mountains and flows down onto the plain. The land slopes down sharply in the mountains. Here, the river is narrow with fast-moving currents. It is bordered by walls of rock. The fast-moving stream cuts down through these walls and carries bits of rock and soil, called **sediment,** as it gushes toward the sea.

At the foot of the mountains, the slope of the land is more gentle and the river slows down. When the river slows down, some of the soil and rocks carried from the mountains drop from the water. Sometimes this sediment becomes a fan-shaped mound of earth, such as the one in the picture.

Have You Heard?

Rain and river water carved a large cave in the bluffs—or rock cliffs—at Cave in Rock, Illinois, on the Ohio River. In the 1700s and 1800s, river bandits used this cave as a hideout. From the cave, they could spot boats traveling up and down the river.

sediment (sed′ə mənt), pieces of rock and soil.

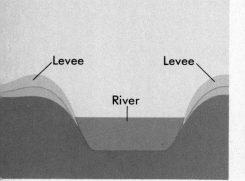

Floods build up levees

Flood plain of a river

How Does a River Change the Land?

A river picks up, carries, and drops sediment as it flows across land. You can feel this sediment squeeze between your toes when you wade through a muddy-bottomed stream.

The photograph shows a **flood plain**—or wide, flat area—that borders a river. During a flood, a river rises above its banks and covers the land. A thin layer of sediment settles out of the water and coats the flooded land. The river sediment contains minerals that enrich the soil. In spite of yearly floods, pioneers in this country settled on fertile flood plains first.

Levees are wall-like hills along a river's banks. During floods, levees build up where sediment drops at a river's banks as shown in the drawing. After repeated floods, some levees are high enough to protect people against rising flood water. When a river is rising rapidly, people often build artificial levees by putting sandbags along a river's banks.

flood plain, the flat land that borders a river and is covered by water and sediment when the river floods.

levee (lev′ē), wall-like structure made of sediment that builds up along a river's banks, or similar structure that is built on river banks by people.

292

The photograph on the previous page also shows curves—or **meanders**—in a river. During floods, a meander might disappear. Notice in the drawings how a river can cut across the narrowest part of a meander and take a shorter, straighter route. As a result the meander disappears. Sometimes, however, a thin, curved lake is left in the old meander.

A river ends at its mouth, where it empties into a lake or an ocean. River water slows down here and drops some of its sediment. The river sediment can build up in the large body of water and create new land at the river's mouth. This new land is a **delta.** The city of New Orleans is built on the Mississippi River delta.

A river builds up and wears down the land. A river often changes its course.

A meander in a river

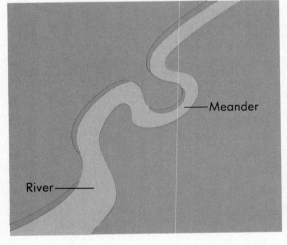

Lake formed from the meander

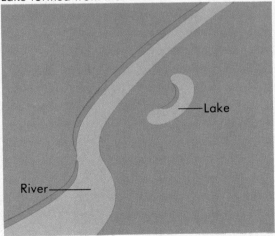

Think About It

1. What is the drainage basin of a river?
2. Explain how rain on the land reaches oceans.
3. **Challenge** If a message placed in a bottle were dropped into the Mississippi River in St. Louis, Missouri, where might the bottle later be found?

meander (mē an′dər), a loop in a river.

delta, new land that builds up at the mouth of a river in a body of water.

3 What Causes Lakes to Disappear?

Lakes form in a number of ways. Glaciers created most lakes in North America. The lake shown below formed when a glacier dug a deep hole that filled with rain and melting ice. Crater Lake in Oregon, shown on the next page, appeared when water filled the hole on top of an ancient volcano. People sometimes make lakes by building dams across rivers.

Water from rain and snow or water in the ground fills a lake. A lake can also be filled by a river that empties into it. Water leaves a lake when it evaporates into the air, sinks into the ground under the lake, or flows out at a low place.

Lake water usually is fresh water that contains only a small amount of dissolved salts. However, the water in a few lakes is salty. The water in Great Salt Lake in Utah is much saltier than ocean water because water evaporates quickly in a dry climate. Very little fresh water comes into the lake.

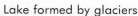
Lake formed by glaciers

Crater Lake in Oregon

Many small lakes disappear during long, dry periods when the ground is dry, rivers are low, and rainfall is scarce. Under these conditions, a lake can become a marsh or can dry up completely. Lakes also disappear when they fill with sediment. In only two or three years, sediment from a river can fill a very shallow lake.

Lakes are not as large or long lasting as oceans. People enjoy lakes. People can go boating, swimming, and fishing in them. Also, lakes reduce flooding by capturing parts of a heavy rainfall that could cause rivers to overflow. The more than 100,000 lakes in North America reduce flooding, provide recreation areas for many people, and increase our supply of available fresh water.

Find Out

On November 20, 1980, Lake Peigneur (pā nyùr′), in Louisiana, drained completely and refilled within a few days. Find out what caused these strange events by looking at a news magazine from 1980.

Think About It

1. List three ways in which lakes form.
2. What can cause a lake to dry up?
3. **Challenge** Suggest two reasons why the five Great Lakes in the United States are longer lasting than many other lakes.

4 What Is Groundwater?

Most people have watered a house plant at some time. They stop pouring when water begins to fill the dish under the pot. The soil in the pot looks packed, but it has tiny openings—or pores—that let water run through.

The soil and rocks of the earth also have tiny pores. Gravity causes water to move downward through the pores in the soil. Notice in the diagrams that the pores in some rocks are connected by cracks, so water can seep through the rock. Other rocks have pores that are not connected, and water does not pass through them.

Rain and snow provide us with water in the ground—or **groundwater.** Some of the water from rain and snow flows into rivers and lakes. But part of the water from rain and snow soaks into the ground. Sandy soil has large pores, so it absorbs water like a sponge. Clay soil has smaller pores, so water does not soak into clay soil as well. Water runs off rocks at the earth's surface faster than the rocks can absorb it. In rocky places, such as mountains, the ground absorbs very little water.

groundwater, water from rain or snow that sinks into the earth.

Water passes through some rocks but not others

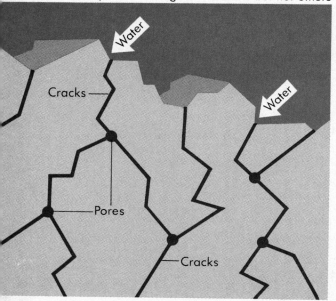
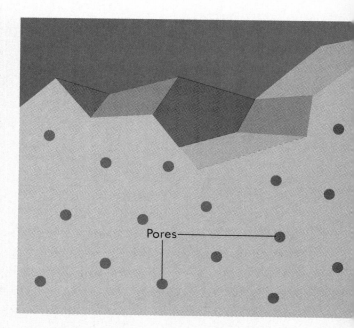

296

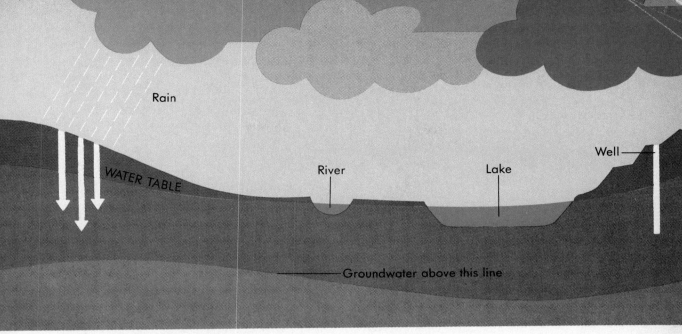

Rain

WATER TABLE

River

Lake

Well

Groundwater above this line

Groundwater and the water table

The diagram shows how the ground stores water. Water sinks into the ground until it meets rock that has no connecting pores or cracks. Water cannot move below this level. Above this level, however, the pores and cracks of rocks are filled with water.

The top of this water-soaked layer is the **water table.** Notice on the diagram how the water table roughly follows the slope of the ground—up under hills and down under valleys. The depth of the water table depends on the amount of rainfall. In moist climates, or when rainfall is heavy, the water table is close to the surface.

The pores in the rocks and soil above the water table are filled with air as well as water. Plants and organisms in the soil soak up some of this water.

Notice in the diagram that rivers and lakes are low places where the water table is near the surface of the ground. Wells that are dug by people give water if they are drilled below the water table. When less rain than normal falls, the water table sinks lower. Rivers, lakes, and wells can dry up when the water table goes down.

water table, the top of the water-soaked layer in the ground.

Find Out
What is an artesian (är tē′zhən) well? Where would you expect to see artesian wells? Use an encyclopedia to find your answers.

What Are Some Problems with Groundwater?

Wastes from towns, farms, and industries often seep into the ground and make groundwater unfit for drinking. The picture shows how this can happen.

Scientists estimate that sixty times more fresh water is stored in the ground than in all the rivers and lakes of the world! However, people have drilled many wells and pumped the groundwater up. As a result, the water table has dropped in many places, and wells have gone dry. Farmers use huge amounts of groundwater for irrigation. Industries use large amounts of groundwater for manufacturing.

People are now aware of our problems with groundwater. They are taking steps to avoid wasting groundwater and to keep it clean.

Think About It

1. How can water move through some rocks?
2. How is water in lakes, rivers, and wells related to the water table?
3. **Challenge** If you are digging a hole in the ground, how do you know when you have reached the water table?

Wastes at a chemical dump

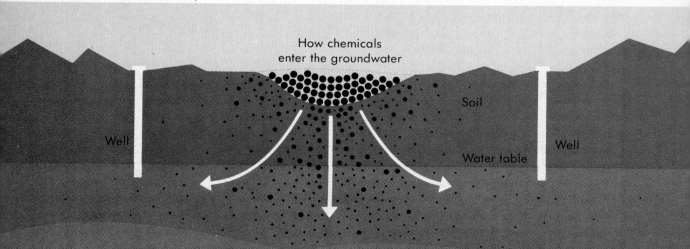

How chemicals
enter the groundwater

Well

Soil

Water table

Well

Do You Know?

Groundwater Can Form Caves

Mammoth Cave in Kentucky

Moving water can change the shape of the land. Mammoth Cave in the picture looks as if it were scooped out with a giant bulldozer. Instead, the steady movement of groundwater formed the cave over millions of years.

A weak acid in groundwater, called carbonic acid, can dissolve some kinds of rock, such as limestone. Groundwater might reach a crack in limestone and dissolve some of the rock as it moves through the crack. In time, the crack gets larger and larger. Finally, the crack becomes a cave. The trickle of groundwater might become an underground river.

Groundwater has made Mammoth Cave in Kentucky the longest cave in the world. No one knows exactly how large the cave is. Many parts are still unexplored. So far, over 200 kilometers of passageways have been found.

The largest cave-rooms in the world are found in Carlsbad Caverns, New Mexico. The Big Room at Carlsbad is 1200 meters long, 190 meters wide, and over 100 meters high. You could put 12 football fields end to end in this room!

Caves have unusual rock formations, such as those in the picture. Stalactites are pillars of limestone that hang from the ceiling of a cave. They form as dissolving limestone drips from the ceiling. When the water evaporates from the dripping limestone, the limestone rock is left hanging. Drops of dissolving limestone often fall from the ceiling to the floor. The limestone forms a mound called a stalagmite on the floor. Sometimes a stalactite and a stalagmite grow until they meet each other and form a pillar of limestone. Stalactites and stalagmites can form many shapes. They can look like icicles, folded curtains, thin wires, or delicate lacework.

5 How Do Glaciers Change the Land?

continental (kon′tə nen′tl) **glacier,** a huge ice sheet that can cover an area as large as a continent.

valley glacier, a glacier that moves down a mountain valley.

A glacier is a mass of ice that moves or that has moved at some time. Glaciers can develop where it is cold—on mountaintops or near the North and South Poles. For glaciers to form, the climate must be cold enough so that snow does not melt from year to year. Just as a person can squeeze snow to make a very hard snowball, the weight of deep snow presses on the snow below and changes it to ice.

Glaciers once covered much of North America. These glaciers melted about ten thousand years ago. Now, glaciers cover only 10 percent of the land on earth. However, huge glaciers still extend across most of Greenland and Antarctica. Glaciers that cover very large areas, such as the Greenland Ice Sheet shown in the picture, are **continental glaciers.** Smaller glaciers, such as the one in the other picture, move down mountain valleys. They are **valley glaciers.**

Continental glacier

Valley glacier

A moraine

The tremendous weight of a glacier causes the glacier to spread out and move. The weight of the ice can also create enough heat to melt ice at the bottom of the glacier. The resulting layer of liquid water helps the glacier slide along just as oil makes a bicycle wheel spin easily.

Glaciers that cover a continent are heavy enough to make the continent sink several meters. These frozen rivers of ice can scrape out U-shaped valleys in mountains or can dig holes big enough to hold lakes.

As glaciers move, they carry along the sediment that they scraped out. When the ice melts, some of the sediment is left on the ground. The dark band—or **moraine**—in the picture is made of sediment carried by glaciers. Moraines develop around the edges of melting glaciers. The power of moving ice to change the land is great indeed!

moraine (mə rān′), a ridge that forms where sediment drops along the sides and edges of a glacier.

Have You Heard?

Two percent of the world's water is found in glaciers. If ships could tow icebergs—or chunks of glaciers—to countries that need water, those countries' shortages of fresh water might decrease.

Find Out

What is a fiord (fyôrd)? Find a book on glaciers in the library to learn how glaciers cause fiords.

Think About It

1. Describe two types of glaciers.
2. Describe how a glacier can wear away or build up the land.
3. **Challenge** Explain one way that a scientist could estimate how far to the south glaciers have moved in the United States.

301

Activity

Adding Pressure to Ice

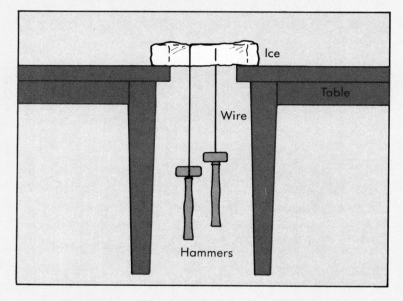

Ice
Table
Wire
Hammers

Purpose
To observe how ice reacts to small, large, slow, and sudden pressures.

You Will Need
- bar of ice
- wire about 80 cm long
- 2 heavy metal objects, such as 2 hammers
- 2 small metal objects of different weights
- ice cubes
- 1 plastic bag and a fastener to close it
- metal pan
- hammer

Directions
1. Look at the picture as you set up this activity. Balance the bar of ice between 2 tables.
2. Tie a heavy metal object at each end of the wire. Wrap one end of the wire around one object and the other end around the other object.
3. Place the wire over the middle of the ice so that the same length of wire hangs down on each side of the ice. Observe what happens to the ice while you are working on the rest of the activity.
4. Put the lighter of the small metal objects on one ice cube and the heavier object on another ice cube.
5. Record how long it takes each ice cube to melt completely.
6. Put 2 ice cubes in the plastic bag, and close the bag with the fastener.
7. Put the bag in the metal pan. Hit the ice cubes once with the hammer.

Think About It
1. Explain what happened to the bar of ice and the wire.
2. How does the amount of pressure acting on ice affect the way ice melts?
3. Describe the way ice breaks when a sudden, heavy pressure, such as the blow of a hammer, acts on it.
4. **Challenge** Suggest a reason why pressures acting on a glacier sometimes cause the glacier to crack and other times cause the glacier to melt.

Tie It Together

Sum It Up

All the boldface words in the story below are in the wrong places. Rewrite the story, and put each word where it belongs. Use each word once—wherever it fits best in the story. Start by making a list of the boldface words. Cross each word off your list after you use it once.

On April 10, last year, the Big Muddy River rose 10 meters in 6 hours. Workers at the scene threw sandbags on the **moraines** that border the river. They hoped to prevent the overflow of the river onto the **rainfall.**

There were several reasons for the flood. In the surrounding mountains the **flood plain** broke up when the spring thaw brought unusually warm temperatures. The **levees** that had built up along the edges of the ice were destroyed by the violent streams of water from the melting ice. The **lake** of the Big Muddy River extends for hundreds of kilometers across the countryside. Water flowed from the river's farthest reaches into the streams that join the Big Muddy. In addition, the rising water destroyed the dam up river. The water from the **drainage basin,** formed by damming the river, overflowed into the Big Muddy.

However, good things can come from a flood of the Big Muddy. The **glacier** in the area was very low before the flood. Little **water table** had fallen to refill the supply of groundwater for nearby cities. When the flood water soaked into the ground, water returned to normal levels in the wells.

Challenge!

1. When does a river deposit sediment?

2. What could prevent the growth of a delta where a large river empties into the ocean?

3. What is a reason for lakes, which were formed by damming a river, to dry up?

4. Explain how plants, concrete, asphalt, and buildings can affect the water table.

5. What signs can warn people that glaciers will be advancing over the earth?

Science Words

continental glacier

delta

drainage basin

flood plain

groundwater

levee

meander

moraine

sediment

valley glacier

water table

Chapter 18
Salt Water and the Oceans

About three-quarters of our earth is hidden under water. Until recently, no one knew much about the hidden part of the world—the ocean bottom. Now, people can explore the ocean bottom without even getting wet. As a result, scientists are beginning to understand some mysteries of the ocean.

The lessons in this chapter describe the oceans of the world. You will read how scientists study the oceans and what they know about them.

1 Estimating the Distribution of Water on Earth

You see large amounts of water in lakes and rivers. When it rains very hard, the sky seems to be full of water. But how is water actually divided among the oceans, lakes, rivers, glaciers, groundwater, and air?

Using a medicine dropper, put 100 drops of water in a small cup. Imagine that these drops are all the water on earth. Get five more cups. The picture shows you how to label each cup. Estimate how many of the 100 drops would be found in each source of water represented by the cups. Divide the 100 drops of water among the cups, using your estimates. Compare your estimates with those of your classmates. Ask your teacher for a more accurate distribution of water on earth.

Think About It

1. Did the more accurate distribution of water on earth surprise you? Explain your answer.
2. Did you think that lakes and rivers held more water than the ground or glaciers? If so, why?
3. **Challenge** From which of the five groups of water can we get drinking water?

2 What Are the Properties of Ocean Water?

Look at the map of the world. Notice that the earth has four main oceans—Pacific, Atlantic, Indian, and Arctic. They are not really separate oceans, because water can move from one ocean to another. They are all part of one large world ocean! This world ocean covers about 70 percent of the earth's surface.

Scientists think that millions of years ago, all water came from deep inside the earth. Gigantic volcanic explosions might have released water in the form of a gas. This gas eventually changed into liquid water.

You may have swallowed a mouthful of seawater by mistake. If so, you do not need to be told that seawater, the water in oceans and seas, is salty. Seawater contains the salt you use to season food. Other kinds of salt are also dissolved in seawater. Since water can dissolve almost all substances on earth, seawater contains small amounts of most substances found on earth.

Oceans of the world

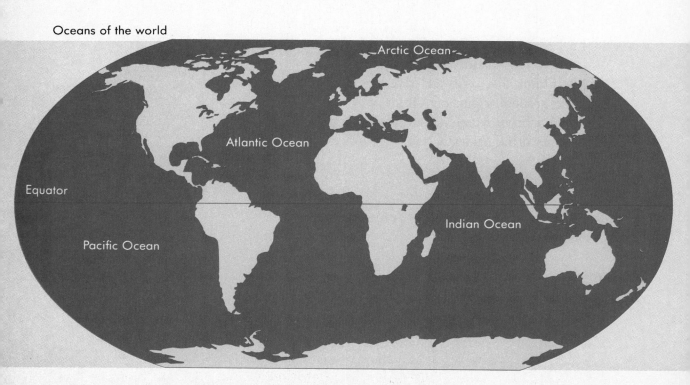

Mississippi River flowing into the Gulf of Mexico

Oceans get their salt mainly from the rocks beneath them. Ocean water seeps down through the rocks and dissolves salts from the rocks. Rivers also wash salts from the land into the ocean. The picture shows river water pouring into the ocean. The color of the river water shows that the water is full of sediment, which contains salts.

Water from the Arctic Ocean has the same salts as water from the Pacific or other oceans. But the amounts of dissolved salts in an ocean can vary from place to place. Where it is hot, the water at the surface of oceans can be very salty. The heat of the sun rapidly evaporates water at the surface. When seawater evaporates, its dissolved salts remain in the ocean and make the surface water saltier.

Think About It

1. What does the term *world ocean* mean?
2. From where do the salts in ocean water come?
3. **Challenge** What could cause surface water in the ocean to be less salty than usual?

3 How Does Ocean Water Move?

current, a river of water that flows unseen through the ocean.

Water in the ocean is never still. Waves, such as the one in the picture, break and foam along the beach. Tides move water higher or lower along the shore. **Currents**—or rivers of water—flow unseen through the ocean. Waves, tides, and currents mix and stir ocean water.

When you throw a pebble into a puddle, waves ripple through the water. Disturbances in the ocean cause waves too. The ocean is rarely calm. Winds are the main cause of waves in the ocean. Steady winds are blowing somewhere on the ocean at all times.

The size of waves depends on the force of the wind and how long the wind blows. Even light winds that blow a long time can cause waves. Large waves can move as fast as the wind.

Ocean waves

For hundreds of years, sailors have known that currents of water flow like rivers through the oceans. These currents can differ in speed, temperature, or saltiness from the water around them.

Currents exist at all depths in the water. Cold polar currents move along the ocean bottom from the poles toward the equator. Warm currents move from the equator toward the poles.

The map shows some surface currents. The Gulf Stream is a warm current that moves in loops through the Atlantic Ocean. Air warmed by the Gulf Stream flows over England and northern Europe. This air warms the climate there.

You can sometimes see the Gulf Stream as it moves north in the Atlantic Ocean. In some places the current looks blue compared with the green water around it. Tiny sea organisms that can make seawater look green are eaten before the Gulf Stream reaches the North Atlantic. Clouds often hang over the warm water of the Gulf Stream as the current moves north. However, scientists usually find currents in the ocean by checking for differences in the temperatures and the speeds of the ocean water.

Have You Heard?

The temperature of the water near the ocean bottom is about the same everywhere in the world. It is a few degrees above freezing. However, surface water, where people swim, changes temperatures with the seasons. In August, swimming along the coast of Florida in the Gulf of Mexico is like swimming in a heated pool. In January the surface water in the Gulf is much colder.

Surface currents in the oceans

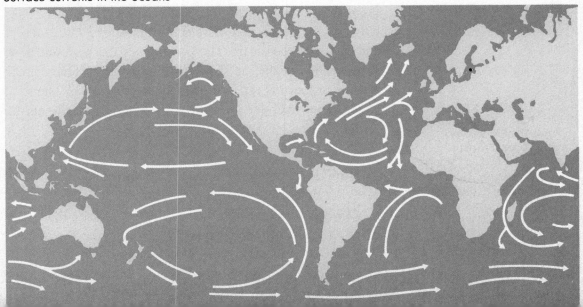

High tide

Low tide

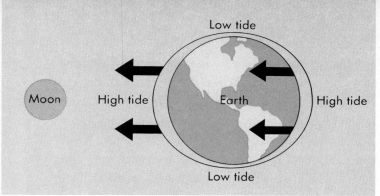

Tides on earth

What Are the Ocean Tides?

Some people like to go clamming on the beach to catch their dinners. They search for clams during low tide, when the water level drops and the water pulls back from the beach. Clams are then exposed in the wet sand at the water's edge. A little more than six hours later, high tide comes up onto the beach, and water covers the clams.

Two high tides and two low tides move onto a beach every 24 hours and 50 minutes. If low tide came at 8:00 a.m. on Tuesday, it would come again at about 8:25 p.m. on Tuesday, and then at about 8:50 Wednesday morning.

The moon has a similar time pattern. Each day the moon rises 50 minutes later than it did the day before. Long ago, people realized that the movement of the moon was related to the tides. The force of gravity between the moon and the earth pulls on the land, air, and water of the earth. The pull causes the high and low tides in the oceans, as shown in the pictures. One set of arrows in the diagram shows the moon's pull on the water. The other set shows the moon's pull on the earth.

Think About It

1. How do waves, currents, and tides differ?
2. What determines the size of a wave?
3. **Challenge** How might a cold ocean current that is moving down the coast affect the climate?

Have You Heard?

People fishing in the Amazon River in South America must be alert when high tide comes in. Near the mouth of the river, high tide occasionally arrives in a wave 8 meters high—about as high as a 2-story house.

Activity

Making Waves and Currents

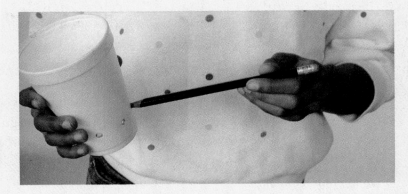

Purpose
To observe the effects of waves and currents on a body of water.

You Will Need
- 1 large basin
- warm water to fill basin
- sharpened pencil
- 1 plastic-foam cup
- small pieces of ice
- food coloring
- small pieces of cork
- 1 drinking straw

Directions
1. Fill the basin 3 cm deep with warm water.
2. Use the point of a pencil to punch 8 small holes near the bottom of the plastic-foam cup, as shown.
3. Fill the cup with ice. Place the cup in the middle of the basin, as shown.
4. Add 10 drops of food coloring to the cup. Observe what happens.
5. Place the pieces of cork in the basin of water.
6. Above the water, blow air through the straw to make waves on the surface of the water.
7. Observe how the waves affect the cork.
8. Observe what happens when the waves meet the colored water.

Think About It

1. Use your observations in step 4 to explain what happens when cold and warm water meet in the ocean.
2. How was the colored water similar to an ocean current?
3. What happened to the cork when you blew through the straw?
4. How did waves affect the colored water in the basin?
5. **Challenge** Explain why currents mix ocean water more than waves do.

311

4 What Is the Floor of the Ocean Like?

plate, a slowly moving piece of the solid, outer layer of the earth.

Mid-Atlantic Ridge, an underwater chain of mountains in the Atlantic Ocean that formed where 2 plates are moving apart and new crust is forming.

trench, a deep ditch in the ocean floor that forms where 2 plates are colliding and crust is being destroyed.

Few people have seen the bottom of the ocean. Yet, scientists have learned a great deal about the ocean in the last thirty years. They learned that the solid outer layer of the earth is divided into a number of large pieces. These pieces, called **plates,** move very slowly over the earth.

Where two plates move apart, melted material rises from deep inside the earth. The material forms new crust, which is the outer layer of the earth. Huge underwater mountains can grow where new crust is forming. Scientists discovered a chain of towering mountains on the Atlantic Ocean bottom. These mountains are the **Mid-Atlantic Ridge.** The map shows that they are part of a long mountain chain, or ridge, that stretches through the oceans of the world.

Where two plates bump into each other, the edge of one plate slowly sinks into the earth, melts, and is destroyed. In the ocean, **trenches** develop where crust is being destroyed. These trenches are deep, narrow ditches in the ocean floor. Trenches more than 10 kilometers deep—the length of about 130 city blocks—have been found in the Pacific Ocean!

Ridges and trenches of the world

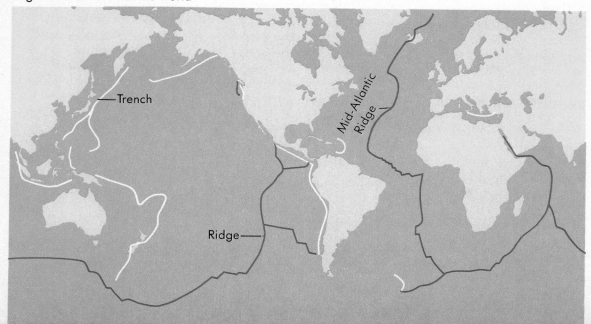

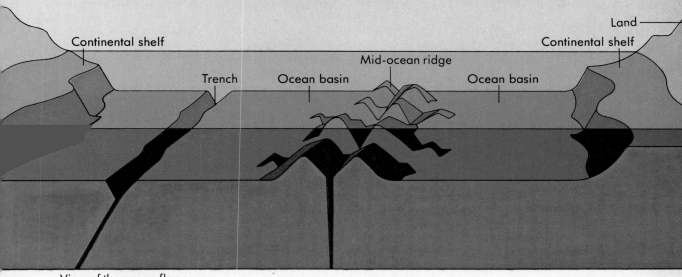

Continental shelf

Trench

Ocean basin

Mid-ocean ridge

Ocean basin

Land

Continental shelf

View of the ocean floor

Find the trenches and ridges on the map on the previous page. Scientists think the Atlantic Ocean is getting larger because new crust is forming there. They also think the Pacific Ocean is shrinking because crust is being destroyed at the trenches in the Pacific. The changes in the size of an ocean are slow—only a few centimeters a year. So millions of years must pass before those changes are noticeable.

The drawing shows what the floor of the ocean looks like. The **continental shelf** is the part of a continent that extends from the edge of the landmass into the ocean. Seawater is rarely more than 135 meters deep on the shelf.

Beyond the shelf the ocean bottom slopes steeply. Sediment that washes off the continent is dumped at the base of this steep slope.

The **ocean basin** is beyond the steep slope. There, the ocean is about 4,000 or 5,000 meters deep. Ridges, trenches, and flat plains make up this part of the ocean floor.

continental shelf, land that extends into the ocean from the edge of a continent.

ocean basin, the deep ocean floor.

313

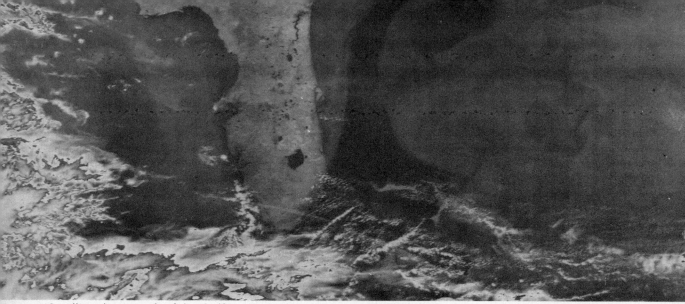

Satellite photograph of the Gulf Stream

How Do People Explore the Ocean Bottom?

Until about thirty years ago, scientists knew more about the moon than about the earth's oceans! Now scientists have many tools to explore the oceans. People can go to the ocean bottom or they can use instruments to look at it.

Satellites that orbit high above the earth are valuable tools for studying the ocean. They take pictures of the earth and collect information that tells about water movements and temperatures. In the satellite picture the warmest waters show up as dark areas.

To make maps of the ocean floor, people need to know how deep the water is. Scientists measure the depth of the water as they move along in ships. Instruments on the moving ships send out signals. When the signals hit the ocean floor, they bounce back like echoes. People measure the time it takes a signal to go to the bottom and return. Then, they divide the time in half to find out how long it takes the signal to reach the ocean bottom. Since people know how fast the signals travel in water, they can calculate the depth of the water.

The photograph shows the *ALVIN*. This ship is a **submersible**—or an underwater research vessel. Submersibles carry scientists and instruments as deep as 4 kilometers into the ocean. The *ALVIN* and other submersibles have dived to the ridges in the Atlantic, Pacific, and Indian Oceans. Scientists have brought organisms, water, and sediment up from the bottom.

Scientists were surprised at what they learned from the dives. Hot water and minerals shoot through chimneylike holes in the Pacific Ocean floor. The worms in the picture grow like thick, colorful plants near the warm chimneys.

Think About It

1. What is happening at the Mid-Atlantic Ridge?
2. What are three tools that scientists use to learn about the ocean bottom?
3. **Challenge** Iceland is an island at the Mid-Atlantic Ridge. What can you guess about the way Iceland formed?

submersible (səb mėr′sə bəl), underwater vessel used to explore the ocean bottom.

Worms on the Pacific Ocean floor

A submersible

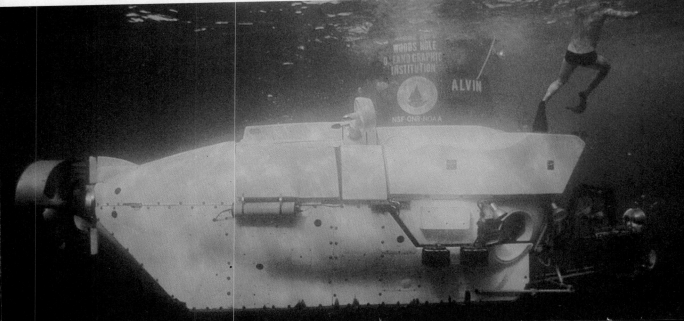

5 Where Is Life Found in the Oceans?

Sea life swarms in the waters on the continental shelf. Notice in the pictures that some organisms, such as the fish, swim in the water. Others creep around or burrow into the ocean floor. Coral is attached to the ocean bottom.

Seaweeds, such as kelp, need the sunlight that can reach only about 100 meters into the water. While plants live only in the sunlit waters of the ocean, animals can live at all levels in the water.

Sea organisms, like land organisms, need nutrients to live. Nutrients for sea organisms come from a number of places. Rivers carry sediment containing nutrients into the oceans. Sea organisms also get nutrients from plants, other organisms, or the remains of organisms.

The tiny sea organisms in the picture on the next page are called **plankton.** They float in the sunlit surface waters of an ocean. If you scooped up a bucket of seawater, you would probably scoop up thousands of plankton as well.

plankton (plangk′tən), floating sea organisms.

Sea urchin

Fish and coral on the ocean floor

316

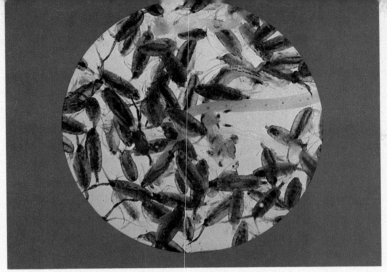
Plankton from tropic ocean

Sea organisms of all sizes eat plankton. Even certain kinds of whales depend on tiny plankton for food. Plankton make the surface water like a rich soup for other sea organisms to eat. As a result, animals are especially numerous just below the sunlit surface water of the ocean.

The cold water near the ocean bottom is also rich in nutrients. When organisms die in shallow water, their remains sink slowly through the water. Fish eat these dead organisms as the organisms sink. Any remains that are not eaten fall to the ocean floor. Organisms that live in very deep water eat some of these remains.

Great currents can sweep deeper water and its nutrients from the ocean bottom to the surface. Experienced fishers search for rising, cold currents. They know that fish can be found where nutrients are plentiful.

Think About It

1. At what depth are seaweeds found in the oceans?
2. At what depth are sea animals most numerous? Explain why.
3. **Challenge** Why does most seafood we eat come from the continental shelf?

Discover!

Hot Springs Are Found on the Ocean Floor

The ocean floor is filled with surprises. The picture shows one of them: a hot spring coming from the ocean floor. Many hot springs were discovered in 1979 near South America. The water pouring out of openings in the ocean floor—or vents—was as hot as 350° Celsius!

Scientists think that the water coming from a vent is heated as it moves through the hot rock which makes up the earth's crust. As the water passes through the crust, it dissolves the minerals from the surrounding rock. Then, when the hot water erupts from the vent, it carries the minerals from the crust with it. The area around the vents contains a great many minerals such as iron, copper, lead, and sulfur.

Scientists were very surprised to find life near these dark, hot vents. The ocean around the vents is 2,500 meters deep, so sunlight does not reach the ocean floor. Most food chains begin with organisms that use sunlight to make food.

Imagine how surprised the scientists were to find a community of sea organisms, such as the one in the picture, living around the vents. Many organisms were similar to familiar animals that live in shallow water: clams, crabs, mussels, and seaworms. But a few were organisms that no one had ever seen before, such as worms nearly 1½ meters long.

How do these organisms live without sunlight? Scientists think that bacteria living around the vents are able to use certain minerals from the vent to get energy. Then, the other organisms feed on the bacteria. The bacteria begin food chains around the vents, just as green plants begin food chains on land.

Some scientists think that underwater vents are one of the most interesting discoveries ever made on the ocean floor. Divers are searching for more underwater vents in other parts of the world.

Underwater hot spring

Organisms living near an underwater vent

Tie It Together

Sum It Up

The words and phrases below describe the parts of the deep ocean shown on the diagram. Write them in your notebook. Next to each word or phrase write the letter from the diagram that best matches the description.

1. light energy _____

2. no seaweed below this depth _____

3. where the remains of sea organisms finally lie _____

4. evaporation _____

5. depth where sea animals are most numerous _____

6. saltiest water in a hot climate _____

Deep ocean environment

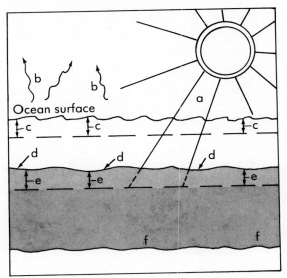

Challenge!

1. The Mediterranean Sea is an enclosed sea with a warm climate. Explain how these conditions affect the saltiness of the surface water of the sea.

2. Explain why a boat trip from America to northern Europe can be faster than the return trip from northern Europe to America.

3. Explain how sediment from the land can be found on the floor of an ocean basin.

4. What would happen to the crust of the earth if only ridges, and no trenches, formed?

5. In some parts of the ocean, especially near the equator, plankton are scarce. How might this affect other organisms in these places?

Science Words

continental shelf

current

Mid-Atlantic Ridge

ocean basin

plankton

plate

submersible

trench

Chapter 19
Valuable Resources from Water

A long time ago, a fierce storm in the Atlantic Ocean sank the ship in the picture. The divers have brought up gold and silver treasures worth millions of dollars. But sunken treasures like these are not as valuable as the other kinds of wealth available in the oceans.

The lessons in this chapter describe some of the important resources we get from the oceans. The oceans are a storehouse of resources for the future.

1 Comparing Food Resources from Water

2 What Is the Water Cycle?

3 Is Fresh Water an Unlimited Resource?

4 What Are Our Seafood Resources?

5 How Do We Get Other Resources from the Ocean?

1 Comparing Food Resources from Water

Food from salt water and fresh water is a valuable resource. Most people occasionally eat some kind of lake fish or seafood. Because so many people like shrimp, you might expect shrimp to be the biggest sea-animal catch. But shrimp are only a small part of the yearly harvest of organisms from bodies of water.

The table shows a variety of organisms that were caught in a recent year. Each group is listed as a percent of the total catch. Make a bar graph that shows the information in the table. Use the graph shown to help you make your own graph. Draw and label one bar for each group of organisms in the table.

Think About It

1. Which kinds of organisms make up the biggest part of the catch?
2. Suppose 500,000 kilograms of a certain type of tuna were caught in one year. If one of this type of tuna weighs an average of 23 kilograms, about how many tuna were caught?
3. **Challenge** Why might a particular type of sea organism be more valuable than another type of sea organism?

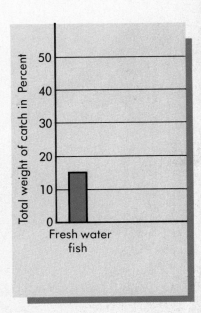

Sea Animals Harvested From Fresh and Salt Water—whales not included

Types of organisms	% of Total Weight
Fresh water fish	15%
Salt water fish	
Herring, sardines, anchovies	35%
Cod, haddock	15%
Unidentified fish	15%
Bass, mackerel, redfish	10%
Tuna, flounder, halibut, sole	5%
Clams, oysters, shrimp, lobsters, crab	5%
	100%

2 What Is the Water Cycle?

Answer this riddle. If rivers flow into oceans, why does the water level in the oceans stay about the same? The answer is in the **water cycle.**

The picture of the water cycle shows the paths that fresh water and salt water follow on earth. Water changes from fresh to salt water and back to fresh water, again and again. But the total amount of water on earth stays the same.

In the water cycle, water evaporates from the ocean, leaving the salts behind. This water, which enters the air as water vapor, is fresh water. Moving air carries the water vapor away. Clouds form when water vapor **condenses**—or changes into tiny drops of water. In time, rain or snow falls from the clouds onto the oceans or land.

Most of the rain or snow that falls on the land or oceans evaporates into the air once more. But some of the rain and snow that falls on the land sinks into the ground and becomes groundwater. Plants use some of this water to live and grow and release the rest of the water into the air as water vapor.

water cycle, the movement of water between the earth's surface and the air, and back to the earth.

condense (kən dens′), to change from a gas, such as water vapor, into a liquid, such as water.

Water cycle

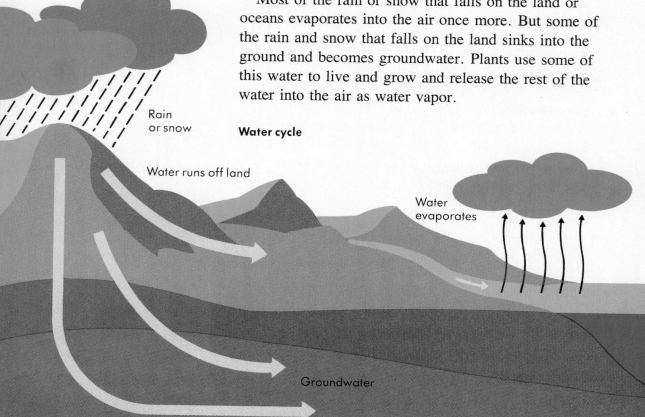

Water condenses in clouds

Rain or snow

Water runs off land

Water evaporates

Groundwater

The rest of the rain that falls on the land flows into rivers and lakes. Rivers then transport some of the water back into the ocean. The ocean water changes into water vapor as it evaporates from the surface of the ocean.

Oceans lose more water by evaporation than they gain from rain and snow. However, water comes into the oceans from rivers and melting glaciers. This water makes up for the large amount of water that is lost from the oceans by evaporation. So the level of the oceans remains about the same.

Energy is needed to evaporate water and to move air. The water cycle uses energy from the sun. The sun's energy is always available. So the water cycle never stops.

Think About It

1. Describe how water can change from fresh to salt water and back again to fresh water.
2. What happens to rain that falls on land?
3. **Challenge** What controls how fast water moves in the water cycle?

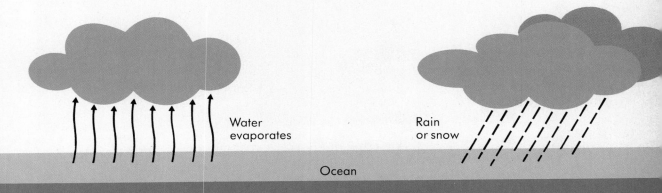

Water evaporates

Rain or snow

Ocean

3 Is Fresh Water an Unlimited Resource?

During a visit to Europe, a desert nomad saw a waterfall for the first time. The astonished nomad refused to leave the waterfall for several hours. He wanted to wait until the water stopped! He had never seen water continuously flowing across the ground.

Fresh water is everywhere. But available fresh water is scarce in dry climates. The total amount of fresh water on earth depends on the amount of rain that falls on the land. So the amount of fresh water is limited.

Fresh water is a valuable resource. People use fresh water in irrigation and industry, as well as in their homes for washing, drinking, and cooking. People can increase the amount of available fresh water by removing the salt from ocean water.

The simplest way to remove salt is to trap water as it evaporates from salt water. In the picture, the plastic covers over the ponds of salt water trap the water vapor from the ponds.

Desalting ponds

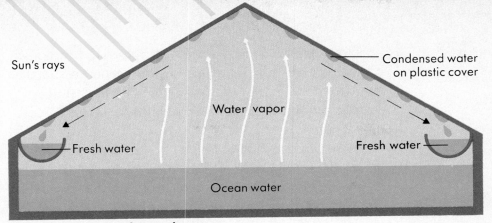

Sun's rays

Condensed water
on plastic cover

Water vapor

Fresh water

Fresh water

Ocean water

Getting fresh water from salt water

The drawing shows how the plastic covers collect fresh water from ponds of ocean water. Water vapor from the ponds condenses as drops of fresh water on the plastic covers. The fresh water eventually collects in containers placed beneath the plastic covers.

Since removing salt from ocean water is not possible everywhere, people have found other ways to increase their fresh water supply. In some places, for example, they have raised the level of groundwater. Some years ago, the water table near Long Island, New York, was so low that wells were running dry. To solve this problem, workers drilled many special wells. Into these wells, they pumped water coming from homes, businesses, and industries. The water was cleaned as it filtered through the ground. Before these special wells were built, the used water went into rivers or directly into the ocean. In a few years, the water table near Long Island was up again, and wells did not run dry during dry weather.

Think About It

1. What determines the amount of fresh water on earth?
2. How can we get fresh water from salt water?
3. **Challenge** What are two reasons the water table might drop?

4 What Are Our Seafood Resources?

Seafood is an important part of people's diets in some countries. Fish from the ocean provide about half of the animal protein eaten in Japan. In the United States, seafood provides only a small amount of the protein people eat.

About seventy million tons of sea animals are harvested in the oceans of the world each year. Fish, such as anchovies, herring, cod, haddock, and tuna, make up most of the harvest. Other kinds of sea animals, such as shrimp, oysters, and lobsters, are a small, but valuable, part of the catch.

People can use nets to catch large numbers of fish at sea because fish swim in groups called schools. At one throw, a net can trap thousands of herring or other small fish. The pictures show a type of net that many fishers use. Pulling a cord on the net closes the net, like a drawstring bag or purse, around the fish.

Fish in closed net

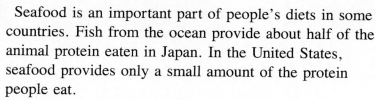

Open fish nets

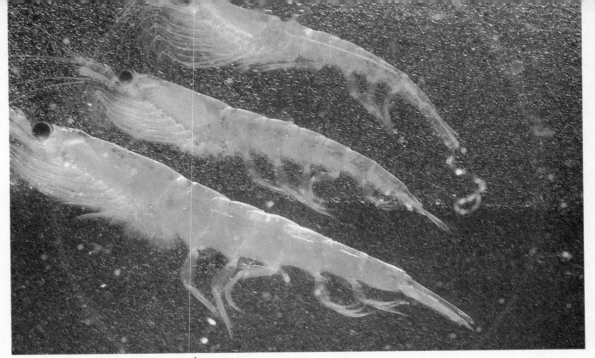

Krill are about three centimeters long

Scientists are looking for ways to get more food from the oceans. Fish that are not usually eaten can be ground into a powder called **FPC**—fish-protein concentrate. This powder is tasteless, does not spoil, and is nutritious. Adding FPC to foods, such as bread, does not change their taste. This powder could be useful in countries where meat and fish are scarce.

Catching **krill** can increase food production from the sea. Millions of krill live in the ocean near Antarctica. The picture shows this tiny sea animal, which is about 3 centimeters long—or half as long as your little finger. The holes in ordinary fishing nets are too large to catch krill. With modern ships and fishing equipment, people can now catch krill in large amounts. But krill are so small that they must be processed into a powder, such as FPC, before they can be used. Because the current demand for FPC is not great, fishing industries are not yet prepared to process large amounts of krill.

FPC (fish-protein concentrate), a powder made of ground fish.

krill, a tiny sea animal that is common in the ocean near Antarctica.

Find Out

Many kinds of sea organisms might disappear from the earth if people from all countries continue to catch as many organisms as they do now. Find out about the future of whales in the oceans by looking in books written about the oceans.

What Is a Sea Farm?

Many countries have "sea farms" to boost seafood production. Sea farms are businesses located on the continental shelf that raise sea organisms to sell. Animals, such as oysters and shrimp, live on the floor of the continental shelf. They are raised successfully on sea farms along the coast.

Oysters have been grown on sea farms for over one hundred years. Now, nurseries, such as the one in the picture, are placed near the farms. In the nurseries, oyster eggs are watched carefully until they hatch. Here, the eggs are safe from rapid temperature changes and predators. Sea farmers make sure the young oysters survive to increase the harvest. When the young oysters get too big for the nursery, farmers place them on the sea floor at the sea farm. Fences do not have to be built around the oyster beds because these animals stay where they are placed.

At some oyster farms in Japan, the oysters grow on long ropes that dangle into the ocean from rafts. Oysters grown this way get very large because they can get nutrients at all levels of the shallow water.

Japanese oyster farm

Kelp harvesting

The picture shows kelp, a sea organism, on a sea farm in California. Kelp can grow to be 60 meters tall—from the sea floor to the surface of the water. Kelp can grow more than half a meter a day. The ship in the picture harvests kelp by mowing it like grass. People use kelp to make many products, such as ice cream, drugs, toothpaste, jellies, and canned meat.

Harvesting of sea life could help feed many more people. Careful ocean management is important today and for the future.

Kelp

Think About It

1. What is our largest seafood resource?
2. What is a sea farm?
3. **Challenge** List some foods to which FPC could be added.

Have You Heard?

About 300 sea farms in Japan grow oysters that make pearls. The farmer puts a grain of sand inside the oyster's shell. The oyster then covers the irritating sand grain with a coating of pearl! Pearls grown in this way are called cultured (kul'chərd) pearls.

329

5 How Do We Get Other Resources from the Ocean?

The variety of resources we get from the ocean comes either from the water itself or from the ocean bottom.

We can get fresh water, a resource, from seawater. Kuwait, a country in the Middle East, has about fifty water-desalting plants. There are about one thousand such plants in the world. Removing salt from ocean water is necessary for survival in Kuwait. The country is rich in oil, but poor in water resources.

We also get many kinds of salt from ocean water. The salt you sprinkle on food is one of these salts. The picture shows beds of salt that were harvested from ponds of Pacific Ocean water on the beaches near San Francisco. When shallow pools of seawater evaporate, beds of salt are left. Sometimes, tiny sea organisms in the water color the salt. These organisms are removed when the salt is treated in a factory.

Harvesting salt

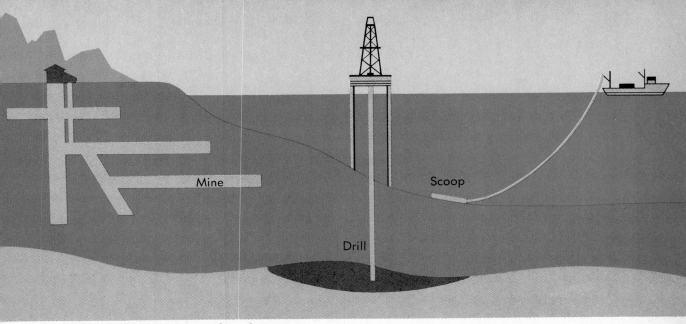

Mine

Scoop

Drill

How we get some resources from the ocean

The drawing shows how people mine, scoop, and drill resources from the ocean floor. As land resources get scarce, ocean resources increase in importance.

Some mines that once began on land near the coast now extend beneath the ocean. Miners work under the ocean near Great Britain, Japan, and Canada. From these mines, people get copper, iron, and coal.

Some of the sand and gravel people use comes from the ocean. Sand and gravel are scooped from the continental shelf. They are needed for concrete, which is used to make roads and buildings.

Lumps—or **nodules**—of metals, such as the one in the picture, are vacuumed from the ocean bottom with huge suction tubes. Right now, it is easier to get metals from the land. But people will gather more and more nodules as metals on land become more scarce.

About a fourth of the petroleum we use comes from wells drilled into the continental shelf. Most of it comes from wells that were drilled where the water is no more than 60 meters deep. When these wells run dry, people will drill farther out in deeper water.

nodule (noj′ül), a lump of metal found on the ocean floor.

Metal nodule

331

Where Is Petroleum Found in the Oceans?

Geologists are searching for petroleum in oceans all over the world. They look for petroleum in places where it could have begun forming millions of years ago. Ancient continental shelves are such places.

Petroleum forms from the remains of tiny organisms, such as those that are plentiful on continental shelves. For petroleum to form, the organisms must be buried by sediment from the continent before the organisms decay. Rivers carry the sediment onto the continental shelf. The water above the sediment must be calm enough so that the sediment does not wash away. The shallow, calm water in a bay along the coast is an ideal place for petroleum to form.

The picture shows an oil rig on the continental shelf. Many of the best petroleum deposits on land are now gone or are not as rich as they once were. People are relying more and more on petroleum from beneath the ocean.

Offshore oil rig

Think About It

1. How do we get salt from the ocean?
2. In what ways do people get resources from the ocean bottom?
3. **Challenge** How do scientists know what conditions were like on ancient continental shelves?

Activity

Observing Groundwater

Purpose
To infer what happens when water passes through the ground.

You will Need
- 2 paper cups, 1 with a hole on the side
- tape
- soil
- clay
- fine gravel
- water
- saucer

Directions
1. Put tape on the outside of the cup to cover the hole.
2. Look at the picture as you make your model. Put a layer of soil 2 cm thick in the bottom of the cup with the hole.
3. Cover the soil with a layer of clay. The clay should be just below the hole, as shown. Carefully press the clay against the sides of the cup to seal this layer.
4. Add a layer of gravel above the clay.

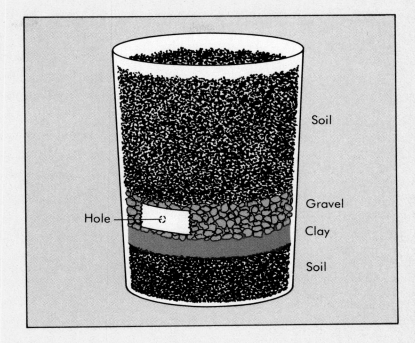

5. Above that, add a layer of soil deep enough to nearly fill the cup.
6. Half fill the other cup with water. Sprinkle soil into the water until it is muddy looking.
7. Slowly pour enough muddy water into the cup with the hole to make the soil thoroughly wet.
8. Put the cup with soil, clay, and gravel on a saucer. Remove the tape, and observe what happens. After a few seconds, pour the rest of the muddy water into the cup.

Think About It

1. Where was the water table in your model?
2. Explain what you observed in step 8.
3. Which part of your model can be compared to a well in the ground?
4. **Challenge** Suggest what might happen if people put poisonous substances, which dissolve in water, on or in the soil.

333

Discover!

Metals in the Oceans Can Be Mined

The treasure is there. Lumps of metals called nodules can be found on the ocean bottom. The nodules contain mostly manganese and small amounts of iron, nickel, copper, and cobalt. People use these metals to make a variety of products, such as steel, batteries, and dyes. Supplies of these metals on land might be gone someday. But some scientists think that the oceans contain enough metals to meet our needs for many years.

How can we get nodules from the ocean bottom? Methods used in mining metals on land will not work 2,000 meters or more below the water's surface. Following are some methods used in ocean mining that have been tested:

1. *Using television cameras to find minerals.* Nodules are not spread all over the ocean floor. They occur together in certain places that are difficult to find. Television cameras dragged on very long lines from ships are used to search for the nodules. The pictures show how the cameras allow miners to observe the ocean floor.

2. *Using giant strainers to separate minerals.* Getting nodules to the surface is expensive. Miners have to avoid dragging up sand, rock, plants, and other unwanted materials too. Giant strainers have been tried to separate the nodules from unwanted materials.

3. *Using long pipes and vacuums to bring nodules to the surface.* The nodules are sucked up through a long pipe. The pipe acts like a giant vacuum cleaner. It moves along the ocean floor, sucking up nodules and bringing them to the surface.

The vacuum method of picking up nodules seems to work well. Some mining companies plan to use this method when they begin mining the metals from the oceans. They hope to begin mining the metals from the ocean floors in the 1990s.

Close-up of the nodules

Viewing nodules with an underwater television camera

Tie It Together

Sum It Up

Pretend that you are in charge of producing a television program about the search for resources in the oceans. Write a short story about ocean resources that can be used by the writers of the television program. Use each of the words listed below at least once in your story. You may reuse a word, if necessary. Underline each of the words as it appears in your story.

rain	copper
fresh water	coal
salts	sand
ocean bottom	gravel
petroleum	continental shelf
gas	water cycle
iron	sea animals

Challenge!

1. Suggest how the water table might be affected by a very cold winter during which the upper 2 meters of the ground are frozen.

2. How does the water cycle affect the total amount of water in the world?

3. Why is getting fresh water from salt water, as described in lesson 3, not practical for a large city located on a foggy coastline?

4. What is a good reason—other than getting nutrients at all levels—for growing oysters up and down on a rope, rather than flat on the ocean floor?

5. Explain why geologists are more likely to search for petroleum in Indonesia, which has a large continental shelf, than they are to search for petroleum off the west coast of South America, where the continental shelf is not very large.

Science Words

condense

FPC

krill

nodule

water cycle

Laboratory

The Water Cycle

Purpose
To make a model that demonstrates the water cycle.

You Will Need
• large clear jar with lid
• centimeter ruler
• gravel
• clay
• potting soil
• water
• spoon
• plastic cup
• food coloring
• masking tape
• paper towel
• scale or balance

Stating the Problem
The amount of water on earth is always the same. Water continuously changes from liquid to gas or solid and back to liquid. As it changes, the water moves over the surface of the earth. The movement of water between the earth's surface and the air is known as the water cycle.

You can build a model that demonstrates a water cycle similar to the water cycle on earth.

Investigating the Problem
1. Study picture *a*. Place a layer of gravel 2 cm thick on the bottom of a large jar. Put a 1-cm layer of clay on top of the gravel. Press the clay against the jar so that water cannot move below the clay. Add a layer of gravel 2 cm thick. Place a 3-cm layer of potting soil on top of the gravel. Soak the soil with water so that it packs firmly. Press down the layers.

a

2. Use a spoon to carefully scoop out a hole 4 to 5 cm wide along the side of the glass as shown in picture *b*. Dig the hole about 4 cm deep. The hole represents a lake.
3. Half fill a plastic cup with water. Add several drops of food coloring to the water. Slowly pour the colored water into the hole until the lake is half full. Mark the water level on a piece of masking tape.
4. Clean the inside of the glass with a paper towel so that you can see through the part of the jar above the soil. Seal the jar with its lid. Try not to disturb the layers of soil and gravel.
5. Measure and record the jar's weight.
6. Place the jar in the sunlight. Observe the jar after several hours. Record your observations. Before you leave school for the day, place the jar in a cool, dark spot.
7. Observe your jar in the morning. Record your observations. Mark the water level of the lake

b

on the piece of masking tape.
8. Return your jar to a sunny spot. Record your observations, as you did in step 6.
9. Weigh the jar, and record the weight.

Making Conclusions
1. Where was the water table in your model on day 1? On day 2? Explain what happened.
2. Explain what you observed on the walls of the jar.
3. Was any water gained or lost from your model? How do you know?
4. Compare what you observed in your model with the process of the water cycle on earth. What provides energy for both water cycles?
5. If the total amount of water on the earth and in the air remains constant, how can a river dry up? Where does the water go?

Careers

Fish Curator

"When you work with animals," says Jim, "your day is never boring."

Jim is the assistant curator at an aquarium. "The first thing I do each morning is make the rounds of the aquarium. We have over 500 species of fish here. That is about 4,000 individual fish. I am just one of four people who check on these fish. We look for signs of illness or injury. If a fish dies, we may examine the inside of its body to find out why it died.

"For about half an hour each day, I take 'fish calls' from the public. People call me up with questions or problems about their fish at home. Sometimes, I have to do some research to answer the question. But I am always glad to help out."

Jim is responsible for new fish at the aquarium. A few times a year, some of the staff take a trip to Florida or the Bahama Islands to collect fish. They even went to South America to get some tropical, freshwater fish.

"When we get the fish back to the aquarium, we watch them closely and make sure they are eating enough. In the meantime, we carefully plan how the new fish's water tank will look. Here, at the aquarium, we try to copy the fish's natural environment." Jim takes a lot of pride in being as accurate as possible in displaying the fish and designing the tanks. "People come to see fish. But they also get a glimpse of the fish's natural environment."

In college, Jim studied biology and aquarium science. "If you are interested in fish, it is a good idea to keep an aquarium at home. But be sure to read some books on the subject. You should know about an animal before you try to take care of it."

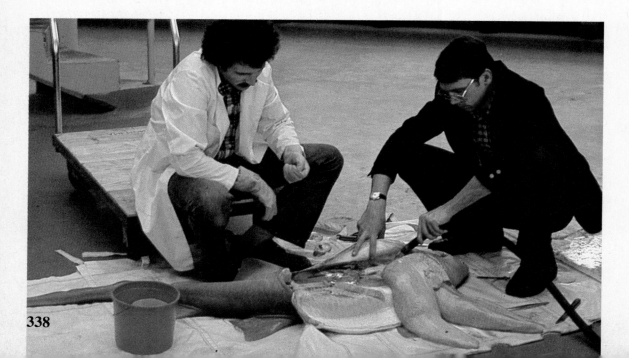

One of the greatest resources that we get from the sea is fish. You may have gone fishing using a pole. But a lot of people who fish for a living use nets. A **fisher** usually catches one kind of fish, such as codfish or sardines.

Shellfishers use wooden traps or rakes to catch lobsters, clams, and oysters. Fishers of all kinds learn most of their skills through experience.

Fish are just some of the things you might study as an **oceanographer.** An oceanographer learns about all areas of the ocean. He or she studies currents, tides, and waves. Some study marine life, while others study mountains and valleys on the ocean floor.

Many oceanographers spend a lot of time at sea and are good divers. A few oceanographers explore the ocean floor in special vehicles. But they also spend time on dry land researching and performing experiments.

To become an oceanographer, you must go to college for four years.

The oceans contain some other interesting things—sunken ships! **Underwater archaeologists** explore these ships of the past.

They search for artifacts, such as pottery, tools, and coins, that might have gone down with the ship. Some artifacts are buried more than a meter below the sandy ocean bottom. But engineers have recently invented an instrument that detects objects beneath the sand.

Students of underwater archaeology study archaeology in college for at least four years.

An oceanographer or underwater archaeologist may request the help of an **underwater photographer.** This person uses special lights, lenses, and cameras to take pictures under water. Like other photographers, they often improve their skills at a school of photography.

Fisher

Oceanographer

On Your Own

Picture Clue

The object on page 286 looks as if it were covered with flowers. But the "flowers" you see actually are corals. The corals are covering the remains of something that at one time floated on the water's surface. What is this object?

Books About Science

The Mysterious Undersea World by Jan Leslie Cook. National Geographic Society, 1980. Discover a new world in the oceans as you read about submersibles, sunken treasures, aquariums, animals, and plants of the oceans.

Seafood by Harry Barrett. Crane, Russak and Company, 1977. Learn how people around the world catch fish.

Water: Experiments to Understand It by Boris Arnov. Lothrop, Lee & Shepard, 1980. Try simple experiments that show the properties of water.

Projects

1. Observe how objects act in water by holding a cork, which floats, at the bottom of a pail of water. Notice how hard you must press to keep the cork underwater. Repeat this activity two more times, first using a sealed, empty glass jar, then a blown-up balloon. Compare the amount of pressure needed to hold each object down. Find out why objects float by looking up *Archimedes'* (är⁄kə mē⁄dēz) *Principle* in an encyclopedia. Relate your observations of the objects placed in water to Archimedes' Principle.

2. Observe what happens when you put a hard-boiled egg in a glass of fresh water. Now, take the egg out of the water. Add salt to the water, stirring as you add it. Continue to add salt until no more salt dissolves. Put the egg back in the glass, and observe what happens. Relate what you have observed to the way a ship floats. Compare how a ship floats in a freshwater lake to the way the same ship floats in an ocean.

3. A film—or thin coating—which you cannot see covers the surface of water and other liquids. Try an activity to see what happens when a lightweight object touches the surface of water. Fill a bowl with water. Dry a needle made of steel. Carefully balance the needle on the tines of a fork. Gently lower the fork and needle into the water so that you just break the surface of the water with the fork. If you carefully remove the fork, the needle will float. Look closely where the surface of the water touches the floating needle. Describe how the surface of the water looks.

Unit Test

True or False

Number your paper from 1–5. Next to each number, write *true* if the sentence is correct and *false* if the sentence is incorrect. Make each false statement true by changing the underlined word or phrase and writing the correct word or phrase on your paper.

1. <u>Tides</u> differ from the ocean water around them in saltiness or temperature or amount of sediment.
2. Most of our seafood is harvested from the <u>ocean basin.</u>
3. <u>Kelp</u> is a sea organism that is used to make ice cream, drugs, toothpaste, and jellies.
4. A <u>moraine</u> is a landform deposited around the edges of a glacier.
5. The amount of groundwater depends on the amount of rain and snow that falls on the <u>oceans.</u>

Multiple Choice

Number your paper from 6–10. Next to each number, write the letter of the word or phrase that best completes the statement.

6. Rivers change the earth's surface by
   a. building levees.
   b. wearing away and building up the land.
   c. building deltas.
   d. all the above
7. Landforms found on the ocean bottom where two plates are bumping into each other are
   a. trenches.
   b. mid-ocean ridges.
   c. deltas.
   d. chimneylike hills.
8. The percentage of the earth that is covered by oceans is about
   a. 10 percent.
   b. 40 percent.
   c. 70 percent.
   d. 90 percent.
9. Metal nodules found on the ocean bottom are collected by
   a. digging into the continental shelf.
   b. drilling into the ocean basin.
   c. filtering ocean water.
   d. scooping them up with suction tubes.
10. Water vapor is
   a. condensed water.
   b. visible.
   c. a gas.
   d. salty.

UNIT EIGHT
THE UNIVERSE

Jewels in the sky
Like silverbursts of fire
As the world
turns around.

Carey Reeves *age 10*

343

Chapter 20
Stars

Years ago, people thought stars had magical powers, such as causing illness or bringing good luck. People looked at the patterns of stars in the sky and gave them names.

The picture shows a region in the sky where new stars might be forming. Although stars seem mysterious, scientists are learning more about them. Today, we know stars are not magical. They are spheres of glowing gases.

The lessons in this chapter describe how scientists think stars glow and how stars change over billions of years. When you look at the stars in the night sky, you will better understand these glowing objects that are all around us.

1 Observing Star Patterns

2 What Do We Know About Stars?

3 How Do Stars Form?

4 How Do Stars Change?

1 Observing Star Patterns

On a clear night you can see some of the stars that fill the sky. Years ago, people imagined that groups of stars looked like objects or creatures. The people named these groups of stars after the creatures or objects they resembled. The pictures show the different patterns people saw in the group of stars that is sometimes called the Big Dipper.

A star pattern is like a picture drawn by connecting dots. The dots shown below resemble the position of stars in a group called Hercules. Copy the dots into your notebook. Try to copy the positions of the dots as accurately as you can. See what star patterns you can find by connecting the dots with a pencil. Then, connect the dots in another pattern, using a crayon or pen. Compare your star patterns with those of your classmates.

Think About It

1. What do some people name groups of stars after?
2. Why might one person call a group of stars *the Big Dipper* and another person call it *the Great Bear?*
3. **Challenge** Why do you think people from different cultures often saw different objects in the sky?

Big Dipper

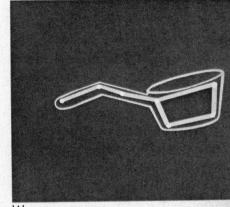

Wagon

Tail of the Great Bear

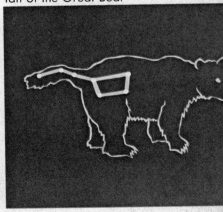

Group of stars called Hercules

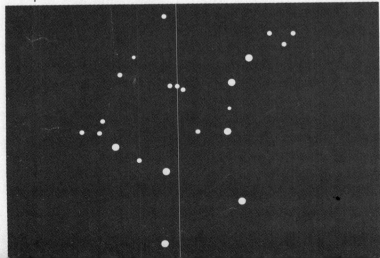

2 What Do We Know About Stars?

Stars make the night sky beautiful. But one star is seen from earth only during the day. This star is important to life on earth. You have probably guessed that this special star is our sun.

The sun is the star closest to earth. Many people have wondered why the sun shines and how long the sun will last. Since the sun is a star, scientists began learning about it by studying other stars. Scientists began their investigations by classifying stars according to their properties.

If you look closely at the stars in the picture, you will notice that some stars are brighter than others. More than two thousand years ago the Greek astronomer Hipparchus (hi pär′kəs) classified stars by their brightness. Sirius (sir′ē əs), the brightest star in the picture, was the brightest star Hipparchus saw in the sky. Today, we still see Sirius as the brightest star.

Sirius—the brightest star as seen from earth

Brightness of light seems to change with distance

When Hipparchus was classifying stars by their brightness, people thought each star was the same distance from earth. They believed some stars appeared brighter because they produced more light.

By the 1700s, scientists using telescopes learned that not all stars were the same distance from earth. They believed all stars produced the same amount of light. The scientists thought some stars appeared brighter because they were closer to earth, just as the light from the flashlight in the pictures appears brighter as the person moves closer to the flashlight.

In the early 1800s the German astronomer Friedrich Bessel (bes′əl) used a telescope to measure accurately distances to some stars. He discovered that both the ancient people and the early scientists were partly correct. Some bright stars were far from earth. Some dim stars were close to earth. Bessel learned that all stars do not produce the same amount of light—or have the same **real brightness.** But a star's distance from earth determines how bright it *appears* to us—or its **apparent brightness.** Although Sirius appears to be the brightest star in the sky, some stars farther away are really brighter. These stars appear dimmer than Sirius because of their distances from the earth.

real brightness, the brightness of a star because of the amount of light it produces.

apparent (ə par′ənt) **brightness,** the brightness of a star as seen from earth.

Have You Heard?

Alpha Centauri (sen tôr′ē) is a group of 3 stars that is closest to our solar system. Alpha Centauri is about 41 trillion km away. A spacecraft traveling at 40,000 km per hour would have to travel about 120,000 years before reaching Alpha Centauri!

mass, the amount of matter an object contains.

Stars with different colors

How Are Stars Different?

After Friedrich Bessel's discovery, scientists began investigating other differences among stars. They used special telescopes to measure the properties of stars. Scientists learned that stars have different temperatures and colors. Try to find stars with a tint of color in the picture. Blue stars are the hottest. Their surface temperatures can be as hot as 30,000° Celsius. Red stars are the coolest. Their surface temperatures are about 3,000° Celsius. The yellow color of the sun means that it is a medium-temperature star—about 5,500° Celsius.

The special telescopes have also helped scientists learn about the composition and sizes of stars. A star is a glowing sphere of hot gases. Some stars consist mostly of hydrogen and helium. Other stars consist mostly of carbon and iron particles that are so hot they are a gas.

Some stars are smaller than the earth. Others are one thousand times larger than our sun. The size of a star is not always related to how much matter—or **mass**—it contains. Some large stars have little mass. In the same way, a cotton ball is larger than a marble, but its mass is less.

Think About It

1. Name properties that you can use to classify stars.
2. What does a star's color tell you about its temperature?
3. **Challenge** Why was it important that Bessel discovered that all stars were not the same?

Activity

Comparing the Distances of Objects

Purpose
To compare the distances of objects by using a simple test.

You Will Need
• centimeter ruler

Directions
1. Close your right eye, and look at your thumb as shown in picture *a*.
2. Close your left eye, and open your right eye. Record what you observed.
3. Use a ruler to cover a distant object. Close your right eye. Hold the left edge of the ruler over the object as shown in picture *b*. Then, close your left eye, and open your right eye. Record the number of centimeters the ruler appeared to move.

a

b

4. Hold the ruler closer to your eyes. Repeat step 3. Record the number of centimeters the ruler appeared to move.
5. Ask a classmate to hold the ruler about 1 m away from your eyes. Repeat step 3. Record the number of centimeters the ruler appeared to move.

Think About It

1. What caused the ruler to appear to shift position when you looked at it with one eye and then with the other?

2. At what distance did the ruler shift its position the most?
3. To learn the distances to some stars, scientists observe the stars at different times of the year when the earth is at different places in its orbit around the sun. How can scientists tell which stars are closer?
4. **Challenge** As you ride in a car, you may notice that trees and people close to the street seem to move past you quickly. Why does the sun not appear to move at all?

3 How Do Stars Form?

fuse, to combine or unite.

nuclear fusion (nü⁄klē ər fyü⁄zhən), the process in which the nuclei of atoms combine and release huge amounts of energy.

Ancient people thought stars were made of burning wood or coal. But early scientists knew such fuels would burn too quickly. They knew that stars shine a long time. The star map in the picture was drawn by people who lived hundreds of years ago. Most of the stars on the star map can still be seen today.

Scientists think that what they know about atoms can help them learn about stars. In the early 1900s, scientists discovered that the nuclei of atoms can combine—or **fuse**—producing huge amounts of heat and light energy. Scientists used this knowledge of **nuclear fusion** to explain how stars form and produce energy for billions of years.

Chinese star map from A.D. 1092

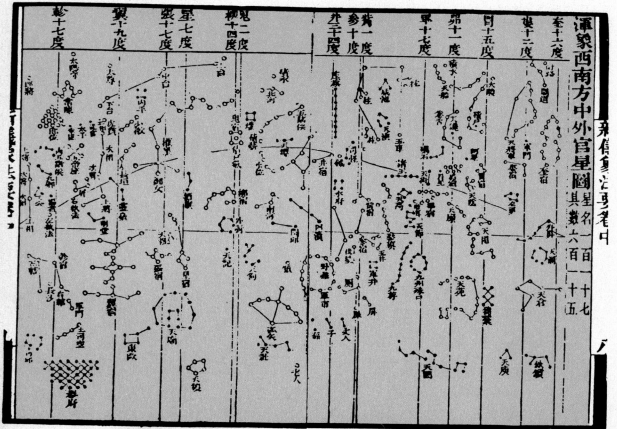

Scientists observed that new stars often appear in cloudy regions in space, such as the one in the picture. A **nebula** is a cloud in space made of dust and gases. Scientists think stars form from gases in some kinds of nebulae.

nebula (neb′yə lə), a cloud of dust and gases in space. [Plural: nebulae (neb′yə lē′).]

Orion Nebula

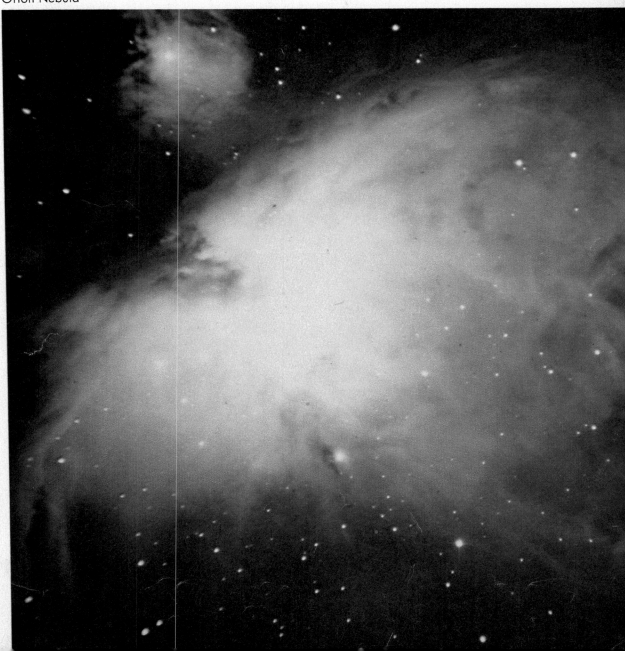

constellation
(kon'stə lā'shən), a group of stars.

Have You Heard?

Stars really do not twinkle. They appear to twinkle because of moving air currents in the earth's atmosphere. Astronauts traveling in space do not see stars twinkling.

How Do Scientists Think Stars Begin?

Over millions of years, gravity pulls together the gases and dust in a nebula into a smaller cloud or clump. As more matter is packed into the clump, the force of gravity gets stronger. Gravity pulls the atoms of the matter even closer together. Most of the matter is made up of hydrogen atoms. The closer the atoms are pulled together, the hotter the matter becomes. Eventually, the matter becomes so hot that nuclear fusion begins. Hydrogen nuclei fuse into heavier helium nuclei. A helium nucleus has four times more mass than a hydrogen nucleus. The nuclear fusions give off large amounts of light and heat. The matter becomes so hot, it glows. A new star begins to shine brightly.

Many of the stars in the picture are newly formed. The stars are found near a group of stars—or **constellation**—called Taurus (tôr'əs). Notice the nebula from which the stars formed.

New stars in a nebula

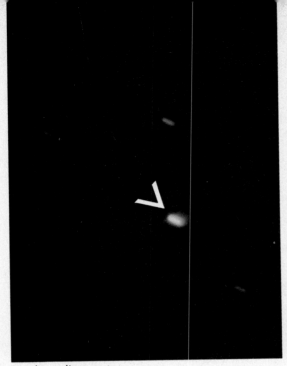

Rigel—a distant star

Sun—the star closest to earth

Young stars have enough hydrogen fuel to last a long time. A star with greater mass, such as Rigel (rī′jəl) in the picture, uses up its hydrogen faster than a star with less mass. Although in photographs Rigel looks like a spot in the sky, it is about 20,000 times brighter and its mass 33 times greater than that of our sun! Scientists think Rigel will take a few million years to use up its hydrogen. Our sun is a low-mass star that formed about 5 billion years ago. Scientists think the sun has enough hydrogen left to last another 5 billion years. When stars use up their hydrogen, they begin to change.

Think About It

1. What is a nebula?
2. How do scientists think stars form?
3. **Challenge** If Rigel is about twenty thousand times brighter than the sun, why does it look like a spot in the sky?

Find Out

A hydrogen and helium nucleus have different numbers of protons and neutrons. Use a chemistry book to find out what the difference is.

353

4 How Do Stars Change?

core, the inner part of a star where nuclear fusion occurs.

shell, the outer part of a star made of hot gases.

Stars change as they grow older. But no scientist can live long enough to observe a star change from a young star to an old star. Stars change over millions of years. But scientists have observed different kinds of stars. By putting together many different pieces of information, scientists have inferred how stars change, grow old, and can eventually explode.

Just as different organisms have different life cycles, different stars grow old in different ways. The mass of a star determines how the star will change. Our sun is a low-mass star. The drawing shows that adult stars, such as the sun, have an inner part, called the core, and an outer part, called the shell. The core is made of closely packed hydrogen and helium particles. Nuclear fusion takes place in the core of the sun. The shell consists of more loosely packed hydrogen and helium particles. Nuclear energy released in the core heats up the shell. The heat moves to the surface of the sun and gives the sun its yellow color.

Atomic particles in a star

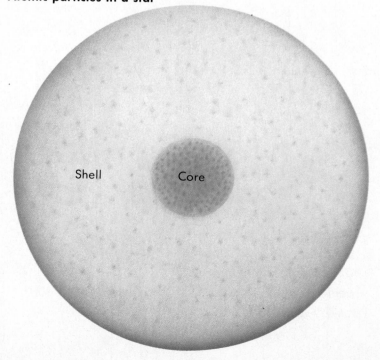

Shell

Core

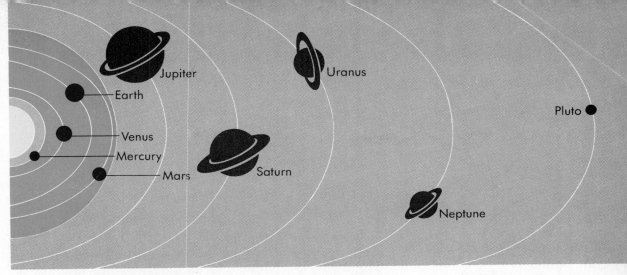

The sun becoming a red giant

Scientists think that in about five billion years, all the hydrogen nuclei in the sun's core will be fused into helium nuclei. This change will cause the core to squeeze more closely together—or contract. As the core contracts, it will give off huge amounts of energy. This energy will push against the shell, causing it to move apart—or expand. These changes will cause the sun to look very different.

The picture shows that the sun will become a giant star much larger than it is today. At first, the sun will reach all the way to the planet Mercury. The temperature on Earth will become too hot for life to exist. After millions of years, the sun will expand beyond Earth, reaching the planet Mars!

As the sun expands, its surface temperature will decrease. The cooler temperature will make the sun look red, instead of yellow. For a few billion years, our sun will be a huge star called a **red giant.** Nuclear fusion in the core of the red giant will change helium nuclei into heavier nuclei such as carbon and oxygen. The red giant will continue expanding until the nuclear reactions stop. Then, it will blow off its shell. The gases from the shell will form a nebula around the star's burned out core. Then the nebula will continue to expand into space.

red giant, an older star that has grown very large in size and has become red in color.

355

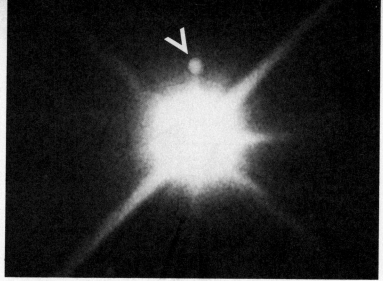

White dwarf near Sirius

What Happens When a Star Explodes?

After the red giant blows off its shell, only the core remains. The core cools and contracts into a small star called a **white dwarf.** The picture shows a white dwarf located near Sirius. The nuclei of a white dwarf are so close together that a spoonful would weigh about 4,000 metric tons! A car weighs only about $1\frac{1}{2}$ metric tons. With time, a white dwarf cools and becomes dimmer. After billions of years, the white dwarf stops shining.

Stars with masses greater than the sun change in a different way. Nuclear fusion in these stars combines carbon and oxygen nuclei. Eventually, very heavy nuclei, such as iron, are produced. At that point, the star blows apart releasing gases into space. An exploding, high-mass star is a **supernova.** People on earth saw a very bright supernova explosion in the year A.D. 1054. Its light could be seen in the daytime during the next two years.

High-mass stars do not become white dwarfs after they explode. Instead, some become **neutron stars.** The nuclei in a neutron star are so closely packed that a spoonful would weigh about 40 billion metric tons!

white dwarf, a small, dim star that remains after a red giant blows off its outer shell of gases.

supernova (sü′pər nō′və), an exploding, high-mass star. [Plural: supernovae (sü′pər nō′vē).]

neutron star (nü′tron), a small, closely packed star that remains after a supernova explosion.

356

A supernova releases gases of many kinds of atoms. These atoms can become part of a nebula from which new stars and new solar systems form.

The supernova explosion seen in A.D. 1054 produced the large Crab Nebula shown in the picture. Stars probably are forming in the nebula right now.

Think About It

1. What property of a star determines how it will change as it grows older?
2. How are red giants, white dwarfs, and neutron stars different?
3. **Challenge** How could some elements on the earth come from the stars?

Crab Nebula

Find Out
Use an encyclopedia or an astronomy book to find out how scientists know that a supernova explosion occurred in the year A.D. 1054.

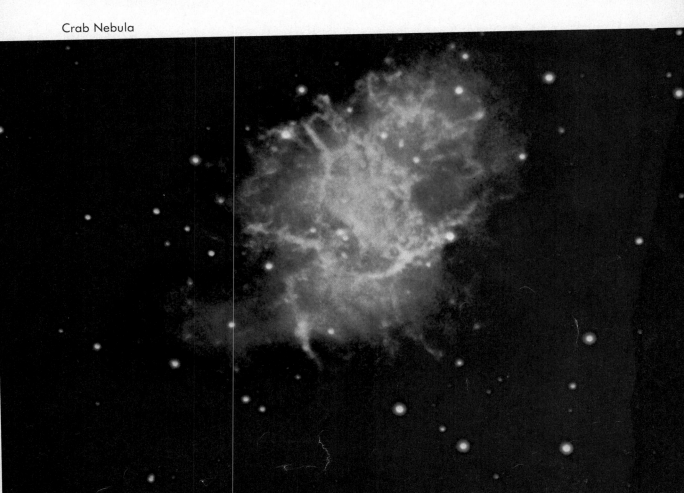

Do You Know?

Astronomers Take Starlight Apart

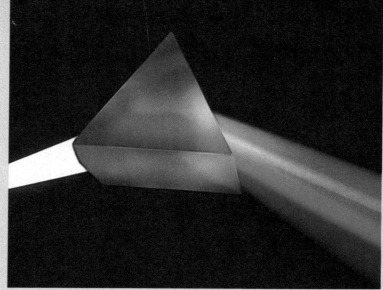

Separating light with a prism

The detectives are astronomers. The mystery is a distant star. The problem—what is the star made of? Is it made of elements that we already know? If so, which ones? Is it made of elements not found on earth? The only clue that astronomers have is the star's light.

Astronomers analyze starlight with a tool more powerful than Sherlock Holmes's magnifying glass. They use a device called a spectroscope, which separates starlight into different colors. The picture shows a prism—or a piece of glass cut in a certain way—separating white light into the colors of the rainbow. A spectroscope also splits light into bands of colors.

How do astronomers use the spectroscope to find out about elements in stars? Astronomers know that elements give off light when heated to high temperatures. When this light passes through a prism, patterns of colored lines form. Each element produces a different pattern of colored lines. The patterns in the pictures were made by neon light and incandescent light that were separated into colors. Notice that the patterns are different for the two sources of light.

When starlight passes through a spectroscope, a pattern of colored lights forms. Astronomers match this pattern of light to the patterns produced by heated elements. Then, the astronomers can identify the elements in the distant star.

With the spectroscope, astronomers can find out what distant stars are made of, how hot the stars are, and how fast the stars are moving. With this information, astronomers can begin to uncover mysteries of the universe.

Neon light

Incandescent light

Tie It Together

Sum It Up

1. Write a paragraph about two imaginary stars named Gamma and Omega that have very different properties. Imagine what might be the properties of these stars. In your paragraph, describe and explain each star's properties, including its color, temperature, apparent brightness, real brightness, mass, and size.

2. Draw diagrams describing how stars form. Use labels and a short explanation with each diagram. Include a nebula, hydrogen atoms, helium atoms, and nuclear fusion in your diagrams.

3. Draw diagrams to describe how a low-mass star, such as the sun, grows old. Use labels and a short explanation with each diagram. Include a white dwarf, red giant, nebula, and an adult star in your diagrams.

Challenge!

1. Star A is larger than star B. Which star has more mass?

2. The star Beta Crucis has a surface temperature of about 25,000° Celsius. What color is Beta Crucis?

3. Could stars form if there were no gravity in the universe? Explain.

4. Why are stars sometimes described as "factories" in the universe that produce heavy atoms?

5. Could the sun become a supernova? Explain.

Science Words

apparent brightness

constellation

core

fuse

mass

nebula

neutron star

nuclear fusion

real brightness

red giant

shell

supernova

white dwarf

Chapter 21
Mysteries of the Universe

This large, bright glow in space is made up of billions of stars. To reach this group of stars, you would have to travel at an incredible speed for millions of years. As you traveled, you would be surrounded by dark, cold space.

The lessons in this chapter describe some mysteries of the universe. You can explore the universe by learning about galaxies, pulsars, quasars, and black holes in space.

1 Comparing the Distances of Stars from Earth

The sun seems very far from earth. But other stars are much farther away. You can compare the distances of some stars from earth.

Using a soft-tipped pen, mark 1-centimeter units on a 1-meter-long strip of paper. Each unit will represent 10,000,000,000,000, or 10 trillion kilometers. Mark earth's location at 0 kilometers. On the strip of paper, mark the distances of the stars listed on the chart.

Distances of stars from earth

Star	Approximate distance from earth
Sun	150 million kilometers
Proxima Centauri	40 trillion kilometers
Barnard's Star	60 trillion kilometers
Sirius	80 trillion kilometers
Procyon	110 trillion kilometers
Capella	420 trillion kilometers
Aldebaran	640 trillion kilometers
Regulus	800 trillion kilometers

Think About It

1. Proxima Centauri is the star closest to our sun. Compared with the sun, how many times farther from the earth is Proxima Centauri?
2. How many times farther from the earth than Proxima Centauri is the star Regulus?
3. **Challenge** A spacecraft orbiting the earth travels a distance of about 40,000 kilometers. How many times would a spacecraft have to orbit the earth to travel 10 trillion kilometers?

2 How Are Stars Grouped in the Universe?

light year, the distance light travels in 1 year—or about 9.5 trillion kilometers.

Although the stars in the picture seem close together, they are separated by billions of kilometers or more of space. Proxima Centauri, the star closest to our sun, is more than 40 trillion kilometers away.

You can easily use kilometers to measure the distance to the town nearest your home. Because objects in space are so far away, scientists have to measure their distances in a different way. They use the speed of light to measure long distances in space.

Light moves faster than anything else in the universe—about 300,000 kilometers per second. If a jet plane could travel at the speed of light, it would go around the world almost 8 times in just 1 second! To reach Proxima Centauri, you would have to travel at the speed of light for about 4 years.

A **light year** is the distance light travels in 1 year. This distance is about 9,500,000,000,000, or 9.5 trillion kilometers. We can measure the distance to a star by the number of years it takes light to travel that distance. For example, the star Rigel is about 8,600 trillion kilometers from the earth. Its light travels about 900 years before reaching us. So Rigel is 900 light years away. When we look at Rigel today, we see it the way it looked 900 years ago!

Stars are separated by long distances

In the 1700s, scientists observed bright, hazy patches of light in space. At first, they thought each patch was a distant nebula. After more powerful telescopes were invented, scientists discovered that the patches actually were groups of billions of stars. The stars appeared as a single, bright patch because they were millions of light years away. The close-up picture of such a patch of light shows the large number of stars in the group.

Part of the Milky Way

Close-up of a group of stars

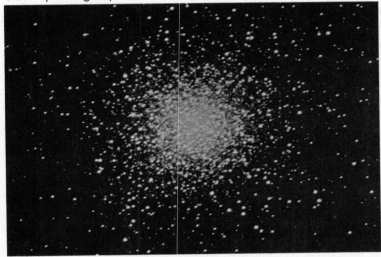

Each bright, hazy patch is a **galaxy**—a large group of stars, dust, and gases in space. Some galaxies have billions of stars. The pull of gravity among the stars holds a galaxy together.

Our solar system belongs to the Milky Way galaxy. All the stars we see at night are part of our galaxy. Notice the "milky" appearance in the picture of one area of our galaxy as seen from the earth.

Scientists estimate that millions of galaxies exist in the universe. To reach the galaxy closest to the Milky Way, we would have to travel for 200,000 years at the speed of light. To reach more distant galaxies, we would have to travel for millions of years.

galaxy (gal′ək sē), an enormous group of stars, dust, and gases in space.

spiral (spī′rəl) **galaxy,** a galaxy with a pinwheel shape.

elliptical (i lip′tə kəl) **galaxy,** a galaxy with an egglike shape.

irregular (i reg′yə lər) **galaxy,** a galaxy with an uneven shape.

Spiral galaxy

What Do Galaxies Look Like?

Stars form different kinds of galaxies. The pictures show that some galaxies have curved arms that give the galaxies a winding—or **spiral**—shape which resembles a pinwheel. Other galaxies have an egglike—or **elliptical**—shape. Still others have an uneven—or **irregular**—shape.

Many galaxies have a center that appears to be packed with stars. The galaxies rotate, with the stars moving around the center of the galaxy.

To see what our Milky Way galaxy looks like from space, scientists would have to travel millions of light years into space. Instead, scientists inferred the shape of our galaxy by studying the stars close to the sun. They noticed that the stars grouped to form arms. Since a spiral galaxy has arms, scientists inferred that our Milky Way galaxy must be a spiral galaxy.

Elliptical galaxy

Irregular galaxy

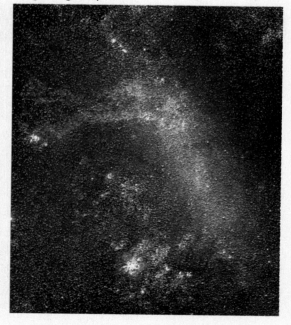

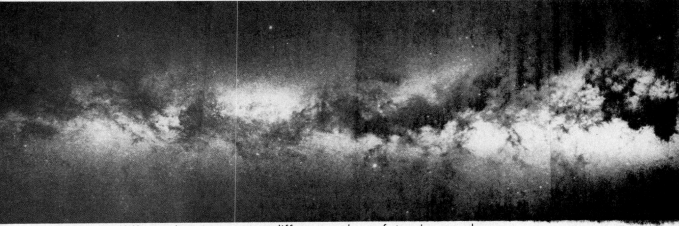

Looking in different directions, we see different numbers of stars in our galaxy

But where is our solar system located in the Milky Way galaxy? If we were in the center of the galaxy—point A on the drawings—the sky around us would be packed with stars. But the photograph taken from the earth shows that we see different numbers of stars in different parts of the sky.

Our solar system must be located away from the center of the Milky Way galaxy, as shown by point B on the drawings. Scientists infer that as we look toward the region of the sky with many stars, we are looking toward the center of our galaxy. As we look toward the region of the sky with fewer stars, we probably are looking at the edges of our galaxy.

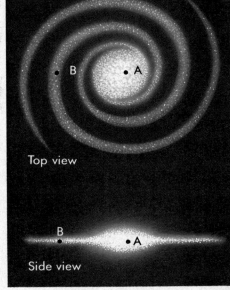

Drawing of Milky Way Galaxy

Think About It

1. What is a light year?
2. Describe the different shapes of galaxies.
3. How can we infer the location of our solar system in the Milky Way galaxy?
4. **Challenge** Suppose a person is traveling at the speed of light from one end of the Milky Way galaxy to the other. The trip takes 100,000 years to complete. How wide is our galaxy?

Have You Heard?

If planets of other solar systems are located in the center of the Milky Way galaxy, they never have dark nights. So many stars surround the planets that starlight keeps the skies bright all the time.

365

3 How Do Scientists Study Mysteries of the Universe?

radio telescope, an instrument that detects radio signals from space.

Radio signals

One day Karl Jansky, an American engineer, tried to get rid of the static on his radio receiver. The static would not go away. In fact, the static returned every day at about the same time. He was surprised to discover it did not come from earth. The static was a radio signal from outer space.

People used to make jokes about "little green men" sending radio signals to earth. We now know that these signals come from stars, galaxies, and other objects in space.

Radio signals from space are like the radio waves that television and radio stations send. But the radio signals from space are weaker. Scientists use **radio telescopes** to detect these faint signals from space.

The first radio telescope was built by Grote Reber in his backyard in 1944. Newer radio telescopes, such as the one in the picture, can detect even weaker signals from space. The large dish collects signals and bounces them to the receiving antenna in the center of the dish. The antenna then sends the signals to an instrument that records each signal.

Radio telescope receiving signals from space

Antenna

Dish

Recorder

Radio telescope

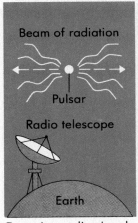

Detecting radio signals from a pulsar

Scientists study the universe by pointing radio telescopes toward different parts of the sky. Some parts of the sky send blinking radio signals. The objects producing these on-and-off signals are called **pulsars.** Scientists now think that a pulsar is a rapidly spinning neutron star which gives off a beam of **radiation**—or energy waves—that includes radio waves. Detecting a pulsar's radio signals is like looking at a beam of light from a lighthouse. Every time the searchlight turns around, its beam of light reaches your eyes. As the beam moves away from you, the light seems to disappear. The drawings show that we detect a pulsar when its beam of radiation is pointing toward earth.

Radio telescopes also are used to study **quasars** in space. Some quasars appear as small, bright spots and give off strong radio signals. Scientists are not sure what quasars are. Some scientists think quasars are the bright centers of the most distant galaxies in the universe. By studying the light from quasars, such as the one in the picture, these scientists have estimated that quasars are billions of light years away. Other scientists think we need more evidence to better understand what quasars are. For now, quasars remain one of the biggest mysteries of the universe.

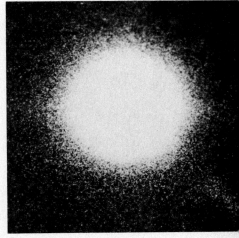

Quasar

pulsar (pul′sär), a neutron star that gives off radio signals as it spins.

radiation (rā′dē ā′shən), energy waves.

quasar (kwā′sär), an unidentified object in space. Some quasars appear as small, bright spots in space and give off strong radio signals.

Artist's drawing showing matter falling into a black hole

How Do Telescopes Detect Black Holes?

black hole, a region in space where gravity is so strong that not even light can escape it.

Have You Heard?

Uhuru means "freedom" in Swahili, a language spoken in Kenya, Africa. The *Uhuru* satellite was launched on Kenya's independence day.

To get more information about the universe, scientists invented new kinds of telescopes. The satellite *Uhuru* carried a telescope that measured X rays from outer space. X-ray telescopes can detect X-ray signals from many stars, galaxies, quasars, and certain regions in space called **black holes.**

Scientists think a black hole is a region in space where gravity is so strong that nothing can escape its pulling force. You might think of a black hole as the funnel-like region in the drawing that pulls in anything which comes near it. A black hole can swallow up the stars around it. Even light, which moves faster than anything else in the universe, does not move fast enough to escape the pull of a black hole. So a black hole can never be seen. But matter spinning into a black hole gets so hot that it gives off X rays. Telescopes pick up these X rays, and scientists can infer where a black hole might be located.

Think About It

1. How do radio telescopes detect a blinking pattern of radio signals from a pulsar?
2. What are quasars and black holes?
3. **Challenge** What do you think would happen if a spacecraft traveled very near a black hole?

Do You Know?

Scientists Are Listening for Messages from Space

A long-distance call from space is waiting for you. Don't miss it! The message traveled 100 trillion kilometers, or about 10 light years, to reach you.

Getting such a message may sound like science fiction, but some scientists hope we might someday. They think intelligent beings besides humans could live somewhere in the universe.

The large number of stars in the universe means there is a chance that intelligent life could exist somewhere besides earth. Our Milky Way galaxy alone has billions of stars. From their knowledge of how stars form, scientists think that many stars besides the sun have planets. Civilizations of intelligent

Message sent from radio telescope at Arecibo

beings might exist on some of these planets.

Scientists have begun searching for intelligent life in the universe by pointing radio telescopes toward different parts of the universe. They listen for repeated signals that might carry messages. So far, no messages have been received.

A second way in which scientists search for intelligent life is by sending messages into space. In 1974 scientists sent a message from a radio telescope in Arecibo, Puerto Rico. The message was a pattern of signals that represented mathematical symbols. If intelligent beings receive the message, they will have to decode the symbols into a picture message. The picture shows what the decoded message will look like. It will include a stick figure of a person and rectangles that represent our solar system and the radio telescope at Arecibo.

Because most stars are so far away, the message might have to travel very many years before reaching other intelligent beings. Then, we would have to wait years for the messages from those civilizations to reach us!

4 What Do Scientists Think the Early Universe Was Like?

big bang theory (thē′ər ē), the explanation that the universe began in a huge explosion.

Some galaxies are separated by millions of light years of space, with very little matter between them. This space seems to be getting even larger.

By studying the light from galaxies, many scientists think that galaxies are rapidly moving away from each other. Distant galaxies are moving away from us at speeds greater than 60,000 kilometers per second! The farther away the galaxy is, the faster it is moving. The universe seems to be spreading out—or expanding.

You can compare the movement of galaxies in the universe to the movement of raisins in a rising mound of raisin-bread dough. Notice how all the raisins move away from each other as the bread rises or expands.

Scientists study the movement of the galaxies in order to understand what the early universe was like. Some scientists think the universe began ten to twenty billion years ago with a huge explosion or big bang. They call this explanation of the beginning of the universe the **big bang theory.**

Raisins moving apart as bread expands

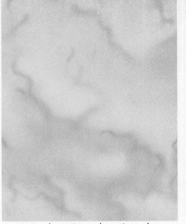

Artist's drawing showing the big bang

Drawing showing galaxies moving away

Drawing showing galaxies moving farther apart

According to the theory, the big bang hurled the matter and energy in the universe in all directions. Gravity eventually pulled some of the moving matter into stars and galaxies. The drawings show how the galaxies might have moved since the big bang occurred.

Scientists who developed the big bang theory looked for other information that could support the theory. In 1965, scientists discovered small amounts of radiation coming from all parts of the universe. The radiation they detected might be evidence of radiation that was produced by a big bang and that had cooled with time. Today, most scientists think the big bang theory is correct.

In the coming years, scientists might find more information that supports the big bang theory. Or new information might suggest that the theory is incorrect. As scientists find new evidence, they will develop a theory that the evidence supports.

Think About It

1. Explain how the space between galaxies might be increasing.
2. What evidence suggests that a big bang occurred?
3. **Challenge** What evidence might suggest that the universe is coming together—or contracting?

Find Out
Not everyone thinks the universe began with a big bang. Use an encyclopedia to find out some other ideas about the beginning of the universe.

Activity

Inferring Characteristics of an Expanding Universe

a

b

c

Purpose

To infer how galaxies in the universe might move away from each other, by using an expanding balloon as a model.

You Will Need

• balloon
• colored markers
• centimeter tape measure

Directions

1. Mark a dot on the balloon.
2. Using a different colored marker, mark 4 dots each at a different distance from the first dot, as shown in *a*. Number the dots.
3. Using a tape measure, measure the distance of each dot from the first dot. Record these distances.
4. Blow up the balloon half way. Close the opening with your fingers, as shown in *b*.
5. Ask your partner to measure the distance of each dot from the first dot you marked, as shown in *c*. Record the distances.
6. Blow up the balloon completely. Tie off the balloon with a knot. Repeat step 5.

Think About It

1. How might the dots on the balloon be similar to the galaxies in the universe?
2. Which of the 4 dots moved away from the first dot the farthest? The fastest?
3. **Challenge** The Andromeda galaxy is closer to our Milky Way galaxy than is the Cygnus A galaxy. Which galaxy is moving away from us faster?

Tie It Together

Sum It Up

Imagine that two space explorers have begun a trip through the universe. Use your knowledge about the universe to complete this story about their trip. Copy the story in your notebook and fill in the missing words.

Anne and Jeff left the earth in a spacecraft. Their spacecraft is moving as fast as anything in the universe can move. It is moving about 300,000 kilometers per second—or at the speed of __1.__ . Anne and Jeff are moving away from our __2.__ ____ galaxy. As they travel farther into space, they can see all kinds of galaxies. They see __3.__ galaxies that look like pinwheels, __4.__ galaxies that are egg shaped, and __5.__ galaxies that are uneven in shape.

Anne and Jeff have a __6.__ ____ on their spacecraft that can detect radio signals from space. They have picked up blinking signals from __7.__ . They also have an X-ray telescope so they can detect __8.__ ____ . If the spacecraft got too close, it could not escape the pull of gravity and would never be seen again!

The space travelers also are studying the light from some galaxies. They noticed that galaxies are moving __9.__ from each other in all directions. They are collecting information to learn whether the explanation that the universe began in an explosion, or the __10.__ ____ ____ , is correct.

Anne and Jeff are continuing their journey through the universe. The more information Anne and Jeff collect about the universe, the better they will be able to understand it.

Challenge!

1. The galaxy closest to the Milky Way galaxy is about 200,000 light years away. How many kilometers away is this galaxy?

2. The supernova explosion that was seen on earth in the year A.D. 1054 produced the Crab Nebula seen today. The Crab Nebula is about six thousand light years away from earth. How many years must have passed between the time when the supernova explosion occurred and when it was first seen from earth?

3. If there were no gravity in the universe, would there be any galaxies?

4. Is a pulsar produced from a supernova explosion? Explain.

5. What evidence could suggest a big bang never occurred?

Science Words

big bang theory	quasar
black hole	radiation
elliptical galaxy	radio telescope
galaxy	spiral galaxy
irregular galaxy	
light year	
pulsar	

Chapter 22
Space Travel

Many stories about space travel that seem impossible today may become possible in the future. People might use spacecraft such as the one in the picture to travel to distant parts of the universe. We might receive or send messages to civilizations on other planets. Today, we do not know enough to make these stories come true. But as long as people wonder, imagine, and explore, the impossible may become possible.

The lessons in this chapter describe space travel in the past and in the future. Learning about space travel can help you imagine new ways of life the future might hold.

1 Making and Interpreting a Space Message

2 In What Ways Would Distant Space Travel Be Difficult?

3 How Do Spacecraft Leave Earth?

4 How Might Space Travel Affect the Future?

1 Making and Interpreting a Space Message

Billions of planets might exist in the universe. Some scientists think life could exist on many of these planets. Some of the planets might be home to organisms that can send messages to us. Scientists use radio telescopes to search for intelligent life in the universe. The radio telescope in the picture can pick up radio signals that are repeated. Such signals might carry a message.

We could learn a great deal by listening to messages from other civilizations. Perhaps other civilizations could learn from us. Make a list of facts about earth that you would like other civilizations to know. Then, include this information in a message that could be sent with a spacecraft traveling through the universe. Organisms on other planets probably would not speak an earth language. So you must prepare a coded message, using pictures.

Trade messages with your classmates. Try to decode their messages. Find out if you decoded the same information they wanted to send.

Radio telescope at Arecibo, Puerto Rico

Think About It

1. How did you decide what facts about earth to include in your message?
2. What questions would you like to ask intelligent life from another planet?
3. **Challenge** How can decoding other people's messages help improve the messages you prepare?

2 In What Ways Would Distant Space Travel Be Difficult?

Inside a spacecraft

Astronaut floating in space

About eighty years ago, Orville Wright became the first person to fly an airplane. People thought he was foolish to try to fly. Now, it is difficult to imagine a world without airplanes. In 1961 Yuri Gagarin, a Russian, was the first person to orbit the world in a spacecraft. Since then, a number of people from the United States, the Soviet Union, and other countries have traveled in space. Someday, people may use spacecraft as much as they use airplanes today.

Space flights often last a few days. The *Apollo 11* astronauts traveled eight days to the moon and back. In the picture you can see how a spacecraft stores food for short trips.

Future trips to planets and other distant places would take many years to complete. New kinds of spacecraft will have to be built for people to travel such long distances. Food might be grown in these spacecraft. Green algae would be a good food source because it grows quickly. Algae also would provide space travelers with oxygen and would use the carbon dioxide the people exhaled. Some scientists think future spacecraft will include small ecosystems. During long trips the ecosystems would cycle resources such as water, oxygen, and food.

Your body is held down to the earth by gravity. But during long space trips your body would have to get used to different kinds of movement and balance. The spacecraft would have too little gravity to hold you down. Your body would have very little weight. All unfastened objects would float in the spacecraft. The picture shows an astronaut and surrounding objects floating in space. Astronauts have to learn how to move in space and how to use objects that have little weight.

Another problem with long space trips is the amount of fuel needed. A spacecraft burns fuel every time it takes off or changes directions. In the future, sunlight might be used to power spacecraft traveling in the solar system. The spacecraft in the drawing has huge sheets called **solar sails** made of a shiny material. Sunlight hitting the solar sails might provide enough energy to push the spacecraft. Scientists are not sure if solar sails will work. But we need to find fuels that are available in space, or can last a long time, if people are going to travel to distant places.

Scientists are now trying to solve the problems of long space flights. Once the problems are solved, people might travel to many distant parts of the universe.

Think About It

1. How might future spacecraft provide people with resources during long space trips?
2. In what ways would having little weight be a problem for people during long space trips?
3. **Challenge** What other problems must be solved before people travel long distances into space?

Drawing of a spacecraft with solar sails

Have You Heard?

The Russian spacecraft *Salyut* was used for 4 years to study how humans respond to long space flights. Some Russian astronauts traveled up to 6 months in space. Scientists learned that people become lonely, bored, and restless when they travel in space for such a long time.

solar sail, a huge sheet of shiny material that might use solar energy to power a spacecraft in the future.

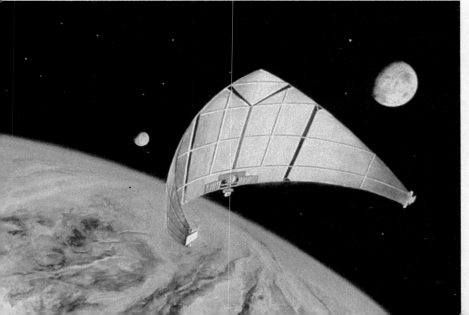

3 How Do Spacecraft Leave Earth?

Have You Heard?

The United States government hires thousands of scientists to work on space exploration. These scientists are part of an organization called NASA. The letters stand for National Aeronautics (er′ə nô′tiks) and Space Administration.

The first spacecraft launched from earth were very small. The astronauts had to squeeze into their seats. Larger spacecraft were built as scientists learned more about space travel and ways of building more powerful rockets. Notice in the pictures how spacecraft have changed with time.

Like the spacecraft on the following page, all spacecraft must be launched before they can travel into space. Rockets accelerate spacecraft, allowing them to overcome earth's gravity. Rockets can be attached either below or beside the spacecraft.

Spacecraft getting larger with time

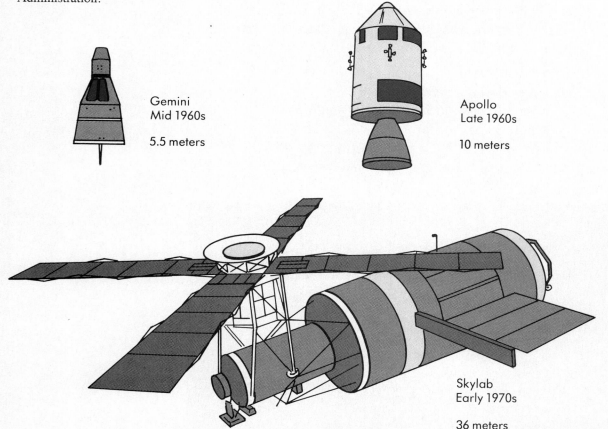

Gemini
Mid 1960s

5.5 meters

Apollo
Late 1960s

10 meters

Skylab
Early 1970s

36 meters

A rocket contains fuel such as kerosene or liquid hydrogen. The fuel burns when it combines with liquid oxygen. The fuel becomes a very hot gas that causes great pressures inside the rocket.

You can see in the picture how these pressures move the rocket. The pressures of the gases moving sideways in the rocket are balanced because they push equally in all directions. But the rocket has an opening in the back, so gases moving backward escape. As a result, there is more forward pressure than backward pressure in the rocket. The unequal pressures produce a forward force—or **thrust**—that moves the rocket forward and allows the spacecraft to take off.

Part of the launching rocket drops off after burning all its fuel. Then, the next part of the rocket ignites and burns its fuel. The speed of the spacecraft continues to increase.

thrust, the force in a rocket that causes the rocket to move forward.

Rocket launching spacecraft

Pressures inside a rocket that produce thrust

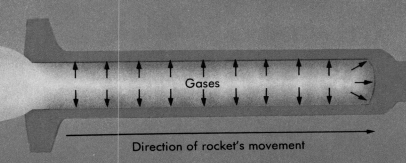

Gases

Direction of rocket's movement

Find Out

Spacecraft returning to earth
are traveling thousands of
kilometers per hour. Find a
book on spacecraft to learn
how spacecraft slow down
before they land.

How Fast Do Spacecraft Travel?

The earth's gravity pulls down on a moving
spacecraft. The diagrams show how the speed of a
spacecraft determines the path the spacecraft will travel.
A spacecraft must move fast enough to work against the
pull of gravity, or it will fall back to earth. A spacecraft
can orbit the earth if the spacecraft is moving 28,900
kilometers per hour. This **orbital velocity** is fast enough
to keep the spacecraft moving in a curved path around
the earth. At 40,200 kilometers per hour or more, a
spacecraft escapes the downward pull of earth's gravity.
With this **escape velocity,** the spacecraft flies into space.

Think About It

1. How do rockets launch spacecraft?
2. What is meant by the terms *orbital velocity* and
   escape velocity?
3. **Challenge** Why would a spacecraft's orbital and
   escape velocities vary on different planets?

Spacecraft moving slower
than orbital velocity

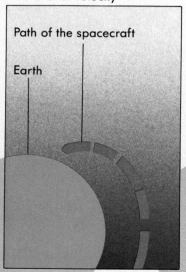

Path of the spacecraft

Earth

Spacecraft at orbital
velocity

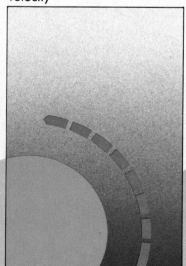

Spacecraft at escape
velocity

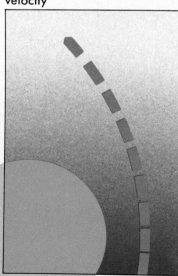

Activity

Making a Space-Rocket Model

Purpose
To infer how a space rocket works.

You Will Need
- spoon
- baking soda
- vinegar
- small cup
- empty medicine bottle
- large pan of water in which the medicine bottle can float
- funnel
- 1-hole rubber stopper that fits into the mouth of the bottle
- 6-cm-long rubber tubing

Directions
1. Add a small spoonful of baking soda and 3 spoonfuls of vinegar to a small cup. Observe what the reaction of the two materials produces. Record your observations.
2. Place a pan of water on your desk or on the floor.
3. Check the rubber tubing to be sure it is not clogged.

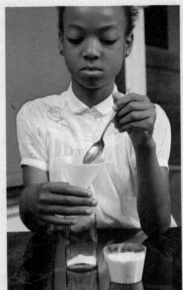

a

b

Insert the rubber tubing into the hole of the rubber stopper.
4. Add a small spoonful of baking soda to the bottle as shown in picture **a.**
5. Half fill the medicine bottle with vinegar.
6. Immediately close the bottle with the rubber stopper as shown in picture **b.**
7. Quickly place the bottle in a horizontal position and put it into the pan of water. Observe what happens to the bottle. Record your observations.

Think About It
1. How was the reaction of the baking soda and the vinegar similar to the reaction that occurs in a space rocket?
2. How was the rubber tubing on the bottle similar to the back end of a space rocket?
3. What caused the bottle to move as it did?
4. **Challenge** How could you control the direction in which the bottle moves?

381

4 How Might Space Travel Affect the Future?

Scientists have had many challenges while exploring the universe. They had to invent better instruments for studying stars, galaxies, and other objects in space. They had to build spacecraft that could travel longer distances through space. Scientists also tried to discover ways in which we could use our knowledge of space to improve our life on earth.

Some materials, such as certain medicines, are difficult or impossible to make on earth. Scientists think these medicines and other materials could easily be made in space, where there is less gravity. Scientists are planning to send small factories into space that will make these materials as they orbit the earth. The space factories will be carried into space by large spacecraft, such as the space shuttle *Columbia* shown in the pictures.

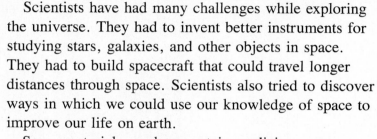

Columbia being launched

Space shuttle *Columbia*

Columbia's cargo space and mechanical arm

The *Columbia* was the first spacecraft that could be reused for trips between earth and space. Notice *Columbia*'s large storage room for carrying cargo such as space factories. The space shuttle's mechanical arm can lift the factories and release them into space. Later, the shuttle can return to the factories and bring back to earth the materials made by the factories.

Scientists have a long waiting list of businesses and citizens who want to send different kinds of cargo in a space shuttle. Some people are interested in learning how animals behave in an environment with little gravity. Others are interested in testing electronic equipment, making new kinds of metals, and sending communication satellites into space.

space colony, a huge spacecraft where many people from earth might live in the future.

Could Space Colonies Be Our Future Homes?

Scientists think that overpopulation on earth might cause people to search for new homes. In the future, people might live in a huge spacecraft—or **space colony**—that will orbit the earth.

A space colony could be a home for thousands or even millions of people. The picture shows how the outside of a space colony might look. A large mirror might reflect sunlight on solar cells to produce electrical power for the colony. The mirror also might reflect sunlight through the windows of the space colony to produce artificial days and nights. By controlling the amount of daylight entering the space colony, people would have winter, spring, summer, or fall whenever they wanted. The space colony would rotate to produce artificial gravity. People inside the space colony could move as they do on earth.

Artist's drawing of the outside of a space colony

Artist's drawing of the inside of a space colony

The picture shows that the inside of the space colony might have homes, factories, streets, and parks. People would go to school and work, much as they do on earth. The space colony also would have an artificial atmosphere and various ecosystems. Some parts of the space colony might have mountains, while others might have rain forests. People could see the beautiful colors of earth by looking through the windows of the space colony.

Nobody is sure how space travel might change our lives in the future. Some people think we can benefit by spending more money on space exploration. Others think we should spend money to find ways on earth to improve our lives. We can only imagine what new ways of life the future holds. But we can learn and work for a better future.

Have You Heard?

Countries from all over the world have written a space law. The law states that all countries have the right to explore space for peaceful purposes. All countries also will cooperate with each other during any emergencies that might occur in space.

Think About It

1. How could space factories help people on earth?
2. What is a space colony?
3. **Challenge** Think of some other things a space colony would need to make it more earthlike.

385

Do You Know?

How Do Astronauts Train for Space Missions?

"Three, two, one, liftoff!" The spacecraft rises in the sky. It is very exciting to watch the takeoff of a spacecraft. Imagine how exciting it would be if you were an astronaut inside the spacecraft!

When the space program first started, only military pilots became astronauts. Today, people of many different backgrounds become astronauts. All astronauts have college degrees in engineering or science. Astronauts also must be in good physical shape.

During training, astronauts learn to live in an environment similar to the environment they will live in while on their space missions. Astronauts learn how to move in environments with little gravity, as shown in the picture. They also learn how to survive in the ocean in case their spacecraft is stranded in the water when it lands.

Astronauts train in models of spacecraft. Movies of views that astronauts might see out of their windows are projected on screens in front of the model spacecraft. As astronauts train in the model, they see movies of takeoff and landing sites, and of the earth, moon, and stars as they will appear in space. These movies look very real. In fact, astronauts have returned from real space flights feeling as if they had gone on the space flights many times before in the model spacecraft.

Astronauts are trained as pilots or as mission specialists. The job of a pilot is to fly the spacecraft. A pilot of a spacecraft must have previous experience flying a jet plane. Mission specialists are trained scientists. A mission specialist carries out scientific research during the space flight. In addition to his or her special job, each crew member learns how to do at least one other crew member's job. This helps ensure that the crew is safe during the flight.

Training to be an astronaut is hard work. But the picture shows that astronauts in training also can have fun.

Astronaut training for space travel

Tie It Together

Sum It Up

1. The astronaut and the spacecraft in the photograph are prepared for a brief space trip. Write a short paragraph describing the changes that would need to be made so the astronaut could travel through space for a long time.

2. Draw a rocket in your notebook. Use colored arrows to show the direction of the pressures inside the rocket. Which way will the rocket move?

3. The diagram shows three different paths, labeled *a*, *b*, and *c*. When a spacecraft is traveling at escape velocity, which path does it take? When a spacecraft is traveling at orbital velocity, which path does it take?

4. Imagine that you are designing the inside of a space colony. Draw your design, including what you think people will need inside a space colony. Write a short paragraph explaining the choices you made in your design.

Challenge!

1. Why do you think astronauts that travel in space for a long time develop weak muscles?

2. What kind of energy source, besides solar energy, might be good for powering spacecraft that travel long distances?

3. If a spacecraft were traveling near earth at 35,000 kilometers per hour, what kind of path would it follow?

4. How will we save money by using the space shuttle to send objects into orbit around the earth?

5. In the future, how might the space shuttle be used to build space colonies?

Science Words

escape velocity

orbital velocity

solar sail

space colony

thrust

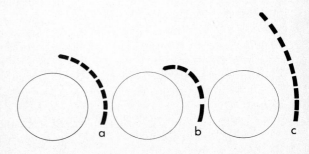

Laboratory

A Galaxy Model

a

Purpose
To construct a model of our galaxy, and to infer the sun's position in the galaxy.

You Will Need
• file folder
• compass for drawing
• scissors
• black marking pen
• 2 paper fasteners
• ruler

Stating the Problem
Scientists have known for about 60 years that our solar system is not in the center of our Milky Way galaxy. Since scientists could not look at our galaxy from space, how did they learn our solar system's location in the galaxy? Scientists inferred the location of our solar system by using a model of the galaxy. They placed the solar system in different positions in the galaxy model. Scientists then compared the number of stars that their model predicted they would see to the number of stars which they actually observed in the night sky. You can make a model of the Milky Way galaxy and infer our solar system's position in it.

Investigating the Problem
1. Use a compass to draw a circle 14 cm in diameter on the file folder. Cut out the circle.
2. Use a black marking pen to draw a spiral galaxy on the disk as shown in picture *a*. The dots represent stars in the spiral galaxy.

3. Study picture *b*. Insert a paper fastener into the center of the disk. This paper fastener represents a spacecraft in the center of the galaxy. Insert another paper fastener in one of the outer arms of the spiral galaxy, as shown in the picture. This paper fastener represents a spacecraft near the edge of the spiral galaxy.
4. Draw a straight line that passes through both paper fasteners, as shown in picture *b*. Label one end of the line *X* and the other end of the line *Y*.
5. Imagine that observers in the 2 spacecraft can estimate the number of stars which they see as they sight along the line. Compare the number of stars each observer would see when looking toward *X* with the number of stars each observer would see when looking toward *Y*. Record your comparisons.

Making Conclusions
1. Which paper fastener most closely represents our location in the galaxy? How do you know?
2. Why would observations from a telescope be necessary in order to infer our position in the galaxy?
3. How is the shape of your model different from that of the Milky Way galaxy? *Hint: Your model has only two dimensions.*

b

Careers

Photograph Interpreter

Imagine someone trying to land a helicopter in a forest. It would be difficult. But a detailed map would show the pilot clearings in the forest.

Now, imagine what it would be like to find a landing place on the moon! "When I started working at the National Aeronautics and Space Administration (NASA)," says Leo, "I was part of a team that helped select safe landing sites for the astronauts."

Leo had been an engineer, working on special projects for the Air Force. Through his work, he became an expert in interpreting photographs taken from airplanes. He could tell what an aerial photograph showed and see things most people would overlook. These skills came in handy for helping to select landing places on the moon for the Apollo astronauts.

"We used photographs of the moon to help choose the landing sites,"

says Leo. "The photographs were taken by cameras on satellites in lunar orbit. The photographs were like detailed maps. We could tell where the rough and smooth surfaces were located."

Leo still works with photographs taken by satellites. But this time, the cameras are pointed toward the earth. "Two satellites, called Landsats, orbit the earth. They take pictures of different areas of the earth. Computers add colors to the photographs which give us a lot of information.

"These photographs can tell us about worldwide farming or insect problems. We can see flood, forest fire, or earthquake damage. The photographs even help locate natural resources, such as petroleum."

Many of the careers at NASA, such as Leo's, require a college education. But Leo has some additional advice. "Learn to communicate well with people. After all, communication is what satellites are all about."

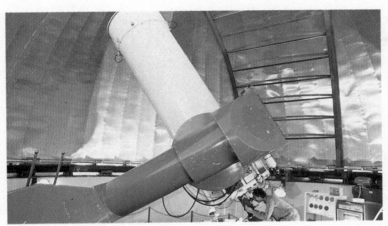

Astronomer

The space shuttle has been very successful over the last few years. This success has helped spark a new interest in careers related to exploring space.

If you are curious about what lies beyond the earth, you may want to become an **astronomer.** This scientist uses telescopes to observe comets, planets, stars, and other objects in space. Astronomers try to understand the past, present, and future of objects in our universe.

Many people enjoy viewing the universe with a telescope. But to become a professional astronomer, you must study math and science in college.

A lot of people work together to build a spacecraft, such as the space shuttle. Although engineers design the craft, it is **aerospacecraft assemblers** who put the craft together. Some assemblers of the space shuttle attach the tiles to the outside of the craft.

An assembler must be very careful in his or her work. Entire space missions depend on the care and skill of the assemblers. They learn these skills during two years of college.

Many of the people who work in the aerospace industry are **technicians** who also attend college for two years.

Technicians work in a variety of areas. Some may operate wind tunnels to test jet aircraft. Other technicians run computers and training equipment that help prepare astronauts for a mission. Still other technicians test satellites and other spacecraft to make sure they will operate correctly in space.

Aerospacecraft assemblers

On Your Own

Picture Clue

Look closely at the photograph on page 342. The streaks of light come from spheres of glowing gases, such as the sun, in space. What are these objects? The photograph was taken with a camera pointed toward the sky. The camera's shutter was left open for a few hours. Why do you think the streaks of light appear to be curved?

Books About Science

Colonies in Space by Frederic Golden. Harcourt Brace Jovanovich, 1977. Explore ways in which people in the future might live in colonies that travel through space.

Galaxies, Islands in Space by David C. Knight. Morrow, 1979. Learn how galaxies were discovered and how scientists think galaxies change with time.

Quasars, Pulsars, and Black Holes in Space by Melvin Berger. Putnam, 1977. Read how scientists try to explain mysterious objects in space.

The Search: Our Quest for Intelligent Life in Outer Space by Frank Stilley. Putnam, 1977. Learn how people on earth have been trying to find out if intelligent life exists in other parts of the universe.

The Space Shuttle by Frank Ross. Lothrop, Lee, and Shepard, 1979. Get more information on the history, design, and operation of the space shuttle. This book also includes instructions for making a paper model of the space shuttle!

The World of UFOs by David Cohen. Lippincott, 1978. Read about unidentified flying objects that have been spotted and what some people think these UFOs are.

Projects

1. Make models of constellations with "stars" that appear to shine. First, use a library to find out the patterns of various constellations. Second, using a small pin, poke a pattern of holes that resembles the pattern of stars of a constellation into an index card. Do this for all the constellations you have researched. Third, get a small box with a lid that is wide enough to let you snugly insert an index card into the box. Punch a hole into one end of the box. Now, tape a small penlight to the opposite end inside the box. Insert one of the constellation cards into the box. Turn on the light, and close the lid. Finally, look through the peephole. You will see the "shining stars" of the constellation.

2. Make a model of a spacecraft that could be used to carry goods to and from a space colony. To help you decide what to include in your model, use a library to find out what some real spacecraft look like. Use simple materials such as cardboard, tin foil, and tape to make your model.

3. Write a letter to NASA officials in Washington, D.C. Ask them to send you information about what kind of cargo the space shuttle is going to carry in the near future, how much it costs to rent cargo space, and how long the waiting list is for renting cargo space.

Unit Test

Multiple Choice

Number your paper from 1–4. Next to each number, write the letter of the word or phrase that best completes the statement or answers the question.

1. Scientists know that star A produces less light than star B. But from the earth, star A appears brighter than star B. Star A probably is
   a. a new star.
   b. farther from the earth than star B.
   c. a white dwarf.
   d. closer to the earth than star B.

2. Which order best describes the life cycle of a star such as the sun?
   a. white dwarf, nebula, supernova
   b. nebula, young star, adult star, red giant, white dwarf
   c. supernova, nebula, star
   d. nebula, young star, white dwarf, red giant

3. How did scientists infer the shape of our Milky Way galaxy?
   a. by studying the position of stars near our solar system
   b. by studying the whole Milky Way galaxy
   c. by traveling in spacecraft
   d. by studying the earth

4. What might limit the distance people can travel in a spacecraft?
   a. the amount of food the spacecraft can carry
   b. the amount of water the spacecraft can carry
   c. the amount of air the spacecraft can carry
   d. all the above

True or False

Number your paper from 5–14. Next to each number, write *true* if the sentence is correct and *false* if the sentence is incorrect. Make each false statement true by changing the underlined word or phrase and writing the correct word or phrase on your paper.

5. The star closest to our solar system is Rigel.

6. A red giant is a unit of measurement used to measure long distances in space.

7. A galaxy with a pinwheel shape is a spiral galaxy.

8. Orbital velocity is the speed and direction at which a spacecraft can escape earth's gravity and fly into space.

9. The hottest stars are red in color.

10. The star Sirius is about nine light years away from the earth. Its light must travel ninety years before reaching the earth.

11. In the future, thousands of people might orbit the earth in a space colony that might have cities, ecosystems, and an atmosphere.

12. A supernova is an exploding, high-mass star.

13. When nuclei in stars split, they release huge amounts of energy.

14. A radio microscope is used to study pulsars, quasars, and stars.

Glossary/Index

atom

and endocrine system, 168–171
in epidermis, 94
guard, 64
muscle, 102, 130, 150
nerve, 150–155
plant, 63–64, 78, 79
receptor, 144–149, 150, 152, 155, 156, 158
and removal of wastes, 114–116
reproductive, 165
respiration, 130–131

guard cells

cell body, 151: part of a nerve cell that keeps the cell healthy and able to transmit nerve impulses

cerebellum (ser′ə bel′əm), 155, 158: the part of the brain beneath the cerebrum that regulates muscle movements

cerebrum (sə rē′brəm), 155, 156–157, 158: the large, wrinkled top portion of the human brain that controls thinking and voluntary movements

charge 215–217

chemical change 67, 71, 108, 130, 152, 254: a change in which one or more new substances are formed

chlorophyll (klôr′ə fil), 62–63, 67, 68, 72: green coloring material found in plants and some other organisms

chloroplast (klôr′ə plast), 63, 67, 68: an oval-shaped structure that contains chlorophyll and is found in a plant cell

circuit (sėr′kit), 222–223: a path for current to follow from a source of electrical energy and back again

circuit (sėr′kit) **breaker,** 225: a switch that opens a circuit when too much current flows through it

circulatory system
and cell respiration, 130–131
and exercise, 129, 183
functions of, 124–128, 131

classify (klas′ə fī), 19, 346, 348: to arrange in groups according to some system

climax (klī′maks) **community,** 49: a stable community that is made up of the same kinds of organisms over a long time

coal, 252, 254, 256, 263: a solid fuel formed by pressure and heat acting on partly decayed plant matter

community (kə myü′nə tē), 13: a group of different populations living together in the same place
and changes in, 46–49, 50
flow of energy through, 26–29
food chains in, 22–25

near vents, 318
and predators, 13–15
See also ecosystem

compete, 10–11: try to get something also needed by other organisms

condense (kən dens′), 322–323: to change from a gas, such as water vapor, into a liquid, such as water

conductor (kən duk′tər), 219, 220: a material through which electric current passes easily

conservation (kon′sər vā′shən), 276–277: using a substance or energy more wisely by not wasting it

constellation (kon′stə lā′shən), 352: a group of stars

consumer (kən sü′mər), 20–21, 23, 27: an organism that eats food

continental (kon′tə nen′tl) **glacier,** 300: a huge ice sheet that can cover an area as large as a continent

continental shelf, 313, 331, 332: land that extends into the ocean from the edge of a continent

core, 354, 355: the inner part of a star where nuclear fusion occurs

current, 308–309, 311: a river of water that flows unseen through the ocean

current
air, 38, 218
electrical, 218–222

cycle, 38–41, 322–323: the continuous movement of resources to different parts of ecosystems to be used again

decomposer (dē′kəm pō′zər), 21, 23, 27, 254: an organism that breaks down the complex chemicals of dead organisms into simpler chemicals

delta, 293: new land that builds up at the mouth of a river in a body of water

dendrite (den′drīt), 151, 152, 153: the end of a nerve cell that responds to stimuli by triggering a nerve impulse

depressant (di pres′nt), 187: a drug that decreases the rate that nerve impulses cross synapses

dermis (dėr′mis), 95, 96–97: the second layer of skin

diaphragm (dī′ə fram), 120: the muscle beneath the lungs that helps you inhale and exhale

diet, 177–181 *See also* health

dietary fiber (dī′ə ter′ē fī′bər), 178: plant material in foods that helps remove wastes from the large intestine

diffusion (di fyü′zhən), 123, 127: movement of particles from an area having more of those particles to an area having less of those particles

starch

stored food

levees

a hat	i it	oi oil	ch child	⎧ a in about
ā age	ī ice	ou out	ng long	e in taken
ä far	o hot	u cup	sh she	ə = ⎨ i in pencil
e let	ō open	u̇ put	th thin	o in lemon
ē equal	ô order	ü rule	ᴛʜ then	u in circus
ėr term			zh measure	⎩

floor, 312–315
food resources in, 321, 326–329
life in, 316–317
resources from, 330–332
tides in, 308, 310
in water cycle, 323
waves, 308
ocean basin, 313: the deep ocean floor
oil. *See* petroleum
oil rig, 257, 331, 332
omnivore (om′nə vôr), 20, 23: an organism that
eats both plants and animals
orbital velocity (ôr′bə təl və los′ə tē), 380: the
speed and direction of a spacecraft that
make the spacecraft travel in a path around
a planet
organ (ôr′gən), 94, 111, 112: a group of different
tissues working together in an organism *See
also* circulatory system, digestion, nervous
system, respiratory system
organisms
and balance of nature, 42–43
in communities, 13–15, 46–49
competition for resources, 10–11
consumers, producers, decomposers, 20–21
and ecosystems, 36–45
and flow of energy, 26–29
and food chains, 22–25
interacting with nonliving resources, 34–37
living together, 5–10
in oceans, 316–317, 326–329
and populations, 12–15, 26–29, 42–44
and predator-prey relationship, 12–16
See also animals, ecosystem, plants
ovaries (ō′vər ēz), 165, 169: female organs that
produce reproductive cells and chemicals
which cause body changes during
adolescence
oxygen (ok′sə jən), a colorless gas in the air that
plants and animals need to live
in cell respiration, 71–72, 130–131
in circulatory system, 124, 127, 128
cycle in ecosystems, 40–41
in leaf, 64, 71
necessary for life, 34, 35, 120
in photosynthesis, 67, 72
in respiratory system, 122–123, 183

in stars, 355, 356

pancreas (pan′krē əs), 111, 170, 173: a large
gland that releases digestive enzymes into
the small intestine
parasite (par′ə sīt), 8: an organism that lives in or
on another organism and feeds on it
peat (pēt), 254: a spongy mass of dead plant
matter that changes into coal under heat
and pressure
pesticides, 30
petroleum (pə trō′lē əm), 255–256, 257, 331–332:
a liquid fuel formed by heat and pressure
acting on partly decayed organisms on the
ocean floor
phloem (flō′em), 78–79: tubes that transport food
in plants
and sap, 82
photosynthesis (fō′tō sin′thə sis), 66–69: a process
by which plants use sunlight, chlorophyll,
carbon dioxide, and water to make food
and respiration, 71–72
pigment (pig′mənt), 62: coloring material
pituitary (pə tü′ə ter′ē) **gland,** 169, 184: endocrine
gland in the head that produces growth
hormone and hormones that control other
endocrine glands
plankton (plangk′tən), 317–318: floating sea
organism
plants
basic needs of, 35
color of light used by, 68
and cycles in ecosystems, 38–41
in food chains, 22–24, 26–29
and fossil fuels, 254–255
hormones in, 172
leaf structure and function, 61–72,
78–79, 80
in ocean, 316–317
and photosynthesis, 66–68, 72
as predators, 14
as producers, 20–21, 23, 28
and respiration, 71–72
and storage of food, 27, 75–77
transport of food, water in, 78–82
use of food by, 27, 70–72
plasma (plaz′mə), 124: the yellow, fluid part of
blood
plate, 312: a slowly moving piece of the solid,
outer layer of the earth
platelets (plāt′lits), 125: cell pieces that release a
substance which helps form a blood clot
pollution
and ecosystems, 44
from fossil fuels, 256

carbon
dioxide →
oxygen
photosynthesis

trench, 312–313: a deep ditch in the ocean floor that forms where two plates are colliding and crust is being destroyed

turbine (tėr′bən), 259, 263, 274, 275: a machine with fanlike blades

universe
    big bang theory of, 370–371
    galaxies in, 363–365, 370–371
    See also space travel, stars

uranium, 263, 274

urine (yùr′ən), 115: liquid waste produced by the kidneys

valley glacier, 300: a glacier that moves down a mountain valley

valve (valv), 126–127: a structure in the vein or heart made of 2 flaps of tissue that prevents blood from flowing backwards

vein (vān), 126–127, 128: a blood vessel that carries blood to the heart

veins, in plants, 63, 78–79

vent, 318

vitamins, 70, 108, 112, 115, 178, 180

vocal cords, 121, 165

voluntary (vol′ən ter′ē) **muscle,** 103, 128, 155, 184: a muscle that you can control

wastes
    in blood plasma, 124
    and circulatory system, 126, 128, 131
    and large intestine, 112
    radioactive, 264
    removal of, 114–115, 116
    and sweat glands, 97
    See also excretion

water
    in cell respiration, 71–72, 130–131
    in circulatory system, 124, 131
    in digestion process, 112
    in ecosystems, 38–39
    as energy source, 258–261
    necessary for life, 34–35
    as nutrient, 108, 178, 180
    in photosynthesis, 66–67
    in plasma, 124
    in respiratory system, 123
    in urine, 115
    transport of in plants, 79–81
    See also fresh water, groundwater, lakes, ocean, rivers, seawater

water cycle, 322–323: the movement of water between the earth's surface and the air, and back to the earth
    in ecosystems, 38–41

water table, 297, 325: the top of the water-soaked layer in the ground

water vapor, 64, 80, 322–323, 324–325

water wheel, 258, 261

watt, (wot), 251: unit of electrical power

watt-hour, 251: amount of electrical energy used

waves, 308, 311

white blood cell, 125: a cell that protects you from disease

white dwarf, 356: a small, dim star that remains after a red giant blows off its outer shell of gases

wind energy, 272–273, 275

work, 202: the result of a force moving an object through a distance along the same line as the force's direction
    and force, 202–203
    and energy, 199, 204–205, 208–209
    See also energy, force

X-ray telescope, 368

xylem (zī′lem), 79, 80: tubes in plants that transport water and minerals

xylem

Acknowledgments

Positions of photographs are shown in abbreviated form as follows: top (t), bottom (b), left (l), right (r), center (c). All photographs not credited are the property of Scott, Foresman and Company. Cover, illustration by William Peterson, photograph by David Muench; **2,** W. H. Hodge/Peter Arnold, Inc.; **4,** Hans Reinhard/ Bruce Coleman, Inc.; **7, (t)** Ron and Valerie Taylor/ Tom Stack & Assoc., **(r)** W. H. Hodge/Peter Arnold, Inc.; **8, (tl)** Runk/Schoenberger/Grant Heilman, **(tr)** Manfred Kage/Peter Arnold, Inc., **(b)** Russ Kinne/Photo Researchers, Inc.; **9,** Michael Ederegger/Peter Arnold, Inc.; **10, (r)** Norman Myers/Bruce Coleman, Inc.; **11,** Grant Heilman; **12, (tr)** B. Mackenzie/Tom Stack & Assoc., **(cl)** Michael Collier/Stock Boston, **(b)** A. Blank/Bruce Coleman, Inc.; **15, (l)** Christian Mundt/Tom Stack & Assoc., **(r)** John Zoiner/Peter Arnold, Inc.; **18,** Grant Heilman; **20, (l)** Wayne Lankinen/Bruce Coleman, Inc., **(c)** Diana and Rick Sullivan/Bruce Coleman, Inc., **(r)** Runk/Schoenberger/ Grant Heilman; **21,** Runk/Schoenberger/Grant Heilman; **22, (all)** Grant Heilman; **23, (l)** Tom Brakefield/Bruce Coleman, Inc., **(c)** Joe McDonald/ Bruce Coleman, Inc., **(tr)** John Shaw/Bruce Coleman, Inc., **(cr)** David R. Frazier, **(br)** Robert Strindberg; **32,** Keith Gunnar/Bruce Coleman, Inc.; **33,** Malcolm S. Kirk/Peter Arnold, Inc.; **34, (tl)** C. B. Frith/Bruce Coleman, Inc., **(tr)** David C. Houston/ Bruce Coleman, Inc., **(b)** Tom Stack/Tom Stack & Assoc.; **35, (t)** Hans Reinhard/Bruce Coleman, Inc., **(bl)** Photo Researchers, Inc.; **36, (t)** G. C. Kelley/ Tom Stack & Assoc., **(bl)** Jane Burton/Bruce Coleman, Inc., **(br)** Terry E. Eiler/Stock Boston; **37, (l)** Rene Burri/Magnum Photos, Inc., **(r)** Tom Bean/Tom Stack & Assoc.; **38,** Tom Stack/Tom Stack & Assoc.; **43, (l)** Brian Parker/Tom Stack & Assoc., **(r)** Steve Solum/ Bruce Coleman, Inc.; **44, (t)** Tom Stack/Tom Stack & Assoc., **(b)** Lionel Atwill/Peter Arnold, Inc.; **47,** John Shaw/Bruce Coleman, Inc.; **48, 49,** Courtesy Dr. Thomas L. Poulson, Professor of Biological Sciences, University of Illinois at Chicago; **50,** Leonard Lee Rue III/Tom Stack & Assoc.; **55, (r)** Fred Bruemmer; **58,** E. R. Degginger; **60,** Peter Southwick/Stock Boston, **(tl)** Elliott Erwitt/ Magnum Photos, Inc.; **62, (bl)** Bob Waterman/ West Light; **62, (br), 64,** Grant Heilman; **66,** David R. Frazier; **68, (l)** Phil Degginger/Bruce Coleman, Inc.; **69, (tr)** Peter Arnold/Peter Arnold, Inc., John Melville Bishop/Bruce Coleman, Inc.; **70,** Craig Aurness/West Light; **77,** John Colwell/Grant Heilman; **79, (r)** Manfred Kage/Peter Arnold, Inc.; **82,** Richard W. Brown; **87, (c)** John Running/Stock Boston; **90,** Manfred Kage/Peter Arnold, Inc.; **92,** Hal Harrison/Grant Heilman; **94,** David Hurn/Magnum Photos, Inc.; **96,** Jacana; **97, (r)** Jeff Jacobson/Archive Pictures, Inc.; **100,** Courtesy Lutheran General Hospital; **101,** Dan McCoy/Rainbow; **108, (l)** Bohdan Hrynewych/Stock Boston; **111,** Lennart Nilsson, from *Behold Man,* Courtesy Little, Brown and Company, Boston; **112,** Elliott Erwitt/ Magnum; **116,** Milton Feinberg/Stock Boston; **123, (l)** Frank Siteman/Stock Boston; **124, (l)** Historical Pictures Services, Inc.; **125,** Courtesy Robert D. Allen; **132,** Ellis Herwig/Stock Boston; **137 (c)** Arthur Grace/Sygma, **(b)** Peter Southwick/Stock Boston; **140,** David Attie/Phototake; **142,** Jim Whitmer Photography; **145,** Lennart Nilsson, from *Behold Man,* Courtesy Little, Brown and Company, Boston; **150,** Tom Stack/Tom Stack & Assoc.; **153,** Gary Milburn/Tom Stack & Assoc.; **155,** Paul Fusco/Magnum Photos, Inc.; **158,** Bruce M. Wellman/Tom Stack & Assoc.; **160,** Jane Burton/Bruce Coleman, Inc.; **161,** David R. Frazier; **162, (l)** Grant Heilman, **(r)** Clyde H. Smith/Peter Arnold, Inc.; **166,** Sanford H. Roth/Rapho Photo Researchers, Inc.; **168, (l)** UPI, **(r)** Wide World; **171,** Norman Tomalin/Bruce Coleman, Inc.; **172, (l)** Courtesy Dr. J. A. D. Zeevaart, MSU-DOE Plant Research Laboratory, Michigan State University; **174,** The Bettmann Archive, Inc; **182,** Courtesy U.S. Naval Medicine; **184, 185,** Michal Heron/Contact-Woodfin Camp; **188,** Courtesy Hinsdale Sanatarium Hospital; **196,** E. R. Degginger/Bruce Coleman, Inc.; **198,** Jacques Jangoux/Peter Arnold, Inc.; **202,** Julian Baum/Bruce Coleman, Inc.; **204, (l)** Joe Dimaggio/Peter Arnold, Inc., **(r)** Bob McKeever/ Tom Stack & Assoc.; **205, (l)** James H. Karales/Peter Arnold, Inc., **(r)** Jeff Jacobson/Archive Pictures, Inc.; **206,** Mark Godfrey/Archive Pictures, Inc.; **210,** Brian Payne/Focus on Sports; **212,** Frank Lane/Bruce Coleman, Inc.; **221,** Courtesy Dr. Glenn C. Landon, Association of Orthopedic Surgeons; **233,** NASA; **237,** Steve Firebaugh/Bruce Coleman, Inc.; **244,** Courtesy IBM; **245, (t)** Edith G. Haun/Stock Boston, **(b)**Peter Menzel/Stock Boston; **248,** David Hurn/Magnum Photos, Inc.; **250,** Owen Franken/ Stock Boston; **252, (l)** Historical Pictures Services, Inc., **(br)** Burk Uzzle/Magnum Photos, Inc.; **255,** John Zoiner/Peter Arnold, Inc.; **257, (t)** David Moore/Black Star, **(b)** Shelly Katz/Black Star; **258, (l)** The Bettmann Archive, Inc., **(r)** Guy Gillette/ Photo Researchers, Inc.; **260, (l)** Fredrik D. Bodin/ Stock Boston, **(b)** Courtesy Power Authority, State of New York; **263,** Chuck Rogers/Black Star; **264,** Matt McVay/Star; **266,** Henry Grossman/DPI; **268,** Wil Blanche/DPI; **272, (t)** Jean Guichard/Sygma; **272.** Peter Southwick/Stock Boston; **272, (l)** Gilles Peress/Magnum Photos, Inc., **(t) (br)** Keith Gunnar/Bruce Coleman, Inc.; **273, (r)** David R. Frazier, **(b)**Lowell Georgia/Photo Researchers, Inc.; **274,** Dennis Stock/Magnum Photos, Inc.; **275,** Costa Manos/Magnum Photos, Inc.; **277, (t)** David R.

Frazier; **278,** J. P. Laffont/Sygma; **283,** Mark Antman/Stock Boston; **286,** Herwarth Voightman/Seaphot; **288,** Clyde H. Smith/Peter Arnold, Inc.; **289,** NASA; **291, (l)** S. J. Kraseman/Peter Arnold, Inc., **(r)** Grant Heilman; **292,** Cary Wolinsky/Stock Boston; **294,** Thomas Hovland/Grant Heilman; **295,** Alan Pitcairn/Grant Heilman; **299,** Russ Kinne/Photo Researchers, Inc.; **300, (l)** Jim Holland/Stock Boston, **(r)** Grant Heilman; **301,** Tom Bean/Tom Stack & Assoc.; **304,** Dale Jorgenson/Tom Stack & Assoc.; **307,** NASA/Grant Heilman; **308,** Randy Hufford/Tom Stack & Assoc.; **310,** New Brunswick Department of Tourism; **314,** NOAA/NESS; **315,** Al Giddings/Ocean Films Ltd. **316,** Ed Robinson/Tom Stack & Assoc.; **317,** Peter David/Photo Researchers, Inc.; **318,(l)** Fred Spiess/SIO/Woods Hole Oceanographic Inst., **(r)** Al Giddings/Ocean Films Ltd. **320,** Bob Abrams/Bruce Coleman, Inc.; **324,** TVA; **326, (t)** C. C. Lockwood/Bruce Coleman, Inc., Jim Holland/Stock Boston; **327,** Tom Stack/Tom Stack & Assoc.; **328,** Dennis Stock/Magnum Photos, Inc.; **329, (t)** Bob Evans/Peter Arnold, Inc., **(r)** Ron Church/Tom Stack & Assoc.; **330,** David Madison/Bruce Coleman, Inc.; **331,** Christopher Springmann; **332,** Shelly Katz/Black Star; **334,** Christopher Springmann; **338,** Courtesy John G. Shedd Aquarium/Patrice Ceisel; **339, (bl)** Bryn Campbell/Magnum Photos, Inc., **(br)** U.S. Navy Photo; **342,** Clyde H. Smith/Peter Arnold, Inc.; **344,** Courtesy California Institute of Technology & Carnegie Institute of Washington; **346, 348,** Courtesy Science Graphics, Tucson, Arizona; **350,** Courtesy California Institute of Technology & Carnegie Institute of Washington; **351,** Courtesy Lick Observatory; **352,** Courtesy California Institute of Technology & Carnegie Institute of Washington; **353, (l)** Courtesy Science Graphics, Tucson, Arizona, **(r)** Tom Stack/Tom Stack & Assoc.; **356, 357,** Courtesy Lick Observatory; **358,** Courtesy Bausch & Lomb; **360,** Courtesy James D. Wray, 1979, McDonald Observatory; **362,** Courtesy California Institute of Technology & Carnegie Institute of Washington; **363,** Courtesy U.S. Naval Observatory; **364, (tl) (bl)** U.S. Naval Observatory, **(br)** © 1975 AURA, Inc., Cerro Tololo Inter-American Observatory; **365,** Courtesy Mount Wilson & Palomar Observatories; **367,** Courtesy Hale Observatories; **368,** Astronomical Illustration by Don Dixon; **369,** Courtesy Dr. Franklin Drake, National Astronomy and Ionosphere Center, Cornell University; **374,** Astronomical Illustration by Don Dixon; **375,** Alon Reininger/Contact-Woodfin Camp; **376,** NASA; **377,** Astronomical Illustration by Don Dixon; **379,** © Washington Post/Steve Szabo/Contact-Woodfin Camp; **382-387,** NASA; **391,** © National Optical Astronomy Observatories/Cerro Tololo

Graph on page 14 adapted from Aldo S. Leopold, *Wisconsin Conservation Bulletin,* No. 321, 1943 Information on starfish population on page 42 from E. O. Dodson, *Evolution: Process and Product,* Reinhold Publishing Corp., 1960

Ligature Publishing Services, Inc.: design implementation, internal art and photographic direction.

We wish to express our appreciation to the following schools for their contributions:

Poems for the series were written by children at Fairfield Public Schools, Fairfield, Connecticut; Greeley School, Winnetka, Illinois; Howland School, Chicago, Illinois; Indian Oasis Elementary District, Sells, Arizona; and Model Laboratory School, Eastern Kentucky University, Richmond, Kentucky.

Cloze reading tests for the series were administered at Banting Elementary School, Waukesha, Wisconsin; and Gospel Lutheran Grade School, Milwaukee, Wisconsin.

Photographs for Book 6 were taken at Orrington School, Evanston, Illinois; and Martin Luther King Lab School, Evanston, Illinois.

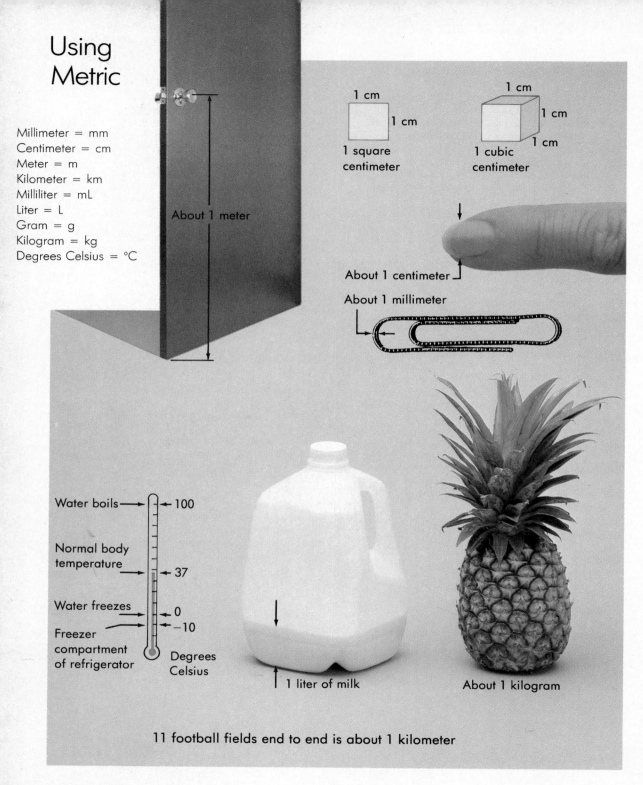

Using Metric

Millimeter = mm
Centimeter = cm
Meter = m
Kilometer = km
Milliliter = mL
Liter = L
Gram = g
Kilogram = kg
Degrees Celsius = °C

About 1 meter

1 cm
1 cm
1 square centimeter

1 cm
1 cm
1 cm
1 cubic centimeter

About 1 centimeter

About 1 millimeter

Water boils ⟶ 100
Normal body temperature ⟶ 37
Water freezes ⟶ 0
Freezer compartment of refrigerator ⟶ −10
Degrees Celsius

1 liter of milk

About 1 kilogram

11 football fields end to end is about 1 kilometer